Edited by Susan Singer and Carol Rutz

D0207866

Reflections on Learning as Teachers

College City Publications, Northfield, MN

Published by:
College City Publications / Ashmore Ink
925 Ivanhoe Drive
Northfield, Minnesota 55057
http://ashmoreink.com

For information on ordering this volume from the Carleton College Bookstore:

E-mail: Carletoninfo@collegebookstore.org

Web site: http://wwwcollegebookstore.org

Phone: (507) 646-4153 or (800) 799-4148

ON THE COVER:

A single circuitous path to the center and out again, the labyrinth on Stewsie Island at Carleton College, Northfield, MN, is a tool for reflection and relaxation. (Photo by Tom Roster)

International Standard Book No. 0-9746379-1-2

PRINTED IN THE UNITED STATES OF AMERICA

Contents

Acknowledgments

This volume began with the exciting teaching and learning environment at Carleton College, a context that informs every word on every page and is exemplified by Carleton's Perlman Center for Learning and Teaching. The LTC, as it is known locally, has fostered faculty development activities at Carleton since 1992. The vision of the LTC's founders continues to unfold, and this volume is just one manifestation of the ongoing culture of collaboration supported by the LTC.

In this intellectual atmosphere, real people still need to get the work done. Therefore, we deeply appreciate the efforts of Jennifer Cox Johnson, who provided administrative support, and Nancy Ashmore of College City Publications, who made our text come to life through her editorial work and book design. The project was supported by a Faculty Career Grant from the Andrew W. Mellon Foundation.

Finally, this volume would never have seen the light of day without the generosity and good will of a group of faculty willing to be bold as well as vulnerable as they reflected on their learning as teachers. We owe our contributors the greatest debt for their willingness to assemble campus lore about teaching and learning into concrete, sensitive explorations of the liberal arts. To our colleagues, we offer our delighted thanks.

Susan Singer and Carol Rutz, editors

Talking about Teaching: The Importance of Colleagues

Susan R. Singer

I t is strikingly naïve to assume that an excellent scholar will instantaneously become an outstanding teacher by crossing the threshold into a classroom filled with students. How do college and university professors become teachers? Most of us learn "on the job." We learn from our teachers, absorbing and emulating how they taught *us*; we learn from the students we work with as graduate school teaching assistants; we learn from the young women and men who have the unenviable experience of sitting in the first classes we teach as members of the faculty. And, we learn from our colleagues.

Writers fueled my aspirations to teach, and the wisdom of colleagues, voiced in text, has been invaluable to me. When I first stepped into a biology classroom as a teacher, however, my intellectualized view of teaching collided with the reality of it. I rushed back to my texts, seeking practical suggestions. I also made a conscious effort to learn on a daily basis from the people I was trying to educate. Shifting from daily conversations with graduate faculty and graduate students to helping undergraduates grapple with new material requires a bit of recalibration.

> Engaging in conversation about teaching and learning issues is crucial for faculty at all stages of their careers. Faculty launching careers, shifting into a mid-career phase, and reflecting back on a full career in the classroom all bring their voices to this volume.

Finally, I gathered up sufficient courage to talk with colleagues at Carleton College in Northfield, MN, and at professional meetings. From

SUSAN SINGER, professor of biology, joined the Carleton College faculty in 1986. She earned her B.S., M.S., and Ph.D. degrees from Rensselaer Polytechnic Institute.

them, I learned both basic survival skills and substantive ideas for engaging students and adjusting the level and pace of my classes and, later, many other valuable lessons. These conversations with colleagues have educated me as a teacher and saved me from reinventing or rediscovering important aspects of pedagogy.

Aware of my debt to those who have willingly shared both their successes and challenges in the classroom with me and others, when I became director of the Perlman Center for Learning and Teaching (LTC) at Carleton, I invited my colleagues to explore the possibility of writing and sharing essays about our teaching lives. I was nervous as I waited, that afternoon in the spring of 2002, in the gathering area of the LTC. Would any faculty members drop by? I breathed a sigh of relief as a few colleagues joined me. Then, more came through the door. Soon our small area was filled with 30 colleagues, and we moved to a classroom to contemplate our venture.

This book is the tangible result of that enterprise, though so much more took place in the course of it than the writing and editing of the essays contained herein. By August 2002, 21 colleagues had prepared essays. In a weeklong workshop that followed, we critiqued each other's work and revised our own essays in response to feedback. Faculty in diverse disciplines discovered common interests. Others uncovered research supporting their own experiences.

> What began as individual metacognitive contemplations of teaching led to deep, meaningful, and sustained conversation about our lives as teachers.

What began as individual metacognitive contemplations of teaching led to deep, meaningful, and sustained conversation about our lives as teachers.

Engaging in conversation about teaching and learning issues is crucial for faculty at all stages of their careers. Faculty launching careers, shifting into a mid-career phase, and reflecting back on a full career in the classroom all bring their voices to this volume. A chemist discovers the power of spontaneity and flexibility in his attempts to replicate a magical, "aha!" moment in teaching. An anthropologist guides introductory students to an understanding of how we know what we know in anthropology through an ethnography project, while a scientist finds the answer to the question "Is This 'Real Science'?" in an inquiry-based curriculum. A professor shares insights into "Teaching and

Learning French without Meta-language, or Re-mapping the World." Essays on rigor in the classroom, civic engagement, and experiential learning abroad have all found their way into this collection. The result is not a patchwork quilt, but rather an introspective view of the teaching life of a faculty. A less visible thread results from the many conversations among the authors as the essays were developed. Our hope is that in some ways the essence of our talking about teaching is reflected in the text.

TEACHING IS LEARNABLE

Learning to teach well is an ongoing challenge. For many of us, our first ventures into teaching are predicated on the assumption that we can learn to be excellent teachers. This assumption is the foundation of programs designed to prepare students to teach and faculty development programs that are growing in number nationally. The research of Travis (1995), Boice (1996), and others validates the belief that teaching undergraduates is learnable. Books and articles on how to teach undergraduates appear on a regular basis, including comprehensive guides for new faculty (e.g., Eble, 1988; Gross Davis, 2001; McKeachie, 2001; Royse, 2001).

Over the past decade support for the development of teacher-scholars has increased exponentially, beginning with graduate students and postdoctoral fellows. Preparing Future Faculty (PFF) Programs, a shared vision of The Association of American Colleges and Universities and the Council of Graduate Schools, began in 1993 to expose graduate students to the multiple dimensions of faculty life (see http://www.preparing-faculty.org for an overview of this program and related publications). One of the major benefits reported by participants is the role of PFF in legitimizing conversations about teaching and learning issues (DeNeff, 2002). My hope is that this reflects a trend towards more teaching conversations at other institutions, like those we have captured in our collection.

Liberal arts colleges also have opportunities and obligations in preparing the next generation of faculty long before they start their first tenure-track position. A piece of DeNeff's research that resonates with me is this statement: "The overall mission of preparing the next generation of academics should not be viewed as falling to the nation's graduate schools alone." PFF programs are set up as clusters of doctoral-degree granting institutions and other institutions of higher education. PFF students often work with a mentor at a liberal arts college to the mutual benefit of the graduate student and the mentor. Their immersion in cutting edge research provides discipline-specific, intellectual companionship that faculty at smaller institutions are often unable to provide for each other with the same depth of understanding. Interactions with PFF students can energize faculty members' research and bring a fresh perspective to their teaching.

The value of discipline-specific collaborations among teacher/scholars at colleges and universities extends beyond graduate student-faculty member interactions. Trish Ferrett (see "Is This 'Real Science'?") reinvented her teaching and her scholarship as a result of collaborative work with a consortium of institutions working on systemic change in chemistry education. Her close ties with colleagues at Berkeley and other institutions have enriched her classroom and her professional life, as well as benefiting others.

TALKING ABOUT TEACHING

Who do or should graduate students and faculty talk with about teaching?

First, the question of discipline is worth considering. As mentioned above, there are times when only someone in your sub-discipline will fully appreciate and be able to offer insight into the complexities of teaching about molecular orbitals or the phenomenology of Husserl. Professional research societies have made huge strides in providing educational forums at national meetings, as well as publishing newsletters with educational information, and more recently, web-based resources. Several years ago a colleague at another institution and I set up a listserv for faculty teaching plant biology. It is wonderful to be able to almost instantaneously reach hundreds of fellow teachers with a question about presenting a difficult concept or trouble shooting a teaching laboratory. Virtual conversations about teaching have enriched my teaching and eased occasional feelings of isolation.

Visiting colleagues' classes, even in different disciplines, can enhance one's teaching repertoire. Much of what I know about creating an interactive learning environment for 100 students is the result of observing and conversing about classes taught by a colleague in the English Department. Students in my small discussion classes in biology started engaging each other in more substantive discussions about journal articles after I consulted with Roy Elveton in philosophy and visited his classroom.

A variation on this theme is to attend talks where others talk about their teaching. Sarah Deel points out how two such presentations changed the way she approached her own teaching in "Finding My Teaching Voice." One source of inspiration for Sarah was Carol Rutz, author of "Civic Engagement through Tragedy" in this volume.

Another approach to enhancing one's teaching is to invite a knowledgeable colleague to visit one's class. John Ramsay, an educational studies professor and then director of our LTC, responded to my panic-stricken call when I could not get students in one of my larger classes to interact with me. I had been happily teaching for over a decade and all of a sudden my questions were being met with blank stares and silence. After sitting through my class, my colleague gently pointed out that, most likely in desperation to get any type of response, I was tossing out dozens of questions without any indication as to whether they were rhetorical or required a verbal answer. During the next class, a few well-placed, clearly defined questions appeared on the board. The atmosphere in the class changed dramatically, and a potentially disastrous term was avoided.

Teaching with a colleague naturally leads to more conversation. At a small institution it is not always possible to establish research collaborations with colleagues, but teaching collaborations can fill a need to connect intellectually with other professors. First-term integrated experiences for students, taught by multiple faculty, are based on sound pedagogical reasoning and are of substantial benefit to entering students (Galotti et al. 1999). Faculty participants, myself included, have found tremendous satisfaction from such interactions with colleagues. In this volume, Clara Hardy in classics and Ruth Weiner in theater describe how they linked two courses and guided students through the production of a Greek tragedy.

Formalized programs for faculty—through centers for learning and teaching or other groups on campus—can provide excellent support for teachers. For a number of years I have facilitated a cross-disciplinary workshop for new faculty. This weeklong workshop occurs after the first term of teaching. Invariably at least one participant is dubious about what they can learn from watching someone teach in a completely different area or what that individual might have to offer them in terms of feedback. For example, I hear that teaching language is very different from teaching science. Yes, to some extent this is true, but evaluations at the end of the workshop confirm my own discovery that you can learn a great deal about teaching from someone in a different discipline. This lesson was reinforced in the creation of this collection of reflective essays on teaching. Mary Savina in geology and Scott Bierman in economics found common interest in ways to help students identify and develop skills that allow them to integrate their experience in their major in a coherent manner. The result of their conversations is the essay "Beyond 'Pizza with the Prof.' "

Formalized LTCs offer the opportunity to sustain conversations about teaching on campus, but success in engaging faculty varies among institutions (Singer, 2002). Research universities and liberal arts colleges face both shared and unique challenges in using such centers as a focus for faculty engagement in exploring teaching and learning.

Some of the challenges at research universities are reflected in the findings of the Reinvention Center at Stony Brook (2002) on the extent to which these institutions had incorporated the recommendations of the Boyer Commission (1998) for *Reinventing Undergraduate Education: A Blueprint for America's Research Universities*. Overall, universities are making substantial progress with many aspects of undergraduate education (e.g., student research, inquiry-based teaching, collaborative learning, integrated first-year programs, written and oral communication skills for students, and teaching assistant training). Almost all of the 90 universities have centers for learning and teaching—but very few faculty take advantage of them. While programs for graduate students are booming, learning and teaching centers are seeking creative ways to assist faculty. Researchers at the Stony Brook Reinvention Center attributed this, in part, to inconsistencies between faculty perceptions of the reward system for tenure and promotion and changes in policy reported by universities that add additional weight to teaching in evaluations.

Certainly the reward system at liberal arts colleges explicitly acknowledges excellence in teaching, and it is possible that our ability to talk with each other about teaching may rest solely upon this distinction. We are not research universities, and cross-disciplinary interactions may benefit from our smaller size as well. I think, however, that there is more to creating a culture where teaching and learning (not just the content of the curriculum) is an ongoing topic of discussion.

The benefits of talking about teaching seem rather straightforward, but what makes such conversations possible? Why did so many of my colleagues respond enthusiastically to a suggestion that we write essays about teaching, gather to talk about our writing, and help each other in this endeavor? Such questions are best addressed in the context of my institution, rather than through a comparative approach. Cultures, even among similar institutions, are idiosyncratic, but my hope is that the reader can find common threads and ideas.

I should preface my "what works" list by acknowledging that Carleton is not a utopia where each casual encounter leads to deep explorations of education. Nor do all faculty find the LTC and other formal teaching and learning forums to be fundamental to their success as teachers. On the other hand, those faculty who participate are not bored and looking for something to do. Heavy teaching loads and a sincere commitment to scholarship leave minimal time to talk with each other about teaching. Clearly, faculty value their colleagues' opinions. During the workshop phase of our project, colleagues commented on other essays and readily engaged each other in conversations about both content and presentation. A candid but supportive environment developed during this process.

One element of successful teaching discussions is trust and a sense of safety. Tenure and promotion are important; professors do not want to advertise that their current class is lacking luster or perhaps bordering on disaster. Ensuring confidentiality is an important step toward some productive conversation. Discovering that others have encountered similar situations may make it possible for faculty to have more open discussions, which then spill over into larger forums. Enthusiastically sharing a teaching experiment that worked well is as important as muddling through a near miss in class. Creating venues where faculty can share these success stories has been particularly effective. (Again, honesty compels me to note that this information, at least at Carleton, is often of even more interest to faculty when offered along with lunch.)

> Enthusiastically sharing a teaching experiment that worked well is as important as muddling through a near miss in class.

Reflections on Learning as Teachers is a means for us to share our successes and challenges in the classroom with a broader audience. As our project grew, a taxonomy emerged that takes advantage of persistent, irresistible themes: collaboration in teaching, the "life cycle" of a faculty member, engagement in the classroom, links between the ivory tower/liberal arts and the world outside college, and teaching traditions—including traditions in the making.

The contributors to this collection sincerely hope that our essays will resonate with or inspire others who are reflecting on the teaching life. Our explorations of the teaching life range from discovering our own teaching voices, to sustaining engagement as a teacher, to guiding students through old, new, and changing fields, and addressing how liberal arts education intersects with life beyond the campus walls. We hope that you will find, as we did, that these essays are a jumping off point for conversations with your own colleagues.

> Our explorations of the teaching life range from discovering our own teaching voices, to sustaining engagement as a teacher, to guiding students through old, new, and changing fields, and addressing how liberal arts education intersects with life beyond the campus walls.

Each of us becomes a teacher through our own circuitous path. Books, model teachers, honest students providing constructive feedback, workshops, and seminars can make all of us better teachers. What we should not overlook, however, is the wisdom of the faculty member down the hall or across campus. Go knock on a colleague's door. ■

REFERENCES

Boice, R. (1996). *First-order principles for college teachers: Ten basic ways to improve the teaching process.* Bolton: Anker Publishing Company, Inc.

Boyer Commission. (1998). *Reinventing undergraduate education: A blueprint for America's research universities.* From: http://naples.cc.sunysb.edu/Pres/boyer.nsf/

Boyer Commission on Educating Undergraduates in the Research University. (2002). *Reinventing undergraduate education: Three years after the Boyer report.* Stony Brook, NY: Stony Brook Reinvention Center.

DeNeff, A. L. (2002). *The preparing future faculty program: What difference does it make?* Washington, DC: American Association of Colleges and Universities.

Eble, K. E. (1988). *The craft of teaching* (2nd ed.) San Francisco: Jossey-Bass Publishers.

Elveton, R.O., Galotti, K.M., Komatsu, L.K., Rand, M.S., & Singer, S.R. (2000). Origins and mind: An integrated academic experience for new students. *Liberal Education*, 86, 32-39.

Gross Davis, B. (2001). *Tools for teaching.* San Francisco: Jossey-Bass Publishers.

McKeachie, W. J. (1999). *Teaching tips: Strategies, research, and theory for college and university teachers.* New York: Houghton Mifflin.

Royse, D. (2001). *Teaching tips for college and university instructors: A practical guide.* Needham Heights, MA: Allyn & Bacon.

Singer, S. R. (2002). Learning and teaching centers: Hubs of educational reform. In J. L. Narum and K. Conover (Eds.), *Building robust learning environments in undergraduate science, technology, engineering, and mathematics* (pp. 59-64). San Francisco: Jossey-Bass.

Travis, J. E. (1995). *Models for improving college teaching: A faculty resource.* Washington, DC: ASHE-ERIC Higher Education Report No. 6.

The Teaching Life

Teaching Journal / Learning Journal

Arjendu K. Pattanayak

S oon after I started teaching, I confirmed my inklings that teaching physics—the teaching, not just the physics—is very challenging. Like most of us, I have had little formal training in teaching and am always looking for ways to improve my teaching, including maintaining a journal. I was reasonably well prepared for this. I have maintained a personal journal since high school; sporadically, I sit with pencil and notebook to write to myself. I don't quite recall why I started this process of recorded introspection, but it is one habit I now value greatly. It seemed perfectly natural for it to spill over into my professional world.

Starting late in graduate school, I began a research journal and, about two years ago, a teaching journal. This journal is not exactly a collection of gemlike insights, of course. The best stuff emerges when I let go and express myself without worrying about the stupidity, pretentiousness, fallibility, or worth of my writing. As I've grown more used to the practice, I find that I can argue with myself in my journal. I value this process greatly.

> This journal is not exactly a collection of gemlike insights, of course. The best stuff emerges when I let go and express myself without worrying about the stupidity, pretentiousness, fallibility, or worth of my writing.

Perhaps the trickiest thing I've had to learn is to find time for this kind of writing. I fell into the habit of writing about teaching sometime after I had started teaching at Rice University in Houston, TX. I had been hired to revamp

ARJENDU K. PATTANAYAK, assistant professor of physics and astronomy, joined the Carleton College faculty in 2001. He earned his B.S. degree at St. Stephen's College (Delhi, India), a S.M. degree at Brown University, and a Ph.D. degree at the University of Texas, Austin.

their introductory physics class—a year-long marathon with about 200 bright but somewhat cranky and demanding students, most of them engineers in the making. Five faculty members, including the department chair and myself, were involved with various sections and aspects of the course over the year. My task was to innovate: to improve the teaching and the learning and eventually to make the course more popular. It was an interesting assignment for a first-time teacher. Most decisions about changes were made collectively; at the least, everything had to be carefully argued and defended, since any change was going to affect many. I learned to write my teaching ideas down frequently and to shape them into coherent arguments. That provided the motivation.

At that time, my teaching schedule allowed me to fly to San Jose, CA (where my wife was working), for a long weekend every other week or so. All that time I spent at the airport and in flight turned out to be the perfect opportunity for writing. Without the distractions of people, e-mail, or phone calls, I would dive into my journals and focus, trying to capture and link the disconnected thoughts running through my mind. Since realizing the benefits of the practice, I have tried hard to keep it up, although there have always been gaps of varying lengths.

> I should be like an engineer when it comes to teaching—
> or a cook, rather. Borrow anything and everything that's
> useful—share tricks, techniques and recipes with other
> cooks. Anything that works.

Entries in my teaching journal are a mixed bag, and, compared to my research journal, my ego is a lot more present in them. For example, consider the notes I made after reading student course evaluations—either at mid-term or term-end. It probably goes without saying that those moments are when my teaching self is most vulnerable. Somehow, I've learned to breathe through that state to write short summaries about what the students saw in the course and in me. Revisiting those notes at a distance is an interesting exercise in itself. Moreover, I've found that I can use these notes to identify changes when I am in my planning phase for the same class next time. That's one way in which my journal has proven a pretty valuable tool for monitoring and changing my teaching.

> Questions to ask for every course: intent, form, content. The intent—particularly figuring out the point of a course and where the students stand in relationship to this point—seems to be the primary problem. And then the details of content and form.

Sometimes my journal serves as a workbook, with short synopses of ideas for classes and extremely useful notes from teaching workshops or school-wide teaching seminars. Once I asked my teaching assistants about their favorite classes and teachers and wrote down their responses. There also are notes from the painful weekend when I was scrambling to make plans for my colleagues to cover for me so that I could get to my father's side as he lay on what turned out to be his deathbed. Other entries in my journal include paragraph-long snapshots of my teaching state of mind—after a good class, a not-so-great class, after a particularly revelatory grading session, after an unusual encounter with a student, after having read a provocative article or note about teaching.

By the time I actually read these entries, most of these passing thoughts and feelings have long faded from my memory. However, I find that while some thoughts prove trite or erroneous on re-examination, sometimes I have stumbled across a useful insight or a clue to a new approach. Mulling over these ideas leads to my favorite writing in my journal, when I'm distilling: looking back with the help of my notes at a week, a term, and attempting to aphoristically capture whatever new thing I thought I had glimpsed about the art and science of teaching. I talk to myself in these, reminding myself of what I have learned. The excerpts scattered around this essay are examples of these distillations—still-raw teaching moonshine, with a lot of the pleasure being in the creation.

> We shouldn't be surprised when students focus on grades and how we grade. Grades and points serve as our currency in our negotiations with our students. We can hold them in reserve as reward at the completion of the course, or sprinkle them like bread crumbs through the forest of the term to show them the paths we'd like them to follow, help them prioritize

> *their time, for example. But not everyone is motivated by grades—that's the good part. Remember that.*

Without this external record of my teaching thoughts, I would definitely be less aware of the changes in my teaching persona. More to the point, I believe that this evolution is enhanced *because* of the external record. I see this as a variation of what happens when I finally get down to writing one of my physics research articles: I clarify a lot for myself during the process of spelling my ideas out on paper, sometimes discovering what yet needs to be done to make a particular argument or conclusion more compelling. As a result, I've begun to try to get to the writing stage well before the project feels complete. Also, the completed written record often becomes the starting point for the next bit of research, providing a much better foundation than the raw material behind the paper.

Similarly, even without my teaching journal, I would probably have come to my present conclusions about, say, the paramount importance of clarifying course objectives (for myself, not necessarily for sharing with students) before I do any planning for the course or the best way to construct a good exam problem. However, it has certainly helped speed things up to write down the most compelling statements I can construct on these issues and then later to find my own handwriting reminding me what I thought about it a few months before.

> *Scaffolding: Good problems have large gaps between the beginning and the end—the facts provided and the question posed. Bridge the gap with simpler leading questions, then go back and knock big enough gaps in the structure. The goal is to stretch students across the gaps in their knowledge. But not so much that they fall in. I wish I could figure out a scheme where I could let them buy a clue from me if they feel too stretched or overwhelmed by the questions.*

It is quite obvious that I have a strong introspective streak and that this is one reason why journaling helps me. This reflective writing practice has been valuable in other ways as well and has changed how I respond, for example, when faced with reports or proposals. As such, I've begun to consider journaling as a teaching/learning technique for almost any new learning experience. In particular, it is natural that I should try to find ways to transfer this impulse to write to my students. I can imagine that it is difficult to reconcile what I've said above about introspection and about journaling with the notions of "cold hard facts" and "sixth-decimal-place accuracy" usually associated with physics. However, I've converged to the following theory about different learning techniques and pedagogical objectives: We can learn facts effectively by reading or listening. However, to learn skills—for example, problem-solving skills—we must practice. Neither reading nor listening helps us in improving our conceptual map

> What are the fundamental elements of a physics education? Of a liberal arts physics education? Of a liberal arts physics education at Carleton? Is there a consensus? Should there be a consensus? And if such a consensus exists, wouldn't it be a shifting, changing one as the years pass? As our knowledge about the material universe grows, clearly knowledge is distilled, new intellectual paths slashed through the growing thickets of facts. At this point in physics, synthesis is at least as important as knowledge production. And the curriculum is an obvious point at which to address this project.

of ideas, particularly in gaining an overview or fresh insights. For this we must participate in discussions, defending our ideas and probing those of others.

It seems to me that journaling helps in creating and owning knowledge—and sooner or later, all of us have to go through this process. Once in a while, this works easily: There is no need for elaborate techniques and we learn rapidly, internalizing knowledge on the fly. While there are undoubtedly times in our lives when we move swiftly with sure-footed instinct, elsewhere we benefit from caution and reflective development. In journaling, we are recording thoughts in a rawer, fresher form than in writing papers or solving problems. Yet the experience is far removed from lecture notes; there is already a considerable amount of processing going on. This is why it is a valuable method in helping us create and own new material. In fact, the more the material stretches us, the more valuable a journal becomes.

That is certainly how it seems to work in my research journal. This journal isn't my research log or a notebook filled with careful calculations. Sometimes there's a listing of present or potential research projects or conversations, followed by doodles about thematic links. For the kind of speculative and abstract theoretical physics work I do, this doodling sometimes yields unexpected insights about directions. In contrast to the "real work" of my papers that focuses on the concrete details, the journal is about my deep map of my research

> How do we reduce the distance between Newton and the 21st century? When we teach, we deepen our field. We give it strength at its core, distilling accumulated knowledge to fundamental wisdom. Else we'd never catch up—our students would never catch up with our incredibly rapidly growing knowledge base. Prioritize. Distill.

world, including how I think I could add to it—or occasionally subtract from it—by integrating seemingly different results. As such, it proved to be a wonderful resource when I was writing my "research statement" for job applications not too long ago and also helped me get started with a recent proposal for research funds. While this is not the kind of journaling I expect from students, it encourages me to believe that I should introduce some variation of this in my classes, if only to seed the habit for the future.

> Flying to a conference: How do I reconcile moving between immersion in my teaching world of younger, malleable, minds with the other world of experts and professional physicists? It seems to take a different mindset, almost a different self. There is an inherent difference between the speed of knowledge transfer and acquisition when we are in a classroom and when we do research. Still, clarity and rigor at all times—make lectures more like research talks and research talks more like lectures and so on. Integrating

> research and teaching. How can I make learning project
> based/discovery based? Search, reach into the ideas and
> construct them—ownership of ideas, not consumption.

There are some definite challenges in implementing this, however. Some of it goes beyond the usual issues of using writing itself in science classes; journaling feels inherently more problematic. For example, when I first thought of this essay, I managed to persuade myself that I could embed examples from my journals within it. As I write, sharing bits from my journal is a source of much greater anxiety than anticipated. This may be attributed to my self-image as a writer. However, I believe I am also experiencing the inherent tension between the freedom to be vulnerable in journal writing and the value of getting feedback from sharing this writing. This is something I certainly need to remember when considering how to get students to write journals freely but yet for a grade. Clearly, I cannot just ask students to maintain journals. I have to provide a structure to seed the habit and it is probably better to start with short, frequent writing.

> Teaching is performance. The larger the class, the more it
> feels like performance—you have to be "on" during the
> classes and it is exhausting to maintain this over extended
> periods of time. I see why it is tempting to lapse into fully
> scripted readings—transcriptions from class notes to
> blackboard to student notebooks. Improvisation is hard!
> I feel like my best classes and seminars contain
> improvisations on top of tightly written scripts. I am going
> to have to deal with this element of performance as part of
> my life from now on.

I know that technology has helped the current generation of learners be particularly facile and quick at short writing—via e-mail, message boards, chat rooms, text messaging, web-logs. So I am trying to take advantage of this to introduce writing into my classes, building towards more reflective journaling. I am coming to the conclusion that journaling in physics is likely to prove most effective at the extremes, by which I mean that I intend to use the following strategy.

> About my seminar class: Why improvise? Because I want you to learn how to talk about physics publicly—defend these strange ideas, engage intensely. For you, every class is improvisation. So, when you see me construct arguments on the fly, fumble, speak unscripted—does this encourage you to speak up? Or does it make matters worse? Irrespective, to truly engage with the material and the class, prepare well.

First, given my growing conviction that journaling is of most value where knowledge is being constructed rather than received, it seems natural to ask my research students to maintain a daily record and then to look back and write about that log weekly.

At the other extreme in scientific sophistication, I am going to push further forward with writing in my classes for non-scientists. Here I am trying to exploit the possible familiarity of writing as a tool—or perhaps only avoiding the fear of mathematics and calculations—to help introduce these students to the subtle ideas and complex intellectual puzzles of science.

I am trying to use the novelty and challenges of the material to get scientists more comfortable with writing and, on the flip side, to get non-science students to appreciate science through a possibly familiar technique. No matter how these efforts pan out, I shall probably learn something about my students, about writing, and about how learning and knowledge construction works in physics. What is even more likely is that I shall learn what I do through writing about these things in my teaching/learning journal. ■

Finding My Teaching Voice

Sarah E. Deel

PROLOGUE: TEACHING FROM SCRATCH

When I began teaching during my first term in graduate school, all I knew about teaching came from watching my own teachers over the 16 years I'd spent in school. Unsure where else to start, I began with the most basic question: How do I teach? I was not sure how loud to talk, how long to talk, or what to say. I was told "good research makes you a good teacher." I pondered this repeatedly as I taught my first 72 students in three lab sections of Human Anatomy and Physiology (a course I'd never taken as an undergrad) and began my research (involving clams). The connection seemed tenuous to me.

I was given little guidance about teaching during graduate school. I got the sense that it didn't matter much; it was how you paid your bills while you were conducting research. I arrived at graduate school from a small, liberal arts college where teaching was given a strong

> I was given little guidance about teaching during graduate school. I got the sense that it didn't matter much; it was how you paid your bills while you were conducting research.

emphasis, and I was unable to let go of the idea that my teaching mattered. I ended up reading what I could find about teaching and collecting hints from anyone who would share them. I learned a lot about techniques and strategies for effective teaching. I used the ones that made sense to me and became a competent teacher. I communicated information about biology to my students reasonably well, and they learned more biology than they would have alone.

SARAH E. DEEL, adjunct instructor in biology, joined the Carleton College faculty in 1996. She earned her B.A. degree at Grinnell College and her M.S. degree at Oregon State University.

QUESTIONING

As I gained experience and improved my teaching, I realized that I was still not very comfortable in the classroom. I was nervous about teaching and had a lot of doubt about whether or not I was doing the best job I could. I was in charge in my classroom but wasn't certain I belonged there. I started asking more sophisticated questions revolving around my direct interactions with students. The articles I was reading didn't seem to cover the less tangible aspects of teaching, like: What tone should I take with my students? And: How do I convince my students to really buy into all those creative classroom activities I'm using? Having students stand up and act out the process of DNA replication is all very well and good but somehow less effective if they're rolling their eyes and acting bored.

I had to go back and look at my experience in college: How did the good professors interact with students? Some of the well-liked profs were comedians; class was lively and amusing. My notes from class were full of anecdotal marginalia—funny quotes I couldn't resist writing down. (Once when our labs were going particularly poorly, a professor quipped "Well, dying cells don't divide, and dead cells divide damn slowly." That was high humor in a biology lecture.) Some popular professors were young, laid-back, and easy to relate to. They could be found at the student union and were often still on campus during student-active hours (11 p.m.–2 a.m.). Because the students liked these charismatic professors, they were attentive and eager to be engaged in their classes.

So, it seemed like a good goal to be a popular professor. But this brought up a less comfortable question: How do I create a professional relationship with my students? Can I maintain authority and treat students fairly while striving for them to like me? Where should the boundaries be? If I become my students' buddy, how can I assess them properly (i.e., give them low grades when appropriate) without compromising our relationship?

Also, most of the popular professors I knew were men; I was a little concerned, as a young woman, about becoming too familiar with my students and losing authority in the classroom. Treating students fairly was a key component of this professional relationship I wanted to cultivate and stemmed from some of my experiences in college. I hadn't liked it when professors gave last-minute extensions to the whole class, particularly if I had already spent time on the assignment and pushed back my other coursework to finish. It seemed to reward students who were less prepared. I made it a goal to treat all my students the same, so no one had an unfair advantage in the course. But I wasn't sure how to do this and maintain the easy-going attitude I was imagining for myself.

FORMULATING ANSWERS

I struggled with these questions and goals for several years; I still revisit some of them. For a long time, I tried to emulate the popular professors, but I was eventually forced to acknowledge that I am neither comic nor laid-back. My attempts at humor garnered me blank looks or an avoidance of eye contact. I couldn't even use canned jokes; the timing was all wrong. People who know me can tell you I have even less of a chance at coming across as relaxed. I am also not a man; I will never have the deep, booming lecture voice I admire. In truth, who I am is rather earnest, intense, and detail-oriented, with just a faint hint of dry humor that goes unacknowledged by my students. When I perceived this chasm between popular teachers and myself, I sighed deeply and resigned myself to it.

That brought me back around to the question of how to engage my students: How could I get them past their reticence and embarrassment so they could learn, especially if I was not charming them into it?

I muddled about until I attended a campus seminar at Carleton given by Carol Rutz (1999). She had interviewed teachers of writing about how they responded to students' assignments. The teachers had very different styles of response; the person sitting next to me during the seminar actually snorted in disgust and shook her head as Rutz described how one of the teachers had a set of formulaic responses for certain errors, even referring students to specific pages of a grammar handbook. I winced slightly at her snort, since I had been thinking that this seemed quite a reasonable option to me. (I have often longed for a rubber stamp which reads "The word 'data' is always plural.") Different writing teachers focused on different aspects of their students' writing (grammar, structure, flow, or content), made different types of comments, and had different priorities generally.

I remember being interested to find out which evaluation techniques were the most effective—and being amazed to find that no such judgment was forthcoming. Rutz's assessment showed that the different response strategies were equally effective. The commonality she noted among all these teachers was this: They explained their strategies to their students. The context of the particular classroom was very important; since the students in each class understood their teacher's philosophy and evaluation style, they were able to learn from the teacher's responses to their writing.

I took two important lessons from this seminar. First, at a practical level, I finally had some help with the question: How do I get students to buy into my classroom activities? In most cases, giving them a brief pedagogical explanation seems to be sufficient. If I can justify to my students that getting up and acting out a process will help them understand it or explain that using a different teaching method will help students with different learning styles, they seem to be more amenable to exploring these activities. I'll often admit to them that what they will be doing is a little silly, so they're prepared for it. They seem more willing to let go of their embarrassment if I remind them that the whole point is to help their understanding of the material.

Second, at a more abstract level, I embraced the idea that there are many ways to be an effective teacher. This realization has been a key turning point in how I see other teachers and how I see myself as a teacher. I'm not sure why it wasn't self-evident to me. Certainly it wasn't something I was learning from reading articles about teaching. It seems like most authors were so intent on supporting their particular theses that they didn't remind readers that there are other, equally effective ways to teach.

> I hadn't considered that certain qualities which described me (like my earnestness or attention to detail) could be a legitimate part of my teaching voice.

In fact, for a long time, I didn't read anything about the relationship of individual teachers to their craft or even think of teaching as a craft. This changed when Parker Palmer visited Carleton in 2000 and gave several seminars. In preparation for his visit, I read one of his books (Palmer, 1998). Here I found guidance I needed and a different way to think about teaching. One of Palmer's major theses is the idea that the more you bring yourself to your teaching, the better teacher you will be. I realized finally that becoming a good teacher was more than just adopting a set of techniques and strategies. I should not have been surprised. Although I was using good techniques and strategies, I wasn't as comfortable in the classroom as I wanted to be. I had tried adopting the teaching styles of the good teachers I remembered, and it had not been an improvement, for me or the students.

I hadn't considered that certain qualities which described me (like my earnestness or attention to detail) could be a legitimate part of my teaching voice. Moreover, I could not construct my teaching voice from other people's qualities, no matter how much I admired them. My encounter with Parker's ideas freed me to try to become a teacher true to my own qualities of self.

TEACHING AS MYSELF

I have been fascinated by this process of figuring out who I am as a teacher. Currently, I would use the terms "approachable," "detail-oriented," "earnest," "enthusiastic," and "uncool" to describe myself as a teacher. That is a rather uncool characterization, but I think it suits me. Being approachable is very important to me because of the subject matter I teach. Although many of my introductory biology students arrive in class feeling confident and well-prepared, I also have students who feel completely daunted by being in a science course. I would like to think at least I am accessible to the students, even if the subject matter is not, initially. Being detail-oriented makes it imperative for me to be well-prepared for my classes; I'm not comfortable otherwise. All my advance preparations have a real benefit for my relationship with my students: Because I am relaxed and comfortable answering their questions, the students get the sense that I know what I'm talking about, and this increases their level of respect for me. Being earnest and enthusiastic helps me to engage the students; if I am not embarrassed by getting genuinely excited about the biology, maybe they will be less inclined to back away from it. I enjoy the freedom that acknowledging my uncool qualities carries with it; I don't spend time or energy trying to be someone I'm not.

As I express more of my individuality in the classroom, I am finding it somehow easier to see my students as individuals.[1] This has helped me reconsider my definition of "fairness." The more I understand of my students, the less important it is to me that I treat them identically. They don't enter my classroom with identical backgrounds, and they won't leave it with identical understanding, no matter what I do. In my individual interactions with students, I focus more on improving their understanding (from whatever their starting point is), and I spend less time worrying if I've made the same particular statement to all the students in the class.

This change in my idea of what is fair was a surprise to me. I was teaching a lab course with a first-year teacher, and we were planning oral final exams for the course. Oral exams are challenging to assess completely equally, but they are an easy way to find out how much a student knows. The professor I was working with was very concerned about assigning points and giving consistent marks for similar responses. As we discussed the exam, I was surprised to find myself relatively unconcerned about the minutiae of the points involved for a particular type of response. This was a definite shift for me from previous courses, and I was briefly concerned that I was becoming apathetic. I think, however, that I had gained confidence in my ability to know when a student was demonstrating understanding. I also was less afraid of letting my knowledge of a student affect how I assessed that student.

Instead of assessing students equally, in some circumstances I have shifted toward assessing students individually.[2] I think this is related to the goals I have for my students. Some goals are easily stated and assessable. Can you dispense 0.1 ml of water using this mechanical pipettor? Can you explain how proteins are made from a gene? I still assess my students equally in these arenas.

It is the more abstract goals I have for my students that I assess more individually. These abstract goals are common in the context of a liberal arts education. Can you use critical thinking skills and creativity to solve this problem? Can you design an experiment or study to get at this issue? Different students are going to express their answers to these types of questions in a very personal manner, and assessing them equally by a common rubric is very difficult. It suddenly becomes relevant to me who that person answering the question really is.

In considering my students as individuals, I am again faced with the issue of maintaining boundaries. I have found that the boundary lines I draw now have a firm footing in mutual respect between the students and me. I think because I share my true self with them in class, they believe that I am genuinely trying to help them learn and respect me for that, even if some of my teaching methods seem odd to them. I am no longer tempted to blur the boundaries between us, because I appreciate that embracing that sort of popularity is not the right way for me to be a good teacher. In fact, I am having to reevaluate my definition of "popular" as I remember other good teachers in college. These were the professors spoken of with respect in the library rather than those praised effusively at the bar. Given the variety of learning styles among students learning at any college, it seems only fitting that professors with a variety of teaching styles are teaching.

ON FROM HERE

In forging connections between my personality and my teaching style, I have become comfortable in the classroom and comfortable dealing with students. Because I am more relaxed about interacting with students, my communication with them seems to go more smoothly. I have more energy to figure out how to teach the peculiarities of my subject; I can develop a larger repertoire of techniques and activities to use in class. I will always be thinking about how to be a better teacher, but this acceptance of my teaching voice as an extension of myself is freeing.

> Given the variety of learning styles among students learning at any college, it seems only fitting that professors with a variety of teaching styles are teaching.

It is encouraging to me that this way of looking at teaching is flexible, and not static. As I grow and change, my teaching voice will change, too. I will not spend my teaching life striving to be the one perfect teacher; I know that there are many ways to be a good teacher, and I will enjoy the freedom to explore them as I choose. ▪

ENDNOTES

[1] For more on teaching students as individuals, see the essay by Tisdale in this volume.

[2] For additional discussion about assessing students, see the essay by Galotti in this volume.

REFERENCES

Palmer, P. J. (1998). *The courage to teach: Exploring the inner landscape of a teacher's life* (1st ed.). San Francisco: Jossey-Bass.

Rutz, C. (1999, October 20). *What does my teacher want me to do? A response-based investigation of the teacher-student relationship in the writing classroom.* Presentation to the Perlman Center for Learning and Teaching, Carleton College.

Relearning How to Teach

Kevin Pettit

The questions "What do you teach?" and "Why do you teach?" seem simple enough at first. For me, however, they are each rather difficult questions. To understand the reasons for my difficulty and to grasp how my experience has influenced my thoughts on the effects of teaching, I'll have to tell you about my background.

I started teaching physics at Carleton College, my alma mater, in the fall of 1997. I loved it and think I did it well. One of the things that helped me do well was encouraging the students to focus on the fundamentals. That's what physics is—the study and science of universal fundamentals.

After starting on my second year of teaching, everything changed. On October 27, 1998, the car I was riding in was struck by a truck that had run a red light. My wife was driving the car, my son was seated in his car seat in the middle of the back seat, and I was in the passenger seat. The truck hit our car exactly where I was sitting.

My son wasn't physically hurt, and my wife suffered a broken rib and a punctured lung. I broke six ribs, fractured my pelvis, lacerated my liver and spleen, and broke my right collarbone. I wish that all my injuries had been so minor.

> The car I was riding in was struck by a truck that had run a red light.... I broke six ribs, fractured my pelvis, lacerated my liver and spleen, and broke my right collarbone. I wish that all my injuries had been so minor.

KEVIN PETTIT, assistant professor of physics, joined the Carleton College faculty in 1997. He earned his B.A. degree at Carleton College and his M.A. and Ph.D. degrees at University of Illinois at Urbana-Champaign.

As a result of sitting exactly where a truck traveling at over 62.5 mph in a 40 mph zone hit our car, I was given a severe traumatic brain injury (TBI). The rapid change of momentum that my body underwent caused a diffuse closed head injury. Just as an egg sitting in a jar of water that is slid across the kitchen counter and stopped suddenly accelerates and hits the inside of the jar, the rapid change of velocity of my head caused my brain to crash into the inside of my skull and shear against the supporting structures that hold the brain in place. The swelling of my brain that resulted from the shearing gave me a severe diffuse TBI and put me into a coma for 11 days.[1]

I'm very thankful that it was me who sustained such severe injuries, not my son or wife. I believe that my character was well suited for this. In recovering from my injuries, I was forced to focus on the fundamentals of living. For example, it wasn't until two months after my accident that my sister, who is the age of my students, could teach me how to use a spoon. Before that, she had to feed me like a baby. I also had to learn how to walk again.

My recovery has gone well. I can now speak. I no longer need a wheelchair or a cane. I think that one of the reasons for my excellent recovery was that I was (and am still) good at focusing on the essentials and my love for learning.

Even though my recovery has gone so extraordinarily well, I still have several difficulties. I have *clonus* in my right calf muscle—an involuntary twitching of my calf muscle in my right leg when it is in a certain position. I have a difficult time with my coordination and thus can't run. I can't sing as rapidly as I used to and I have a difficulty in speaking that is called *disfluency*. In addition, my speed of neural processing is much slower than it used to be. I see it this way: I used to be a 650 MHz Intel Pentium computer, whereas because of the accident I am now a 66 MHz Intel 486 computer.

But my main problem is with my memory. I have a very difficult time remembering things that happened only one day ago. I score around the 3rd percentile in the country on tests of my short-term memory. In medical-speak, my short-term memory is termed "moderately impaired." To me, that means that the RAM in my head went from 128 megabytes to 4 megabytes.

In one of the hospitals I was in, as part of my cognitive therapy, I was asked to give a lecture. Preparing for the lecture wasn't very difficult; I could remember quite well the physics that I learned years before my accident as an undergraduate at Carleton College and at graduate school. But I had real difficulties with my short-term memory. These difficulties are a result of *anterograde amnesia*. Back then I could still work with quantum mechanical wave functions, but I had difficulty completing sentences. The problem was that I'd forget what I was talking about before I'd get my thought out. Yet, since I could write down every step of a derivation, I wouldn't forget what I was proving.

After a half a year as an inpatient in two hospitals, two and a half years as an outpatient at a third hospital, and two years of teaching as a teaching assistant at the University of Colorado in Boulder, I returned to Carleton to try to restart my teaching career. However, considering that I receive from insurance 60 percent of my salary for doing nothing (which is all that I used to be able to do), you might wonder why I choose to teach again. For about two years after my injury, I would occasionally wonder the same thing.

About three years ago, almost nothing brought me happiness. I couldn't work. My therapies were difficult. It was demanding and frustrating to learn to speak again. It was even harder to learn to walk. I had to be taught how to cross roads safely, just like my son who was two and half years old. I had a very poor self-image and had a difficult time seeing a good reason to continue using up the Earth's resources. I decided that what made me happy was teaching.

Teaching—a way of helping the students and professor climb toward a heightened understanding—is a very pleasing thing for me to do. Sometimes it can be uncomfortable for the students (or for their teacher), but learning—gaining knowledge and understanding—is one of the few things in life that is always good.

In this last year, I've become happier and I now value myself more. When I see the "ah-ha" look on my students' faces in class or lab or when their self-confidence and their knowledge of their own limitations evidences a firm understanding of a subject that they value, I know that I've helped my students. I get a positive self-image and validation when I help others understand things more fully and when I help them enjoy the learning process. It gives me the feeling that even though my brain is like an out-of-date 486 computer, I still am a good, valuable person. It is because I feel that I bring happiness and understanding to others (and also because I value my influence on my son) that I choose to live.

Okay, that's a rather long winded answer to the question "Why do I teach?" Next I need to answer the question "What do I teach?" The easy answer is that I teach physics. But, the actual answer is much more complex.

I think that when we teach, we are helping students construct specific neural patterns in their brains. I do this by giving my students texts, laboratory exercises, homework, and tests that help them to organize the electrical impulses and chemical elements of their neurons in a very specific pattern in their brain. That is the one common thing that all professors at every institution do: We help our students develop specific fixed neural patterns in their brains. However, some professors at some schools do more than just deliver content and help their students form specific neural patterns: They help their students construct neural pathways specifically designed to help the students construct new neural pathways again, now by themselves.

An image that I find helpful is of a house. We teach our students and help them construct beautiful houses in their heads. Like a drawing plan of a house, we teach them the content of our discipline. By studying different subjects, our students construct different rooms of a house and learn to construct complete and well-furnished abodes.

However, teaching is much more complex than that, and, teaching at a liberal arts college, I am asked to do much more than that. Professors can help students learn architecture and the process of fine carpentry. It is not enough for us to simply help them build a specific pattern; we also have to teach them how to fashion. It is not enough to teach a particular subject. We must help them learn how to learn.

An image I have is of an art teacher. Art teachers don't paint for their students and expect their students to mimic them. Art teachers help their students learn how to express themselves with paint. Similarly, as a collection of faculty and individually as teachers, we don't ask our students to mimic our understandings. We should help them learn how to learn. Not everything to be taught or learned is a subject or a concept; we should remember to also teach them the process of learning.

I think that struggling to learn has made me a better teacher. It has helped me stay sensitive to the challenges my students are experiencing—particularly my students with disabilities and those who are having difficulty in my classes. Having undergone similar challenges so recently, I can share the techniques that have helped me learn more easily.

I believe that this is the reason that the college encourages professors to do research: The struggle to learn makes their teaching better. We each may learn well by different methods—close reading, analytical thinking, or expressive and clear writing—but, in the end, we are good teachers because we remain good learners. We can explain to our students what we find works for us. We can help them become better architects who can fabricate and design complex, beautiful, and purposeful neural patterns in their brain.

> This is the reason that the college encourages professors to do research: The struggle to learn makes their teaching better. We each may learn well by different methods—close reading, analytical thinking, or expressive and clear writing—but, in the end, we are good teachers because we remain good learners.

Just as research keeps us always learning, my brain injury has forced me to relearn much. Learning so much again while having an awareness of the possibility that someday I might possibly teach others, I was quite conscious of my re-education. I was re-learning how to learn. Having done so quite recently, I think that I use this experience to help my teaching. I share with my students in my introductory classes simple tips. For example, after reading a chapter of their textbook, I tell them to write a summary of the chapter, then skim through the chapter again and check to see that they remembered and included all of the key points in their summary. I also encourage active reading, a very useful technique that I was taught as part of my cognitive therapy (Pauk, 1997). Simple things that I learned while recovering from my brain injury are a tremendous help for students.

After waking from my coma, my short-term memory was very drastically affected. For about 15 days, I could remember nothing from second to second. I had a very severe case of *anterograde amnesia*. After a while, my short-term memory got a little better. I could still remember everything that I had learned years before my injury. If asked I could probably work with Schrödinger's wave equations. However, I couldn't tell you what activity I had done an hour ago or what I had for dinner just one night before.

As I slowly recovered, the nature of my understanding changed. When presented with a picture, we all notice particular things about the picture—the subject, the colors, the paints used in the painting, or possibly the perspective. In a similar way, as I recovered the things that I was aware of and the things that concerned me changed.

In addition to forcing me to answer the questions "What do I teach" and "Why do I teach it," my injuries and recovery were also a rather forceful introduction to an understanding of metacognition. As I understand it, metacognition is thinking about thinking. It is an evaluation of the modes of thought, their usefulness and weaknesses, and consideration of thinking and the effect of beliefs themselves. (In a way, this book represents metacognitive reflections on the teaching process.) Because of my injuries, I have become acquainted with the concept of metacognition because my thinking was so changed by my injuries. During my recovery, I became aware of this change.

One way that my thinking has changed is my ability to conceive of the severity of my injuries. This has a technical term of *anosognosia,* an organically caused unawareness of illness. It is the inability of the brain to conceive of changes it or another major body part or function has undergone. Anosognosia commonly occurs in people who suffer from schizophrenia and people who have had strokes or any type of TBI. Some brain-damaged patients are entirely unaware of the existence or severity of their deficits, even when they are easily noticed by others. I, too, was unable to comprehend the severity of my injuries for a while. My accident happened in October 1998. At the end of that year, about two months after my coma, I was still planning to go back and teach during the winter term that began in early January of 1999!

I am now aware of the shifting of my consciousness. I know that I had anosognosia and may still have it. This is a rather dramatic change in my thinking during the process of my recovery. Now, I am able to think about how I see myself and the effect my thinking has.

Similar and related to this ability to see myself more accurately is my awareness of the effects my own thinking has on me. My injuries forced on me a heightened awareness of my own cognition and an appreciation of how my thinking affects my own thoughts. Now I have a metacognitive understanding of my own thoughts.

This metacognition has helped me with my teaching. My awareness of how I used to think and the usefulness and limitations of my own thinking and attitudes has heightened my awareness of the use and limitations of different models of the atom. I teach an introductory class for sophomores on atomic and nuclear physics. I have chosen to have the class focus on the historical development of the concept of the atom. I start out with the Greeks, the four elements they believed in, and the Greeks' conception of the atom first developed by Democritus, jump to Millikan's proof that quantified electric charge in atoms exists, then progress slowly to Niels Bohr's planetary model of the atom. We then slowly advance to the understanding of the inability of humans to picture the atom in three dimensions. We learn the usefulness and limitations of different models of the atom and develop a metacognitive understanding of the atom. I hope and believe that my awareness of the use and functioning of models—made more sensitive by my experiences with a TBI—helps all of the students, whether they major in physics or not.

This understanding of the functioning of models is an important realization for all scientists, since that is what we commonly do in our work—create a picture in our mind's eye of the effect that we're studying. It is also an understanding that few students enter an introductory class with. They believe that only one way of conceiving and only one picture is "right." I hope that when they leave their undergraduate studies and possibly become practicing scientists, they will carry with them a metacognitive understanding of the power, limitations, and usefulness of models we use to picture reality.

> Although my injuries very nearly killed me and the consequent recovery was the hardest thing I've ever dealt with, I think that they have helped me teach better. I have had to relearn how to learn ...

Although my injuries very nearly killed me and the consequent recovery was the hardest thing I've ever dealt with, I think that they have helped me teach better. I have had to relearn how to learn, so I pass to my students what for me were recent discoveries. I am thankful and hope that others can learn from my experience as I have. ■

ENDNOTES

[1] Although many might consider my experiences extraordinary, they are not. While my injuries were severe and are not very common, there is only a loose correlation between the severity of the initial diagnosis of a TBI and the eventual outcome. According to the Center for Disease Control, traumatic brain injuries occur to 1.5 million people every year and about 2% of the population of the United States currently live with disabilities resulting from a TBI. See "Traumatic Brain Injury from the Injury Fact Book" published by the Centers for Disease Control and Prevention. This publication can be obtained from the CDC at http://www.cdc.gov

REFERENCES

Pauk, W. (1997). *How to study in college.* Boston: Houghton Mifflin.

Prigatano, G. P., & Schacter, D. L. (1991). *Awareness of deficit after brain injury: Clinical and theoretical issues.* New York: Oxford University Press.

Staying Focused on What Matters: A Vision of Teaching at Midlife

Louis E. Newman

Sometimes our most telling insights dawn on us when we least expect them. My most significant experience of this sort occurred a few years ago during a seminar I was teaching to 15 very bright, particularly delightful Carleton students. This was their first term of college—they were incredibly eager and unusually engaged with one another. The subject—"Faith, Hope, and Love: Religious Responses to Suffering"—was one I had never taught before, so I came to the course fresh and open to going wherever this material might lead us. And because I was also the academic advisor to these first-year students, we very quickly developed unusually strong relationships.

About midway through the course I decided it was time for a social event outside of class, a chance to eat and play and just "hang out" together. We met in the student union, I provided the subs for dinner, and we talked about school and families and life,

> With several decades of life experience behind me, this is the time to distill the lessons I've learned, to pay attention to the patterns that I see unfolding in my life, and to seek some sense of wholeness.

much as I do with friends. Conversation flowed, my rapport with the students was great, I was "in my element." How wonderful, I thought, to be so connected to these kids. I was feeling like a young prof, really "cool."

After dinner, we moved upstairs to play some games. That's when I made my fatal mistake. Confident that I could be one of the gang, I challenged

LOUIS E. NEWMAN, the John M. and Elizabeth W. Musser Professor of Religious Studies and director of Judaic studies, joined the Carleton College faculty in 1983. He earned his B.A. and M.A. degrees at the University of Minnesota and his Ph.D. at Brown University.

one of the students to a game of ping-pong, something I was once fairly good at. With the first volley, though, I knew I was in trouble. The problem was that each time the ball sailed across the net toward my side of the table, it kept getting fuzzier: "ping"—in focus, "pong"—out of focus.

Damn, I thought. *This is what my ophthalmologist meant when he warned me that as we age our eyes don't refocus as quickly as they used to, that it might be time to consider bifocals.*

And then I had a second, sinking realization, almost worse than the first: How was I going to explain to this 18-year-old punk across the table that I was too old to focus clearly on the ball.

No, forget that—I'm still too proud to admit my weakness so openly. But inside I know the truth—that I'm really not as young as I used to be. No, worse yet, I'm not as young as I imagine I am, as I wish I were, as I felt I was just moments ago.

I recount this story because it is emblematic for me of several aspects of middle-age, as I experience it. It is customary, of course, to talk about midlife as a time of losses, and not without good reason. First, of course, there are the physical changes, the myriad of little (and not so little) ways in which I am not as strong or as quick or as agile as I once was. The little aches and pains I regularly experience remind me that my body has slowed down. I forget things that I used to be able to remember, I sometimes lose my train of thought in the middle of a lecture or struggle to find the words I'm looking for. Though I still think of myself as fairly active and energetic, I know that 10 years ago I was more so, and 10 years hence I will be still less so. On the physical level, middle-age is undeniably about loss and gradual decline.

But the psychological adjustments are no less dramatic than the physical ones. The legendary "midlife crisis," though we exaggerate its importance in our culture, does represent a genuine shift in consciousness. By this point, we have come far enough to know that, in all likelihood, we will not achieve all that we once hoped for; some of our dreams really never will come true. And we have learned, sometimes the hard way, that life is not as full of promise and opportunity as we once believed or wished it to be. For all of us, I suspect, there is something—fame or fortune or happiness or success—that has eluded us. In any event, we are almost certainly not living the lives that we imagined for ourselves back when we graduated from college.

And that leads to perhaps the most basic of all experiences of midlife—the one I confronted across that ping-pong table from my student—we are not as young as many of us believe (or should I say "pretend") that we are. In a culture that glorifies youth and bombards us daily with images of adolescent sexuality, we cling (sometimes desperately) to the illusion of our own youthfulness. But in our heart of hearts, most of us know that those days are behind us, indeed, that most of our days are behind us. Much as we might wish it were otherwise, we are closer to the end of this journey than to its beginning. And that realization brings with it a host of questions—about what our life has amounted to, about our priorities for the time that remains, about the legacy we will leave behind us.

Middle-age, I think, is inevitably a sober time of life, a time to take stock as we look backward and forward in our own lives, as we find ourselves poised between our aging parents and our maturing children. In reflecting on this stage of life, I am reminded of a bit of ancient Jewish teaching about King Solomon. There are actually three books in the Hebrew Bible attributed to Solomon and, though modern scholars conclude that in fact he wrote none of them, the ancient rabbis regarded them as representing three distinct stages in his life. Song of Songs is a book of sensuous love poetry, filled with the imagery of spring, the exuberance of young love and sexual longing. It is the product of Solomon's youth. Ecclesiastes is marked by resignation and cynicism, full of admonitions that everything we do ultimately comes to naught, is "emptiness and a striving after wind." This is the voice of Solomon in his old age. In between, we find the curious book of Proverbs. It is less a book, really, than an anthology of aphorisms and reflections on how to make the most of life. It is the work of a man who has lived long enough to have learned a good bit about how the world works, but not so long that he has grown weary of life. Proverbs, a book of wisdom and insight, captures the perspective of Solomon at midlife, expressing the sort of discernment that grows from sober reflection on decades of life experience.

So, I ask what to me is the central question of midlife: Amid the losses and adjustments that mark these years, how do we find *our* wisdom? At this juncture, what have we learned about ourselves, about life, that can guide us in the years that remain and, perhaps more importantly, that we can bequeath to those who follow us? Each of us will respond to these questions differently, for our lives have followed different trajectories. I can respond only for myself, out of my own experience as father and son and husband and teacher.

From this vantage point it is clear to me that my life has been shaped most decisively by several experiences of loss and tragedy. My oldest brother died quite suddenly 19 years ago, when he was 39 and I was only 28. His death shattered my sense of family, and in the months that followed I found myself aware that I was holding my breath, wondering when tragedy would strike next. Never had I questioned that we would grow old together, and now I realized that any of my most cherished dreams for the future could evaporate in the blink of an eye.

Several years and two children later, my first marriage ended, once again shattering my sense of family and my dreams for the future. It propelled me to open an entirely new chapter in my life, one that, I am pleased to report, has brought me much fulfillment and happiness. But, at the time, this was the defining crisis of my life. As a single dad in my 30s, I was forced to forge a new identity, to reassess my relationships with others, and, especially, to create a new kind of family with my two small children.

Then, seven years ago, my mother succumbed to cancer and, with one parent gone, it was clear to me that an era in my life had come to a close. Reflecting on her life and all the love she gave me, I knew that it was now up to me to carry on her values and transmit them to my children.

And, last but not least, my sister has been living for the past nine years with a form of leukemia for which, as yet, there is no cure. Being as close to her as I am, I know first-hand something of what it means to live every day with a life-threatening illness.

How shall I describe the cumulative effect of all these losses? In part, they have taught me to expect the unexpected, though not in an anxious or bitter way. I simply know that life is not predictable and no longer assume that things will work out as I have planned. More importantly, it is now clear to me how much of life is not in my control; indeed, the things I care about *most*— like the health and life of those I love—are *least* in my control. As a result, I no longer take them for granted.

In the process, I have discovered a new appreciation for the traditional Jewish practice of reciting blessings on all sorts of routine occasions—on opening one's eyes in the morning and on closing them at night, when one sees a storm, or meets a friend one hasn't seen in a long time, even when one wears a new article of clothing. Of course, I have long known about this ritual practice, and even taught students in my Introduction to Judaism class about it, but only recently have I understood its wisdom. It is a wonder each morning that I can breathe in and out, that I can open my eyes and see the world. By reciting a prayer at such moments I cultivate the habit of being thankful for these every-day miracles. In short, each experience of loss has brought in its wake a deeper awareness of what I have *not* lost, and with it a deeper sense of gratitude.

Midlife, for me, has also been about growing comfortable with ambiguity. When I was 20, I was clear about what was right and true and so too certain of which moral and political views I could dismiss out of hand. Today I feel

> I have come to see that it takes still greater courage to live with uncertainty. Those who see things in "black and white" terms, I now think, probably haven't looked at them very closely.

certain only that most things are uncertain, that the truth lies almost invariably in that vast gray zone between the extremes. When I was younger I admired those who had the courage to take a radical position and defend it. Now I have come to see that it takes still greater courage to live with uncertainty. Those who see things in "black and white" terms, I now think, probably haven't looked at them very closely. But precisely because truth rarely appears to us so pure and unadulterated we frequently pretend to see clearly what is, in fact, rather fuzzy and indistinct. Today I readily sacrifice ideological purity for a more pragmatic approach to the world that can adapt to life's ever-changing challenges. Seeing clearly requires a willingness to explore the subtleties and nuances of situations and to entertain multiple perspectives at once.

Midlife is, above all else, a time of transition. The path of wisdom is not to resist all this flux and uncertainty but to embrace it. On my most optimistic days, I believe it is even possible to live creatively in the midst of all the ambi-guities that midlife brings.

Perhaps the overarching themes in all these reflections on midlife are balance and integration. With several decades of life experience behind me, this is the time to distill the lessons I've learned, to pay attention to the patterns that I see unfolding in my life, and to seek some sense of wholeness. By this point, I have had time to find myself and lose myself and find myself again, to learn from my mistakes, and all with enough of life still ahead (I hope) that perhaps I can yet put these lessons into practice. No wonder that Solomon is supposed to have written proverbs at this point in life. Just now the impulse to consolidate what we have learned, to put the pieces of the puzzle together and to record them for ourselves and others is strongest.

I am most aware of this impulse in relation to my children, as I try (like every parent, I suppose) to steer them away from the mistakes I have made. Perhaps this too explains my impatience with those who *fail* to learn from their mistakes, or who are disingenuous enough to suppose they haven't made any, or who just pretend they are something they are not. I have come in these years to value integrity above all other virtues, because it now seems clear to me that without it none of the others endures.

In a sense, much of what I have been trying to say here was expressed far more eloquently and succinctly by the eminent Christian theologian Reinhold Niebuhr in his now famous serenity prayer, which can only have been the expression of a man at midlife: "God grant me the serenity to accept the things I cannot change, the courage to change the things I can, and the wisdom to know the difference." What I think we hope for at this stage in life is precisely this—to make our peace with all the things in the past that we cannot change, to bring our accumulated experience to bear on the problems that surround us in the present and that loom ahead, and to have enough discernment to sort through all life's ambiguities. Solomon, when *he* was our age, would surely have concurred.

Of course, all these reflections shape my experience as a teacher and express themselves in my relationships with students. It is a standard joke among faculty that, as we say, "the students keep getting younger and younger." There really is something peculiar about working year after year with 18- to 22-year-olds; certainly, it has given me plenty of opportunities to reflect on what it means to be middle-aged. On the one hand, of course, it is positively maddening—they have so much energy, they have expended so little of their capital, they have the freedom to choose among so many paths. It is enough to make one appreciate George Bernard Shaw's quip—youth really *is* wasted on the young.

I confess that I frequently look at my students with a combination of envy and nostalgia. They travel to distant parts of the world I will never see, embark on adventures of all sorts that I am now too old to have.

On the other hand, they are so very young and unformed, naïve in so many ways, largely untested by life's adversities, so uncertain about who they are. They come to college with little idea of why they're here and where they're headed. They are still years away from acquiring the sense of balance or integration or discernment that I have talked about. At those moments, I look at them with a combination of amusement and compassion. And I wouldn't for a moment consider changing places with them.

But there are times when I move beyond both envy of and sympathy for my students to what I think is a deeper appreciation of what it means to be a middle-aged teacher of young people. It gives me, almost daily, opportunities to share with them something of my experience, to give them some perspective on the challenges they face and perhaps to ease their way in the world just a bit. The student who is dealing with his parents' divorce, the one who is terrified that she is failing and has convinced herself that her admission to Carleton was a cruel mistake, another who is in a near-fatal car accident during winter break, and another who is in tears because the only serious relationship she's ever had just ended—all are looking for support and guidance, a bit of empathy or some words of advice from someone "older and wiser."

> No wonder that Solomon is supposed to have written proverbs at this point in life. Just now the impulse to consolidate what we have learned, to put the pieces of the puzzle together and to record them for ourselves and others is strongest.

I find that my role with these students is almost as much parental as professorial; indeed, the difference between these roles has faded over the years, for my oldest son and my youngest students are now virtually the same age. Many students are open to being mentored in this way, even eager for it, and I treasure the chance to engage them on this level. What an extraordinary privilege it is to encounter students in this way, helping these exceptionally gifted young people make their transition to independence and maturity. When I make those connections, I feel as though I have made the best possible use of my middle-age. They are genuinely grateful that I am willing to bring my life experience to bear on theirs, and I feel certain that these are the lessons they will remember long after my brilliant lectures have been forgotten, along with the grades they received and pretty much everything that appeared on the syllabi of my courses.

But this sort of engagement has something in it for me, too. I derive a vicarious satisfaction through my connection with their youthfulness. Their energy and creativity feed my own, their idealism (even when it is naïve) restores my faith in humanity, their willingness to challenge every received truth forces me to reassess and defend my own values. I never feel more vibrant or alive than when I am engaged in animated conversation with these students, now less than half my age. Through them, I find that I keep in touch with that youthful part of myself that recedes farther and farther out of reach.

So, in truth, I need their youthful exuberance at least as much as they need my middle-aged wisdom. I sometimes think that if we have to be middle-aged (and who among us has a choice?), there is surely no better way to spend it than in dialogue with the young.

All of which brings me back to that fateful game of ping-pong. One of the defining characteristics of middle-age is that we are neither here nor there. Just as our children begin to need us less, our parents need us more. We live betwixt and between, for unlike the young, we are not defined by what lies *ahead* of us, and unlike the elderly, we are not defined by what lies *behind* us. We are defined, instead, by the particular dual vision that marks this time of life—our ability to look back at the distance we have traveled and ahead at the challenges we still face—and by the ability to embrace the very ambiguities of this transitional time.

This is a time for grieving our losses, consolidating our gains, and distilling our experience for whatever lies ahead. It is a time when we have learned what matters and how to keep it in focus, a time for cultivating our wisdom. And the path of wisdom lies, I now think, in being able to keep in touch with the youthfulness both within and around us and integrating it with the life experience we have gained in all the intervening years. It is the hope of achieving that integration that keeps me here, interacting with young people, sharing with them. and being inspired by them. At times, it even misleads me into thinking that I can be one of them again, if only for an evening. The fact that I cannot, however, will not prevent me from teaching them or playing with them. But there are some lessons I have learned along the way. Next time I will probably stick to playing pool. ■

The Engaged Teacher

Engaged in Thought: Teaching the Hard Disciplines of Seeing and Thinking

Neil Lutsky

> . . . we teachers do not automatically deserve a future. We must earn it by the skill with which we disorient our students, energize them, and inculcate in them a taste for the hard disciplines of seeing and thinking. (O'Donnell, 1998, p. 123)

Why do I teach? What are my goals as a teacher of these students, eager people giving four precious years and all that money to be here? Their assumption is that I know what I am doing—that I am an able college teacher of psychology—and, more importantly perhaps, that I know *why* I am doing what I am doing and believe sincerely in the value for them of dedicating themselves similarly, if temporarily.

I *do* believe in what I am doing, of course. My teaching is anchored in a venerable tradition (Newman, 1899/1996), one my increasingly aged appearance suggests I may have initiated personally. It's just that my goals as a teacher keep changing under the pennant of my sincerity; that anchor keeps dropping in

> My teaching is anchored in a venerable tradition .... It's just that my goals as a teacher keep changing under the pennant of my sincerity; that anchor keeps dropping in fresh waters ...

fresh waters. This year international understanding and quantitative reasoning are the *causes célèbres*, but the year prior to that technological proficiency was my foremost concern. Fortunately—or unfortunately—students don't typically

NEIL LUTSKY, professor of psychology, joined the Carleton College faculty in 1974. He earned his B.S. degree at the University of Pennsylvania and his M.A. and Ph.D. degrees at Harvard University.

have the kind of contact with me that would allow them to recognize such variability of purpose. These shifts of my attentions are a source of the discomfort I feel whenever I am asked to state my goals in some planning or self-assessment report or whenever I consider how I might measure the impact of my teaching on students' growth toward a set of concrete end states. My aspirations are always in play.

Have I ever known definitively what my reasons for being a teacher are? I've been discovering, testing, and adapting goals throughout my career, all the while I have been acting *as* a teacher. And that process continues while events in the world, currents in higher education, initiatives at the institution where I teach, changes in my areas of specialization, reading and research, the sincere endorsements of my teaching friends and colleagues, or the changing realities of an individual life prompt new recognitions and evaluations.

In January of 2001, for example, a serendipitous opportunity came my way to participate in a multi-university grant to establish a research center on "building vulnerability." Despite what you might associate with psychology, the focus of that grant was *not* on the means by which we might help people become more psychologically vulnerable but rather on the vulnerability of buildings and their occupants to attack. Post September of 2001, of course, that concern took on new meaning and significance.

Am I as protean as this sounds? There *is* a core to my teaching, but I work to discover or recognize it as my teaching is reshaped or not by the influences and educational fads tumbling around me. Perhaps what I have identified above are simply the temporarily salient concerns of a deeper but occasionally occluded vision. For nearly 30 years, for example, I have taken up arms (and correcting ink) against student writing that is wanting. Although I may marshal my resources against that foe only periodically, in response to some noticeable breaching of the standards, perceived weakening of or call to institutional resolve, or diminution of painful memories of past campaigns, I have nonetheless maintained the watch over the long haul.

This suggests variability and focus both characterize my purposes in teaching. Might my awareness of my own unsteadiness of purpose simply be demonstrating a staple of my field (social psychology), that individuals are more likely to recognize variability in their own lives than in others' (and that others will be less likely to appreciate the complexities that characterize us)? I have come to believe (sincerely) in certain core values in teaching that embrace my inconstancies or that, at least, thrive amid them. We teachers do have significant purposes driving our work, and, if we believe we deserve a future, we ought not shy away from articulating and risking that sense of purpose. What follows is the story I would now offer on behalf of one educator's commitment to teaching an academic field—here psychology—entwined in the liberal arts.

The purposes of my own teaching are rooted incompletely in the particularities of the discipline of psychology, although the path by which they took that root was, possibly, atypical. Most academics are drawn to teaching via a commitment to a field of study; I suspect I was drawn to teaching *prior* to that. I was taken with the pleasures of thinking, whether modeled by a rabbi discussing moral questions in early religious school, an elementary principal instructing her young charges in arithmetic shortcuts, secondary teachers of government and geometry, or college professors of political philosophy, French literature, Russian history, and education. All introduced me to the power of seeing the obvious reconfigured (Alexander, 1964), whether that object of attention was a knotty multiplication problem that, when reorganized, could be completed easily or was a signal world event of my youth, the Cuban Missile Crisis, that, when viewed analytically from multiple perspectives (Allison, 1971), revealed just how complex and fragile human affairs are.

I understand well Mark Edmundson's testimonials to the formative impact of his own teachers (e.g., Edmundson, 2002) and the artist Josef Albers's observation that "the example, the indirect influence of the teacher's being and doing is the strongest means of education, that the unintentional influence of the teacher's being and doing is more effective than many like to believe" (1969, p. 14). My teachers, both the flesh-and-blood people with whom I interacted as well as the authors of the books and articles I read, demonstrated the value and pleasures of knowledge and knowing, thinking and the play of ideas. They drew me to teaching, and psychology emerged, late in my undergraduate career at the Wharton School, as an exciting although for me barely understood venue within which I might pursue the call of ideas.

Each of us who teaches, I assume, appreciates the special significance of his or her field of endeavor; each discipline is, in his or her own eyes, a first among equals. (This belief in the superiority of the self and its extensions, which social psychologists call "pipping" after the Latin *primus inter pares*, is another well-documented finding in psychology, clearly one of the most illuminating of all the liberal arts disciplines!) In part, then, teaching at a college is justified by the sum of the worth of these fields of study.

I certainly believe in the value of learning about the great achievements of psychology, those concepts, findings, and theories that constitute the core of the discipline. What students learn from this body of knowledge may serve as a basis of human understanding, promote human health and well-being, stimulate intellectual curiosity about life, and prepare students for the worlds of work and citizenship they are approaching. Psychology's study of mental disorders provides one illustration of a field's potential practical, cultural, and self-reflective significance. Mental disorder touches so many lives personally and interpersonally, has implications for social issues such as health care funding and employment practices, and raises questions about how we might understand and possibly change or adapt to given human tendencies.

> One of the goals that has energized my teaching in psychology for 30 years is to show students reasons why what they take to be so concrete, real, familiar, and generalized may permit and be challenged by alternative readings.

Exposure to psychological knowledge also has the potential to unsettle students' naïve psychologies, their comfortable ways of seeing themselves and others. One of the goals that has energized my teaching in psychology for 30 years is to show students reasons why what they take to be so concrete, real, familiar, and generalized may permit and be challenged by alternative readings.

So, for example, I can cite the findings of research on helping behavior (Latane & Darley, 1970) to suggest that the person who shows apparent indifference to the plight of another in one set of circumstances may have acted quite altruistically under only slightly different social conditions and that our own behavior (and the judgments of others about us) would probably vary similarly.

Or I can review research on memory to reinforce the writer John Wideman's disorienting claim that "Memory, then, isn't so much archival as it is a seeking of vitality, harmony, an evocation of a truer, more nearly complete present tense" (1994, p. 36).

Or I can challenge students to reevaluate personal stories and individual cases by showing them that we pay inadequate attention to how statistically unrepresentative those experiences might be (Tversky & Kahneman, 1974).

In sum, I can strive to show students how our judgment and behavior may be characterized by psychological tendencies, how to see as a psychologist sees.

Psychology's body of knowledge and ways of seeing are no more fixed than my teaching persona, however. A truly great teacher at Carleton, the late Professor Owen Jenkins, mused about sending out recall notices to former students to correct misreadings or to update the information with which we equipped graduates. Fortunately, if we've done our jobs well, those former students would not be surprised by our notices and may even have anticipated them.

When I cover a particular subject, my intent, at least, is that students will do more than master relevant vocabularies and bits of knowledge. I want them to come to appreciate the complexities and controversies that surround knowledge in an area, to be able to weigh for themselves relevant evidence and arguments in the discipline, and to recognize that knowledge and practice have changed and will continue to change over time. I try to force them to pose questions and seek answers, in discussions, assignments, and examinations, in the hope that they will gain the skill, practice, and confidence to exercise their own abilities to reconfigure the evolving body of convention in psychology. I even want them to call seeing and thinking *psychologically* into question, for example, to consider how external realities constrain subjective experience and the psychological constructions we might otherwise impose on reality. My hope is that I leave students more critical of—by which I mean *both* more appreciative and more rigorously attuned to the shortcomings of—psychology's newfound approaches and insights. Peter Gray (1993) captured my aspirations well when he advocated teaching psychology as a set of ideas aimed at fostering "reflective skepticism."

A great responsibility of teaching, one we risk shirking for the sake of students' comfort and our own ease, is helping students to exercise *discipline* in such reflective criticism. That discipline involves acuity, knowledge, training, and judgment. I don't find it difficult as a teacher to prompt educational experiences that leave students feeling as if they're capable of considered thought (and as if I'm capable of stimulating and/or reinforcing their thinking). What I do find challenging is to help students develop sober assessments of their own skills and backgrounds. What mirrors can I hold up to students to stimulate them to recognize and engage the techniques, knowledge, and appreciations they need to discipline their own thinking? How can I help them develop a more mature sense of the responsible caution and confidence they ought to voice and demonstrate as they address important intellectual, social, and personal issues? What might help shape better preparation for and riskier participation in the now more self-consciously complex disciplines of seeing and thinking?

Addressing these tasks is what I take to be a goal, not only of individual courses but of coherent majors, judicious requirements, challenging capstone experiences (at Carleton in the form of an integrative exercise), and, in fields that invite this, substantive student-faculty collaboration in research. Here, again, it may be easy to involve students in senior projects or in student-faculty research without accomplishing much except to bolster student, faculty, and institutional pride. The challenge is to engage students in a way that effectively introduces them to the important disciplines of a field, motivates and furthers mastery of those disciplines, and strengthens judgment and perspective about the value and limitations of those disciplines.

Although students sign up with the intent of taking my courses in psychology, my purposes as a teacher are far broader ones. A few years ago I chaired the internal review committee for Carleton's outstanding geology department, and what the geology faculty wrote in their self-study report captures, I think, the character of teaching at our college. Here is what they said:

> Though all of us on the faculty are enthusiastic, perhaps even passionate, about our discipline, we tend to view the earth sciences primarily as an extraordinarily powerful tool for educating our students rather than as an end in itself. (Geology Department, 2001, p. 2)

And I view my teaching in psychology similarly. But to what general ends, and for what reasons, do we educate our students?

I have a snapshot of my own general educational goals, taken at a time I was looking back over my first 25 years of teaching. It took the form, appropriately I think, of a series of questions. Here is that list:

> After my classes, do my students think more coherently and systematically? Do they appreciate the insights and perspectives of

various historical and contemporary traditions and communities? Are they more likely to evaluate claims on the basis of argument, evidence, and reason rather than authority, stereotype, and popularity? Do they seek to voice and test their ideas? Do they recognize and challenge what is spurious and injurious? Do they respect uncertainty? Do they express themselves more clearly, effectively, and engagingly? Do they appreciate quantity, complexity, time, and beauty? Are they better prepared to lead grounded, honest, responsible lives? Do they leave with a deeper sense of perspective and a richer sense of humor? Are they any more likely to rely on sober and expansive reason, despite its frailties, in the years ahead? Do they find pleasure and value in their lives by engaging life in thought?

And ever since I encountered it in Henry Rosovsky's (1990) book on universities, I've found inspiration in the following 1861 remarks of William Johnson Cory, a master at Eton:

> You go to a great school, not for knowledge so much as for arts and habits; for the habit of attention, for the art of expression, for the art of assuming at a moment's notice a new intellectual posture, for the art of entering quickly into another person's thoughts, for the habit of submitting to censure and refutation, for the art of indicating assent or dissent in graduated terms, for the habit of regarding minute points of accuracy, for the habit of working out what is possible in a given time, for taste, for discrimination, for mental courage and mental soberness. Above all you go to a great school for self-knowledge. (Rosovsky, 1990, p. 108)

The manner in which faculty approach a field of study—whether geology, economics, studio art, history, mathematics, or some other discipline—yields extraordinarily powerful opportunities for addressing the above goals. I'll try to illustrate that by discussing how my own discipline, taken as an example, can be deployed to promote functionally significant epistemological values and, second, an appreciation for the interrelatedness and openness of knowledge.

The British psychologist Nicky Hayes (2002) suggested "one of the things that makes psychology unique is that it makes the whole scientific process so clear." Well, psychology is probably not unique in doing so, but it is an effective vehicle for teaching science and science's larger values. For example, it reinforces the value of inquiry, of evaluating possibilities by seeking to test their plausibility. Timothy Ferris recently described this characteristic of science beautifully:

> Science is not a collection of facts, any more than opera is a collection of notes. It's a process, a way of thinking, a method, based on a single insight—that the degree to which an idea seems true has nothing to do with whether it is true, and that the way to distinguish factual ideas from false ones is to test them by experiment. (1998, p. 5)

Because students are so often interested and confident in their assumptions about and judgments of human behavior and functioning, they are commonly fascinated by research findings that call their beliefs into question. And these findings, in turn, draw students' attention to the characteristics and virtues of the processes of inquiry putting ideas to test. In addition, involving students more actively in framing research questions, identifying how data could be collected or evaluated to address those questions (Lutsky, 1986), and participating in the design of studies in laboratory courses (Lutsky, 1993), senior projects, or collaborative research with faculty brings the process of inquiry to life.

Tests of claims, in research and even in demonstrations in class, put ideas at risk and show students the wider importance of viewing their beliefs as hypotheses. Inquiry also reinforces the act of grounding beliefs and aspirations in reality. Often, students treat what they wish were true as if it were true or, at least, easily achievable. Their recognition of obstacles and complexities in the worlds they see or envision is often narrow. At the same time, grounding beliefs and aspirations in the reality of historical or cross-cultural or theoretical alternatives may help students see that it is nonetheless possible to help reconfigure some constantly evolving practices. In sum, I hope my teaching in psychological science may provide students with a more expansive sense of what it means to "be realistic."

It is precisely this grounding in the practical world that the liberal arts are rather stereotypically viewed as lacking. Although it is true that the liberal arts may have been conceived as philosophical or mystical in character (O'Donnell, 1998) and that our teaching is not specifically geared to career preparation, how we teach at Carleton nonetheless yields much of substantial practical value. What we teach is grounded in disciplines, and most of those disciplines are grounded in the world—whether in behavior, the physical universe, commerce, culture, or history.

Although I am most concerned that what and how I teach advance the disciplinary and general goals I've described, my teaching is also sensitive to what I take in a larger view to be desirable for responsible lives of citizenship and work. So that, although I use technology in my teaching primarily to help students express and discipline their curiosities, seek sound information, test ideas, and communicate effectively and responsibly with others, I'm also aware of and promoting the practical value of learning a statistical program or exercising informational literacy.

> My teaching is also sensitive to what I take in a larger view to be desirable for responsible lives of citizenship and work.

Moreover, I believe our disciplinary and general goals coincide to a significant degree with the needs of human striving. Appreciating and risking inquiry illustrate this. In a wide variety of applied domains, inquiry has proven to be a productive tool of understanding, a scrupulous basis for decision-making and practice, and a rich stimulus for creativity.

A second hallmark of a liberal arts community is that it recognizes how fields of study may be related. This is obvious in the existence of interdisciplinary programs and often even more surprisingly and compellingly demonstrated in individual disciplines. Psychology, for one, emerged from philosophical and scientific traditions and now interacts with other disciplines as diverse as mathematics, biology, English, history, economics, and engineering.

I try to discuss links like these in my teaching and to show students how our thinking may be informed and challenged by contributions from other fields. For example, in a social psychology course, I commonly assign a short story by Raymond Carver and pieces from economics, history, and anthropology. I hope to reinforce the value of reading widely, often far afield. Doing so often gives credibility to phenomena of interest by providing some independent recognition of their existence, stimulates new thinking about those phenomena, and presses a field's current boundaries.

One of the fundamental methodological and, hence, cognitive norms of psychological science is that hypotheses—or beliefs and practices—ought to be evaluated in comparison to their alternatives. Interdisciplinary contexts provide a means of putting psychology in perspective, of highlighting taken-for-granted assumptions in psychology's approach to understanding or claims of understanding, for better and worse. Virginia Woolf wrote "truth is only to be had by laying together many varieties of error" (1929, p. 105). That is an insight interdisciplinary perspectives in the liberal arts reinforce, and those perspectives may help strengthen students' openness to diverse views, willingness to test their ideas against alternatives, powers of imagination and synthesis, and sense of humility.

No less real than the above practical and cognitive appreciations are the aspirations we all share for pleasure, awareness, meaning, and dignity in life. In the *Phaedrus*, Socrates observes, "Lucidity and finality and serious importance are to be found only in words spoken by way of instruction or, to use a truer phrase, written on the soul of the hearer to enable him to learn about the right, the beautiful and the good."

What kind of teaching can be written on the soul of our hearers? I believe teaching in the liberal arts can do so because of its potential to recognize and address the conditions and wonders of life, the fleetingness and vulnerabilities of our individual lives—and human dignity in the face of these hard facts. This is teaching that embraces the constant change we witness and study and that accepts the contingency of beliefs, that is, our inability to know with certainty until tomorrow. And this is teaching that evinces the genuine pleasures and fundamental seriousness of rigorous thinking and imaginative seeing. In the end, the difficult challenges of these purposes keep me engaged in thought and, if I am fortunate, may do so for the students with whom I work. ■

REFERENCES

Albers, J. (1969). *Search versus re-search*. Hartford, CT: Trinity College Press.

Alexander, C. (1964). *Notes on the synthesis of form*. Cambridge, MA: Harvard University Press.

Allison, G. T. (1971). *Essence of decision*. Boston: Little, Brown and Company.

Edmundson, M. (2002). *Teacher*. New York: Random House.

Ferris, T. (1998, July 20). Not rocket science. *The New Yorker, 5*.

Geology Department (Carleton College) (2001). *Review Document*. Northfield, MN: Author.

Gray, P. (1993). Engaging students' intellects: The immersion approach to critical thinking in psychology instruction. *Teaching of Psychology, 20*, 68-74.

Hayes, N. (2002, June). *The value of teaching psychology*. Paper presented at the International Conference on Psychology Education, St. Petersburg, Russia.

Latane, B., & Darley, J. M. (1970). *The unresponsive bystander: Why doesn't he help?* New York: Appleton-Century-Crofts.

Lutsky, N. (1986). Undergraduate research experience through the analysis of data sets in psychology courses. *Teaching of Psychology, 13*, 119-122.

Lutsky, N. (1993). A scheme and variations for studies of social influence in an experimental social psychology laboratory. *Teaching of Psychology, 20*, 105-107.

Newman, J. H. (1899/1996). *The idea of a university*. New Haven: Yale University Press.

O'Donnell, J. J. (1998). *Avatars of the word: From papyrus to cyberspace*. Cambridge, MA: Harvard University Press.

Plato (1973). *Phaedrus* (W. Hamilton, Trans.). Harmondsworth, England: Penguin.

Rosovsky, H. (1990). *The university: An owner's manual*. Cambridge/New York: Norton & Company.

Tversky, A., & Kahneman, D. (1974). Judgment under uncertainty: Heuristics and biases. *Science, 185*, 1124-1131.

Wideman, J. (1994, August 1). Personal history: Father stories. *The New Yorker*, 36.

Woolf, V. (1929). *A room of one's own*. New York: Harcourt Brace Jovanovich.

Teaching and Learning French Without Metalanguage, or Re-mapping the World

Christine Lac

Dear students: This is the first day of class, and about 20 of you are gathered here to start on your language requirement. You have chosen a French class to do so. Some of you have had French in high school; some of you have already studied another language, while others in this class have never experienced this type of learning. You know Carleton requires you to learn a language, and you may wonder why or how it fits in a liberal arts education.

The goal of the language requirement is often seen as utilitarian—a well-rounded person should be conversant in more than one language in order to allow direct communication (spoken or written) with members of at least another culture. Pushed to the limit, this reasoning leads people to choose a language based on the number of people who speak it and on the social situations where that language may be used. For example, you may have heard that French is a language used for diplomacy, international relations, and research, and that Spanish is the other almost-official language of the U.S. and therefore "immediately useful." These assumptions hide the fact that there are no guarantees that you will use this language in future endeavors—you may have to or want to work with Hopi and have to become cognizant of a language spoken by just

> I have often wondered if my students would learn French better, were I to explicate the process and the goals to them .... I may yet send this letter to my students the first day of class.

CHRISTINE LAC, lecturer in French, earned her B.A. degree at Université de Metz-France and her M.A. and Ph.D. degrees at the University of Nebraska. She joined the Carleton faculty in 1997.

over 5,000 people, for example. Moreover, these assumptions minimize or forget altogether that learning any language, be it German or Bambara, will prepare you to learn Hopi, Japanese, or Arabic faster and better. In this sense, the higher purpose of the language requirement is not to reach a basic utilitarian goal, but to help you, if you have not yet had the experience of confronting another linguistic reality (or have not reached a certain level of competence in so doing), to navigate the waters of this mind-boggling journey.

I use the term "mind-boggling" because my field, that of language acquisition, is very concerned with the many ways the human brain processes linguistic knowledge. I am, and I hope you will be, fascinated by the way your mind will respond to this type of knowledge and method of learning. I hope it will be a profoundly significant experience for you, disturbing enough to create new means of looking at words and their relationship with the world.

In this adventure, you will be stripped of the most basic shield that protects and defines you, your familiarity with the language with which you apprehend and comprehend knowledge. In most disciplines, you are able to negotiate the difficulties you encounter through English, our main language on campus (a native language for most of you, but a second or third language for others among us). The subject—chemistry, art history, or ballet—is explicated within the familiar structures of English, albeit with a specific jargon. When you face a problem you painstakingly formulate questions to ask for clarification; you know that sometimes, after you are able to pose a question clearly and precisely, you can answer it yourself.

But in the language class you will not have access to this most basic of resources, because we will use only French in our class. I will use it to explain assignments, model structures, and communicate with you. You will use it to work with each other as well. Once in a while, I know one of you will ask if she can pose a question "*en anglais, s'il vous plaît.*" Most of the times, the response will be "no." Sometimes you might question this choice, quipping that "we could go much faster" on some topics in English. Today I want to show you what you are learning as you hear, repeat, and utter French words. I want to show you that even though we teach and learn in a way that seems very experiential, we try to attain the overarching goals of shaping your mind by laying the foundation of a bilingual and bicultural consciousness.

I can wax passionately verbose about this topic and will discuss it at length with you outside of class, but now is not the time. Now is the time for French. Yet, today only, I will let you hear, as a translation of sorts, the metalanguage that remains tacit in the classroom and yet informs its discourse as a constant humming sub-text. Let us start.

"Il faut que vous étudiiez le français."

You will not learn to manipulate this structure for a few months, but already you can be acquainted with the famed subjunctive, which indicates the necessity of an action. Were I to write this sentence on the board (note that "were" here represents as much of a subjunctive as you'll ever find in English), you would notice the double vowel "i" in the verb. This may surprise you visually, because English does not make use of "i" in this fashion. Moreover, you will not hear a double sound when I pronounce the word, but there they are in the graphic form of the word.

Their presence attests to the logical beauty of language: *étudiiez* follows regular patterns of formation of the subjunctive. The verb's root that is used to form the present tense, third person, plural and the ending comes from the regular paradigm of subjunctive endings (-e, -es, -e, -ions, -iez, -ent). The second "i" signifies that the writers are aware of the complex logical process at work in language, by recognizing particular syntactic constraints calling for the subjunctive mood and morphological rules to produce such form.

Today, you will not dissect this phrase and learn its secrets, but you will hear it. I do speak fairly slowly (it just seems fast to you today), so this phrase will take about three or four seconds of our class time. During that time your ears will get attuned to its music, and your brain will attempt to parse it. The language centers of your brain will store something of this process that you will retrieve at some point in our second term, when you are finally exposed to these rules more intentionally and learn to manipulate them. Yet, you will need to engage in linguistic studies to analyze fully these patterns and understand their systemic logic, because in our language class you will learn to internalize these structures, not to treat them as objects of study.

"Il faut que vous étudiiez le français."

Why am I not pronouncing the two "i's" if they appear on the page? A better question might be: Why do they appear on the page at all, as they seem to serve no purpose as guide for pronunciation?

As I noted above, their presence signifies an awareness of the language on the writer's part. In this case, the spelling represents the phonetic history of the language. In general, in modern French, diphthongs are not part of the general phonetic system (diphthongs are what you pronounce after the sound /b/ in "buy" unless you use an American southern pronunciation of the word). So, digraphs (or double graphic symbols) are pronounced as a single sound in French: "au" in *"il faut"* is pronounced like "o," for example.

Yet, at some point in the life of the French language, each letter represented a sound. You will understand where these extra letters come from—vulgar Latin, transformed by the stress pattern of Germanic invaders' pronunciation, reviewed by academic rules, etc.—when you study the early history of the birth of France. It may take you several terms of history or political science to appreciate fully the linguistic sediments that appear in the graphic notation of the language to carry the story of its people and its land.

"Il faut que vous étudiiez le français."

To be accurate, I need to let you know you may hear some speakers pronouncing those two "i's," more like a longer sound rather than the repetition of the same one. Teachers, for example, may be exaggerating a certain pronunciation to help students internalize a rule. Very self-conscious native speakers of French may also use this pronunciation in a sort of hyper-correction.

The same phenomenon occurs in English when speakers feel compelled to say "between you and I" instead of "between you and me." What the speakers are signaling with this is that they are so aware of rules and pay attention to them to such an extent they make a mistake by over-generalizing them. Other users of this pronunciation may want to portray themselves as members of a select educated class aware of and defined by adherence to strict linguistic rules.

Our short sentence today does carry the potential for such observations; through it, your mind has direct access to this type of information. You will study such linguistic markers in psychology in order to understand how people perceive themselves and create their identity in relation to others through various linguistic and non-linguistic means. Sociology will help you analyze social variations in speech as indicators and reinforcers of social strata. And yet, I will take a point off if you do not write in that second "i," even if it violates your personal socio-political convictions!

"Il faut que vous étudiiez le français."

We have two interesting sounds to work on here: "ou" or /u/ in phonetic symbols and "u" or /y/ in phonetics. These are a bit challenging for a native speaker of English, because they don't quite match sounds we use in English. English speakers tend to substitute a /U/ sound for either.

Working on /u/ and /y/ poses some very interesting questions. One deals with the value of trying to approximate native speakers' pronunciation. Some argue that we should not try to pretend we are native speakers if we are not. The pronunciation of a non-native speaker is then perceived as part of that person's identity and demands that the listener adapt to it. This point of view is congruent with values supported by a multicultural society.

Yet, we must understand the constraints of the language and make sure that our pronunciation does not erase meaningful opposition of some linguistic features. For example, if you use an English /r/ instead of a French /r/, people will probably understand your words because /r/ and /R/ do not differentiate words in French. But if your neck hurts and you talk to a triage nurse in France while not making a clear distinction between /u/ and /y/, using the phrase "*j'ai mal au cou*" may send you to a proctologist.

> Working on /u/ and /y/ poses some very interesting questions. One deals with the value of trying to approximate native speakers' pronunciation. Some argue that we should not try to pretend we are native speakers if we are not.

Listen carefully, repeat carefully, work on it. When you were an infant, you would have picked up on the difference between these sounds immediately. Now your language system is so efficiently tuned to English that you may have trouble hearing the difference and then reproducing it. However, you soon will be able to do so, and, because of that, you will regain some of the brain plasticity you have lost while becoming so efficient in your first language. You will regain that sound you had lost; you will be able to hear it and use it again. Thus, while working on how much you need and want to differentiate /y/ and /u/, you will be working on your current identity as a language learner, an English speaking (as a native or not) college student in an American college and reconnecting with the babbling infant you once were.

Researchers in language acquisition like Stephen Krashen note that these choices may lead to some anxiety, which in turn will create affective filters impeding learning. To lower these affective filters, remember to keep a sense of humor. Do look up "*cou*" and "*cul*," masculine both, in the dictionary and have fun with these words outside of class, my little joke of the day for you. Expand to other minimal pairs—"*tu*" and "*tout*," "*pou*" and "*pue*," "*roue*" and "*rue*," etc.—and play with them. You will probably encounter similar exercises in a more systematic way in voice or speech when you work on pronouncing foreign sounds and imitating accents.

"*Il faut que vous étudiiez le français.*"

At some point you will wonder who or what "*il*" means. In this context, "*il*" means nothing. In an impersonal phrase, it fills the place of the subject pronoun but refers to nothing in particular—although it sounds just like the "*il*" and "*ils*" meaning "he" and "they (masculine)" respectively.

Context will allow you to define the referent of a given pronoun. It is helpful to realize that words do not have an intrinsic meaning but derive their meaning relatively to others in the language in general and to others within a singular utterance. That particular linguistic feature means that you must pay attention to the words and their context at the same time in order to understand their meaning and or function in a given narrative.

It also means you will not be able to translate word for word from one language to another. English speakers would probably use the phrase "you need to study French" to translate the above French sentence, and yet that translation would refer more literally to "*vous devez étudier le français.*" Some may see a stylistic difference in "*il faut que*" and "*vous devez.*" The choice of an impersonal structure may be seen as more forceful, as it removes any notion of agency in the obligation. This point may lead you to want to study stylistics as it pertains to the expression of authority or socio-political hierarchies in France or elsewhere.

"*Il faut que vous étudiiez le français.*"

In France or elsewhere "*vous*" is an interesting term, in the context of our previous discussion, because of the relationship it implies between the speaker and the listeners. "*Vous*" could mean "all of you" in the classroom or a formal singular form of "you" used to address an adult one does not know very well.

You will need to understand the social context of our classroom to understand what I mean. Usually, in our language classes at Carleton, professors will address you individually with the informal form "*tu*," thus "*vous*" here means all of you. You may question this choice when I tell you I would like to be addressed as "*vous.*" There are compelling reasons for us to use the same term, to show the same type of respect or the same kind of connectedness that cements our social microcosm in our classroom. But, with all due respect to such egalitarian views, that would mean that you would not be exposed to both linguistic varieties of address. So you shall be "*tu*" to me, and I shall be "*vous*" to you.

"*Il faut que vous étudiiez le français.*"

Why "*le*"? English does not use an article, but you need one (*il en faut un!*) in French. It must be definite ("the") because we are referring to a general truth and masculine because that is the way it is. "It" here refers to grammatical gender. It means all words in French are identified as masculine and feminine, although not male and female, because grammatical gender is a completely arbitrary linguistic category and does not at any point reflect reality.

> There are compelling reasons for us to use the same term, to show the same type of respect or the same kind of connectedness that cements our social microcosm in our classroom. But, with all due respect to such egalitarian views, that would mean that you would not be exposed to both linguistic varieties of address. So you shall be "*tu*" to me, and I shall be "*vous*" to you.

Even though I will make that point often—we will learn the word "*arbitraire*" early on—I will acknowledge that language may alter one's perception of reality. (One day, I might share with you my childhood view of the animal world when I was growing up in France, where all mice were girls (*la souris*) and all rats (*le rat*) were boys.) You may want to analyze this phenomenon while reading philosophers and linguists such as Ludwig Wittgenstein, Edward Sapir, and Benjamin Whorf, who studied the relationship between perception, reality, and language. Of course, after our class, you may need a few courses in biology to help you readjust your perception of gendered species on our planet.

We are coming to the end of our 3.57 seconds. You will feel you did not hear anything but a strange string of sounds and yet, in a nutshell, you have been exposed to all the processes your brain uses to work on French and the reality it delineates . . .

This is the process that I mean to teach you. It is similar to the one you underwent as an infant, yet much more condensed and faster because you have access to that previous experience. Thus, this class lets you tap into the most defining human experience there is, learning a language, mapping the world with words. (Some may argue this point, but I will stand on my bias.) Distilled in each sound or phoneme, each word, sentence, or text that you will encounter lies the seeds of human knowledge, embedded in our mind in such an intricate way it will take you all four years of fascinating classes at this college and then the rest of your life to attempt to understand part of it.

Of course, this class represents a daunting task; most of you will struggle in ways that are novel to you, intense, pleasant, and yet challenging. I will help you figure out if your difficulties are within a normal range or not. You will need to remember we are condensing in four terms what it took you 10 to 15 years to achieve in your native language. So you will have to be more intentional in your work with the language. Because adult learners have more difficulty than infants in learning the phonetic system of a language, you will have to use the lab and listen and repeat to perfect your understanding of how these sounds work in opposition to each other to create meaning. It is conscious work you must do. Indeed, you could learn French "just by listening and speaking with people." That might work, but it would take you several years; you have 40 weeks. Ready yourself for that intensity.

By now, I hope you understand what is unique to the language class. Language is the most intricate, developed, flexible map of our world we have. So much so that we have trouble reading it. Our native language has become so habitual we are not conscious of reading a map, not conscious of the knowledge we have encoded in our words.

My hope is that by learning French, you will catch a glimpse of the map your own native language provides you to navigate the flow of reality. This endeavor seems almost mystical, doesn't it? It is. You may be chomping at the bit when we rehearse simple situations about meal times, and you will want to get to the literature planned for the term. But pause and marvel at the complexity of a phrase like "*j'ai faim*" ("I have hunger," literally) and the fact that in

French being hungry is something a person *has* rather than something that person *is*, a structure more closely related to the world of ailments (to have the flu or a cold), or example. Is hunger seen as the symptom of a disease in French? It is always dangerous to generalize from one example, and yet there is an old saying in French stating that "*la faim est une bonne maladie*" ("hunger is a good disease to have"). Wonder about the etymological and historical roots of such a phenomenon. Ask yourself if there are implications in such a worldview. Then appreciate the ingenuity of authors using this phrase in their text.

The language will seem elusive at times. I will answer your questions by "*ça dépend*" ("it depends") many a time. It depends on what you truly want to say. The speakers transform speech, and as they translate their perceptions into words, these will in turn transform, refine, obscure these perceptions. And you will start wondering if you are having problems with a linguistic structure or with a whole society altogether. In order to address this issue, we will use language in a French cultural context. We will look at pictures of French houses to learn about domestic vocabulary, we will read short stories about people and events in French and francophone countries, and we will watch movies about such places as well. Do not be surprised if our cultural information comes from Québec or Zaïre. The use of French in these locations will help you think about its value in different contexts.

Let's take it from the top:

"*Il faut que vous étudiiez le français.*"

TO WHOEVER READS THIS OPEN LETTER TO MY STUDENTS:

It is my hope that I was able to share some of the practices and tools of my trade in this letter while presenting the exciting endeavor of language learning in immersion and its frustrations. I have often wondered if my students would learn French better, were I to explicate the process and the goals to them. Often, while I keep our class as sacred space for French, I do engage in some metalinguistic discourse in a parallel zone, on the Internet, and I may yet send this letter to my students the first day of class. ■

In Search of the Magical Moment

Will Hollingsworth

Algorithm: A step-by-step problem-solving procedure, especially an established, recursive computational procedure for solving a problem in a finite number of steps.[1]

I have taught for more than 15 years, long enough to have transcended the beginner's level of teaching skills. In the first few years, simply surviving was my primary thought. It was only after a few years that I was able to start comparing different teaching strategies. By then, I'd had some truly magical moments in class. I wanted more. I set out to discover ways to make the magic happen on a regular basis. I believed that a class replete with magical moments would optimize student learning. This essay discusses what I learned in searching for guaranteed ways to create them.

Once I had taught each type of class I offer a few times, I started to develop the impression that I could really steer the dynamic in my classroom, in terms of the order of the topics I chose, the way I presented them, etc. The implication was that

> I began to feel that all I had to do was discover the correct algorithms in order to understand how to teach my subjects once and for all and be done with it.

I would likewise be able to control student learning. This is an understandable assumption, given that I was progressing from rank novice into higher levels of

WILL HOLLINGSWORTH, professor of chemistry, joined the Carleton faculty in 1986. He earned his B.S. and B.A. degrees at University of Texas, Austin, and his M.S. and Ph.D. degrees at the University of California, Berkeley.

expertise in my craft. And things **were** going better—as I discovered my unique skills as an instructor, I probably was becoming more effective. How many of us think back nervously to the poor souls who happened to have had us in our very first classes? Over a few years, I had progressed past the absolute fear factor style of teaching where I was in perpetual agony that my notes, so desperately developed well into the wee hours the night before, would either run out 10 minutes early or be lost or left behind, leaving me stranded in front of my class without even a good singing voice with which to pass the time.

Once the issue of mere survival receded and the balance of time evened out a bit, I began to find the energy to work on details and nuances. In addition, comparative aspects of teaching were becoming the mid-career norm, as I was called upon to review and judge younger colleagues' teaching. Reviewing others' teaching is an act that starts out absurd and becomes only slightly more normal with the sheer rote practice and repetition of it—but it never feels quite right. It is hard for me to forget feeling like a charlatan as I was forced to pass judgment on colleagues' teaching when I hadn't even really figured it out for myself. I wondered how in the world I was able to scrape through and how I could possibly live up to the standards being set by my junior colleagues. This is an opinion that I have often heard expressed among my teaching cohort.

My colleagues had started assuming that I knew how to teach. That must mean that I had learned how to steer the dynamic on particular days in class, right? This impression is probably especially strong for those of us who teach in the sciences. Day after day, we imagine that we are revealing a little bit more of the mystery of nature to our students. I began to feel that all I had to do was discover the correct algorithms in order to understand how to teach my subjects once and for all and be done with it. An algorithm, defined above, is a term borrowed from mathematics and computer sciences. It is taken here to mean the sequence of steps, as in a flow chart, that would take me through a class in the precise way that optimized the potential for my students to learn. Armed with my favorite examples and the ordering and presentation of topics that I found worked best, I began a search for the winning formula that would enable me to teach every class the very best it could be taught.

Each instructor develops an individual style of teaching, and I suppose each must be searching for his or her own algorithm. For me, the transition began right away; the contents of those notes that I had so carefully prepared became a little less important each time I taught. Teaching in a quantitative area does require clear checkpoints—those exact equations, magnitudes, correctly worked examples, and negative signs mustn't fail to appear at the proper time—even if such checkpoints might be needed at a moment when the excitement of the classroom or my own stage performance might make it hard to remember such details correctly. Year after year, I found that I was expending less and less energy recopying or otherwise working on my notes, attempting to integrate the different versions to produce the one masterpiece. With experience I found that the details in my notes became merely a template for the more expansive story that I was trying to tell.

Today, at this point in my teaching career, the transition is nearly complete. The days where I attempted to go through the exact content of my notes in a very deliberate way are long gone. What has replaced it is a more general adherence to the content of my notes and, in particular, knowing which stories, case-studies, and extended examples contained within them will work the best in my own form of teaching and for the current class in question.

Classes come and go. Some of them, as well as students in them, inevitably became my favorites. Every so often, an extended discussion with such a class would go particularly well—to the point that the moment seemed downright charmed. The exchanges with the class were lively, natural, and unforced. The points raised that day, in the specific order they came up, seemed to resonate perfectly with the plan I had for my class. The topics became almost vivid enough to hold. Upon reflection, the moment seemed nearly frozen in time, colors were brighter, and the exchanges on both sides positively brilliant. At moments like this, teaching never felt like a higher or more noble profession.

Because I was searching for algorithms, these magical moments had to be considered to be an important part of the puzzle, a discovered keystone link in my own developing algorithm. The teaching quest had to be nothing more than finding the correct number of these moments, gathering them up, bundling them together, sealing the process shut, and calling upon these moments forever more into the future. As these magical moments happened, therefore, I was careful to note them down. In an attempt to replicate them, I got into the practice of making specific comments in my notes about how exactly to stage the same event the next time the class was taught. If the next class responded in the same way, I would move on to the next set of steps in the chain of events leading to the creation of my master algorithm.

Imagine my surprise when, at precisely the correct moment the next year, I set up the class with care for their own magical moment—only to have it fail to recapture any magic whatsoever. Polite acceptance (not to mention even cool indifference) was not the response I was after! Where were the brilliant colors and sparkling repartee from last year? After going through this process for several years, hoping to weed out the results from aberrant classes, I was shocked to learn that the magical moment would, in fact, typically not repeat. It's not that I had managed to eliminate all such moments from my teaching, it's just that they would happen at different times on different subjects in a way I found impossible to predict.

> Imagine my surprise when, at precisely the correct moment the next year, I set up the class with care for their own magical moment—only to have it fail to recapture any magic whatsoever.

It wasn't even that I felt like a failure or that the students didn't learn much the day the special moment failed to return. It was more a feeling that I wasn't going to be as good at steering the dynamic as I had thought and that creating algorithms for teaching was not going to happen. In fact, if algorithms were possible to develop, then there would probably be a rather narrow set of specific teaching plans that would be developed to reflect the basic types of teaching styles. Imagine the catastrophic way in which our entire academic pursuit would be affected: The seemingly endless string of workshops and teaching initiatives, some useful and some not, would soon be a thing of the past and a small set of surefire lesson plans would be rewarded with teaching immortality.

Teaching, after all, is a human enterprise, even if it is science that is being taught. A general conclusion from studying complex systems in nature, even systems well short of the complexity of human behavior, is that they are defined by nonlinear behavior. Nonlinear behavior is the unfortunate type of mathematics that makes it very hard to predict specific outcomes based on initial conditions. Algorithms can handle simple linear systems because they have built-in well-behavedness, yielding a proportionately bigger effect in response to a bigger initial impetus. But complex systems are not linear. Nonlinear systems have intricate accelerating behavior that can rise up to overwhelm predictiveness. Science teachers are chagrined that the very complexity that makes some examples really interesting and relevant for teaching makes them too hard to teach in any detail to our students. Instead we inform them of the basics and hope an understanding of the true underlying complexity emerges later in their own quest for learning.

Because teaching is a human enterprise, I finally realized that there is not much chance that simple algorithms based on linear models of learning can be developed that will work so well as to create a class that is composed of a chain of predictable magical moments regardless of the particular students. What a fitting comeuppance for this uppity scientist! I'm sure some readers will think that I have merely discovered an obvious point. Perhaps I have, but along the way, in the process of searching for my own algorithms, I learned a lot about my own abilities and motivations as a teacher, as well as about the art of teaching itself. I feel that I have some points to offer that might be helpful to others who are developing their own teaching styles, especially those who recognize themselves in the style of teaching described here. The rest of this essay contains those observations, suggestions, and cautionary notes. This is probably more helpful than ending with a detailed discussion of different magical moments I have either had or failed to recreate in the fields of general chemistry, quantum mechanics, spectroscopy, and environmental chemistry and science!

Recognize that each time you teach is different. Once you gain some freedom from your notes and the tight script they can impose on you, you find that each time you teach does vary, often in surprising ways.

Remember that the social dynamic within your class can have significant effects on teaching and learning. Whereas this scientist started out by pretending that social interactions weren't that crucial to teaching, in some cases it can seem like everything. Moreover, as professor, you may not even be aware of some aspects of these dynamics. This is especially true in a small, relatively cloistered community where rumor can spread faster than wildfire. There have been a few notable times where the interactions within my class misfired even to the point of derailing the entire day's teaching. Here I will just note that what students bring into class (e.g., feeling overworked, simply tired out from the pace of college, or from too many competing extracurricular activities) can significantly affect their time in class as well as the time they spend outside of class to consolidate what is being taught. The professor's focus is on the special time with students, the 70-minute period. What is hard to appreciate is the impact the rest of their lives has on what they do in your class.

Don't micromanage the dynamics of your class. I often feel that I am too aware of how students are responding to the time they are having during my class. Stoic or unresponsive classes that are especially hard to read have always made me feel uncomfortable. What I might be interpreting as boredom or a failure of the day's teaching may instead be distraction or even a moment of cognitive challenge that could possibly lead to revelation. Colleagues often remark how hard it is not to fill an uncomfortable silence. Yet it can be important to linger on such uncomfortable moments for the chance of a revelatory moment. With more experience, I have become less aware of and enslaved by the applause meter that is ever running inside my head.

Focus on the big picture of the story you are trying to tell each day. We all teach different aspects of the liberal arts and we all have our different stories to tell. Focus on the larger themes before immersing yourself and your class in the necessary details. Each year, I find that the notes that accompany different units within my classes get used in a different order, an order in keeping with the way the story is being told that year. Loose ends can be brought up next time or resolved in an e-mail if they are of critical timed value.

Accept chaos. Because there are no algorithms and because learning occurs in unexpected ways, embrace the fact that your time in front of your class is not totally yours to control.

Be adventurous and even risky in your teaching. Learn the hard skill of allowing yourself to be vulnerable. Do not be afraid to let your personality shine through in your teaching, because you are an important part of the complex system of your class.

Watch out for an overreliance on teaching aids that separate you from your class. I know that tools such as presentation software, overhead projection, and transparencies have their place, but it is important not to rely on these devices any more than you would your notes. Using these teaching aids too heavily can lead to overly scripted strategies, which may not resonate well with a particular class. Do not let these tools lead the story that you are trying to tell or prevent you from departing for an unplanned teachable moment. The point is to remove as many layers as possible between you and your class so that your focus on the class is as direct as it can be.

Avoid the arrogance that can come from the feeling that you know it all. First, you probably don't. Second, even if you do, that knowledge doesn't necessarily mean that your students will learn, especially if your own arrogance creates a barrier between you that cannot be breached. Our students start out convinced that we do indeed know it all. To bring them up to the level of independent learning that we expect of them, we need to disabuse them of this notion as quickly as we can; we may know a lot about our fields, but we certainly don't know it all.

Seize on the unique dynamic presented by each class. Use your key players for what they can do to achieve magical moments. The impulse to be egalitarian can be taken too far. For a short period of time in my own teaching, in response to recommendations from my senior colleagues, I would call on students in large classes no matter if they were volunteering or not because, in principle, everyone should be ready to contribute. However, I have learned that some people are simply more or less comfortable to be on show in front of the group. Let the livewires and the open and expansive personalities contribute to the class dynamic in ways that benefit all and catalyze others to respond. Don't cling to a strict egalitarian spirit by failing to recognize that different people do possess different personalities.

The above observations should reassure those who worry about the future of liberal arts education and how it can possibly compete with the efficiencies offered by distance-learning strategies. Because there are no algorithms that capture the high-quality teaching moments, especially from a distance, liberal arts colleges—where so much attention and thought goes into teaching that is specifically tailored—should be ensured of a healthy future after all. Whew!

— — —

I have addressed some key aspects that relate to my own development as a teacher in my early years and mid-career. I'd like to conclude this essay by anticipating what the later years of teaching will be like.

A common nervous thought often expressed among professors is to wonder how fresh teaching will seem after having taught the "same" class so many times. My own stage of intense course development is done for now and I have wondered the same thing. However, my failure to find algorithms for teaching actually turns out to be a source of great comfort. It means that each new class will be unique with plenty to be discovered. Not only will I continue to understand my field in evolving ways, I shall always be confronted with a new nonlinear human system to explore and challenge. Whereas I cringe to think about the years left of the aspects of teaching that I don't particularly enjoy, such as the time pressure of making ever more new exams and then having to grade them, the process of unlocking the exact nature of each new class is something that I anticipate with freshness and joy. Even though I do not feel that I will ever be able to dictate the dynamic of my classroom, perhaps through my experience I have gained the ability to read each unique class somewhat better and, in so doing, offer a smaller set of strategies that I feel might work for them. At least that is what I hope is happening. Since the whole teaching affair is so unpredictable, who really knows what is going on?

> My failure to find algorithms for teaching actually turns out to be a source of great comfort. It means that each new class will be unique with plenty to be discovered.

While I have let go of the idea of making algorithms, magical moments still come and go in my classes at their own stubbornly unpredictable frequency. My failure to get the magic back upon demand happens to me more often than not. This tells me that much of the specialness of teaching is created at the moment for the moment, a one-time event between me and the unique set of individuals who find themselves in my class. It argues for keeping far from my classroom the arrogance in the belief that I could ever control it all, while leaving the classroom door wide open for spontaneity, flexibility, and occasionally a little magic. ■

ENDNOTE

[1] *The American heritage dictionary of the English language* (2000, 4th ed.), Boston: Houghton Mifflin, from http://dictionary.reference.com/search?q=algorithm

Reflections on the Art of Teaching and the Teaching of Art

Clifford Clark

One of the big surprises in trying to learn how to be a more effective teacher on the collegiate level is to discover that both the students and the subject matter are moving targets, continuously changing. As a teacher of American history for more than three decades who tries to keep up on the latest scholarship, I know that historical knowledge expands daily as historians reframe their questions, discover overlooked sources, and publish their findings. Student background and expectations about how classes should be conducted, whether they be lectures or discussions, shift as well, as new generations graduate from secondary school and bring with them new ideas and assumptions. Even the attitude toward what constitutes authority and what should be questioned or accepted changes. For those of us who started teaching in the contentious 1960s when students seemed to question every statement made by a teacher, the contrast to today is dramatic. The challenge remains: finding ways to engage student attention and enthusiasm and to channel that energy into new ways of understanding traditional fields of inquiry.

> The challenge remains: finding ways to engage student attention and enthusiasm and to channel that energy into new ways of understanding traditional fields of inquiry.

Given the reality of changing student expectations and changing fields of knowledge, I set out two years ago to redesign a course on the history of American architecture and material culture that I had given, in different ver-

CLIFFORD CLARK, professor of history and M.A. and A.D. Hulings Professor of American Studies, has been a member of the Carleton faculty since 1970. He earned his B.A. degree at Yale University and his M.A. and Ph.D. degrees at Harvard University.

sions, for more than two decades. The objective of the course had been to introduce students to the history of the built environment around them, ranging from the history of houses and public buildings such as prisons, schools, museums, and zoos to the design of furniture, appliances, and cars. In refocusing this course, I retained the original objective and added additional ones: to discover a way to teach students how to think three-dimensionally so that they could conceptualize better the nature of spatial relationships and the impact of these relationships, historically, on social interaction. As director of a new cross-cultural studies program, I was also interested in the question of how one society borrows from another.

This essay provides a brief account of the new course that resulted, as well as an evaluation of its successes and shortcomings. The course, titled "The Zen of Asian and Western Woodworking," added field trips and a hands-on "laboratory" experience—in this case, working in the Studio Art Department's woodshop—to the usual classroom readings and discussion.[1] The 18 students were asked to study the influence of Asian designs (particularly those of China) on the evolution of American furniture, from the 17th century to the present. In addition to writing the usual analytic history papers, however, students were asked to make some simple tools—a marking knife and a marking gauge—and to design and build a small project using dovetails. (Dovetails, a joint used to connect two boards together, have been used since ancient times. The "pins," which consist of wedge-shaped projections, are cut into one board and fit into a corresponding notch between the "tails" on the other board. When the boards are slid together, often at a right angle, they make a very strong joint.)

> In redesigning this course, especially in terms of the woodshop part, I intentionally became a co-learner with the students. It reminded me of one of my first teaching experiences ...

The idea behind this latter feature of the course was that to learn to think conceptually in three dimensions, students had to test and build their own three-dimensional project. In doing so, they would not only gain a new appreciation of the stunning craftsmanship of earlier furniture makers but would also expand their understanding of spatial relationships. I hoped that they would also gain knowledge of how objects and material culture studies might influence their own lives.

The workshop experience was also a manifestation of my uneasiness with the ways in which high schools track some students into "academic" pre-college areas and others into the "manual arts." By separating so-called academic subjects from practical hand skills in working with tools, secondary schools in my opinion have done a major disservice to both categories of students.

Another way to understand the goals of the course would be to see them as related to what anthropologist Clifford Geertz has called "alienating the familiar."[2] By creating a new context and asking new questions about commonplace things, the course would strive to teach students to see everyday objects in a new way. In the process, students might also come to understand the outlook of past generations of furniture makers. As the historian James Axtell has put it,

> . . . our task [as historians] is not only to "alienate the familiar" but to "familarize the alien," to introduce our classes to the strangers and fellow travelers who have once inhabited the worlds that we have largely lost. (Axtell, 2002, para. 7)

In short, by placing students in a position where they had to make their own piece of furniture, I hoped that they would gain a new appreciation of the skill exhibited by earlier furniture makers. By having to choose their own materials and tools, they might also enter into the contemporary debates over design, craftsmanship, functionality, and form.

In redesigning this course, I found myself drawn to some extent to Larry D. Spence's argument in *Change* magazine that college faculty need to shift the focus from "teaching" to "learning" and that they should "work to design learning experiences where students learn on their own, at their own pace, and guided by their own interests" (Holbrook, 2001, p. 2). In redesigning this course, especially in terms of the woodshop part, I intentionally became a co-learner with the students. It reminded me of one of my first teaching experiences where, as a historian of American history, I was asked to teach a freshman seminar on the Middle Ages, a subject which I had never studied in either college or graduate school. By deliberately revealing my lack of expertise in the field and by identifying with my students at the start of that course, I stumbled onto an approach that proved then and more recently to be an effective means of working with them.

Although I would accept Spence's argument that faculty should redesign student learning experiences, I should also admit that I disagree with two other parts of his argument (a disagreement that would play out in my own course as well).

First, I believe that some teaching is necessary in the sense that while learning on one's own is important, it is also often frustrating and excessively time-consuming (as those who have learned new computer programs on their own will attest). As John Dewey explained nearly a century ago, the map of previous experience that the teacher provides "serves as a guide to future experience: it gives direction; it facilitates control; it economizes effort, preventing useless wandering, and pointing out the paths which lead most quickly and most certainly to a desired result" (Dewey, 1902, p. 20). Given the limited amount of time that any course can require, I believe that it is important to teach some of the concepts and knowledge that the student needs to work on his or her own.

I would also disagree to some extent with Spence's argument that *faculty* need to design the "learning experience" for students. I would suggest that it is even better, where possible, to have the students design *their own* learning experiences. Spence's approach seems to assume that faculty *know* what student interests are and understand the pace at which they can learn. Both assumptions are problematic. My own thought is that it is better to provide a place within the curriculum where students can design their own learning experience than to try to design these for them. Students often learn most effectively when they have a personal investment in the process.

With this in mind, let us turn to my redesigned course. Unlike the original course which primarily emphasized domestic and civic architecture, the new course was more narrowly focused on furniture. But while the range of objects was narrowed, the time frame was expanded. In both courses, I wanted to have students see how certain classes of objects, such as Victorian hall stands for umbrellas or, more recently, computer tables, come into existence for certain purposes and then may disappear. I also wanted them to explore how objects are classified and evaluated, how they shape patterns of social interaction, and how designs originate and continue.

The course was divided into four parts: an initial section on recent debates over furniture design from the 1970s to the 1990s; a second section that focused on Ming Dynasty Chinese furniture design and construction, and its influence on English and American furniture in the 18th century; a third section that examined the influence of Asian design motifs on the American Arts and Crafts movement at the turn of the 20th century; and a final section that asked students to use what they had learned so far to evaluate the furniture sold in the IKEA catalog in terms of style, construction, function, and social significance.

Paralleling each of these sections, students worked in the woodshop. While reading in the first section of the course the debates over the role played by hand tools and machine tools, the significance assigned in recent years to custom-made and handmade objects, and the debate over craftsmanship, they made their own marking knife and marking gauge. While examining the complex joinery of Ming Dynasty Chinese furniture in the second part of the course, they learned how to mark out and cut dovetails and to use the bandsaw, table saw, and router in the woodshop. In the third and fourth sections, while examining the philosophy and objects produced by the Arts and Crafts movement, they traveled to a saw mill, picked out their own lumber, and designed and made a small project with dovetails—usually a box, shelf, tray, or basket. In addition, the class included a field trip to the Minnesota Landscape Arboretum of the University of Minnesota to see furniture designed in the 1960s by the Japanese-American architect George Nakashima and to the Minneapolis Institute of Arts to see their Ming Dynasty collection and their American Decorative Arts collection. Two contemporary craftsmen, Yeung Chan and Arthur Gropen, also visited the class, talked about their design philosophy, and brought with them some of their own work.

My goal in each of these sections was to enable students to discover that everyday household objects do not exist in a vacuum. Instead they reflect a complex set of assumptions about design and function. They also carry implications for social status, cultural borrowing, and materialism. Ultimately, they provide a commentary about a society's self-image, values, and openness to change.

Although I had tried to anticipate the student response to this class, several features of the course proved surprising to me. One was the high level of student interest, both among males and females, despite the unfamiliarity of most with woodworking. Both times the course was offered, it filled before most other courses in the department and had long waiting lists. The unconventional nature of the course seemed to attract students from a variety of disciplines, from history and economics to chemistry, physics, and geology. Most students were seniors, but each year I also had one or two sophomores and juniors. Mixing the younger students with the older ones in this case did not seem to make any difference.

Given the initial student enthusiasm for working with their hands, I was also surprised when relatively simple processes such as cutting with a hand saw or grinding a knife blade proved difficult for them to do. Part of the problem was that some students were not very coordinated. Some students also misjudged the amount of time that it would take to complete their project. A few who were used to doing their written work the night before the assignment was due failed to realize that the sanding and finishing of projects could not be completed at the last minute.

I was also surprised at how difficult it was to make students take safety issues seriously. Using power machine tools is inherently dangerous. Although I spent time going over each tool, students often lacked the most basic common sense about securing loose clothing or long hair. Sharpening also proved to be a challenge, since learning to hone knives and chisels razor sharp made it easy for students to cut themselves if they were not careful.

Levels of patience also varied quite dramatically. For some students, the course's expectations about the level of care and attention to detail proved frustrating. Although most students started with so little knowledge that there was little need, unlike in some American history classes, to dismantle simplistic and misleading stereotypes, one student did exclaim that only "Asians" would be willing to measure wood to such close tolerances. He, being of European descent, could never match their achievements, he insisted, in complete ignorance of the high skill levels evident in European furniture design, watch-making, and stonework.

But most surprising was the difficulty that students had in conceptualizing an object in three dimensions. This became especially evident when they tried to measure and cut the dovetails, a very simple joint that proved very difficult for them to make. Nowhere in their educational background had many of them ever had to measure and build anything. Even constructing a cardboard model and drawing their project to scale on a piece of graph paper seemed difficult for them.

Given these problems, how did I assess the final outcome? To what extent had I succeeded in achieving the goals that I set out and to what extent did the course provide a learning environment where students could learn at their own pace?

In terms of the traditional goals mentioned above of learning to understand the cultural context in which objects are made and function, I was reasonably pleased with the results. Although some students mentioned in their evaluations that the readings sometimes went into too much detail about methods of construction and finishing—particularly, the material on colonial American furniture, the students generally wrote papers that displayed a grasp of the basic ideas in the field. They were particularly pleased with their final paper on the IKEA furniture catalog which displayed the idiosyncrasies of the present age—the obsession with storage, the proliferation of furniture to house computers and sound systems, the simplicity of joinery and construction, the juxtaposition of wood and metal, and attempt to combine functionality with aesthetic standards.

> Most surprising was the difficulty that students had in conceptualizing an object in three dimensions .... Nowhere in their educational background had many of them ever had to measure and build anything.

I was also pleased to see that the students were able to examine the idiosyncrasies of cross-cultural borrowing. They noted, for example, the popularity of Chinese designs in English Chippendale furniture but then recognized that the intricacies of Chinese joinery had been simplified. As in other cases of cultural borrowing, objects from one culture were redesigned and altered to fit the needs of another culture. In this case, an emphasis on the exotic other replaced any genuine desire to understand Chinese society.

In terms of the goals of my original course on architecture and material cultural studies, I felt that the general concepts of that course had been met in the new course, despite its more limited focus. But the new course proved even better at getting students to take on responsibility for their own learning than the previous one had. And this occurred in ways that were not foreseen by me but which evolved from the woodshop projects.

Early on in the process of making the tools, those students who were more proficient in using the machines began to help those who were struggling. Since the end product—the marking knife or the mortise gauge—was shown to the others in one of our discussion sessions, the students found themselves working not so much as to impress me as to impress their peers. During the construction of their final project, they also shared materials with each other and helped each other out. At the very last session where they passed around the objects that they had made and explained what they had done, their pride and satisfaction in their own accomplishments was evident.

The project itself provided me with a collaborative learning opportunity that I had not anticipated. I remember that one of my colleagues in the Chemistry Department had once told me that the best teaching opportunities came when an experiment went wrong and they and the student had to try and figure out why it had failed.[3] The same opportunity took place when I looked over the initial plans for the project that the students intended to build. Often, the student had been overly ambitious or had failed to work out how two parts would fit together. In these instances, I frequently found myself in the role of a co-learner, trying to problem-solve collaboratively with the student.

> In the end, therefore, I was reasonably pleased that I had helped the students themselves create a new learning environment for themselves—one in which my role of teacher shifted somewhat from that of expert to that of a resource...

In the end, therefore, I was reasonably pleased that I had helped the students themselves create a new learning environment for themselves—one in which my role of teacher shifted somewhat from that of expert to that of a resource and co-learner. I was particularly happy to see the ways in which some of the student projects, a small shelf in once case, a pencil box in another, had picked up on the debates at the start of the course among James Krenov and other furniture-makers about using woods' natural forms, distinctive grain, and imperfections and incorporating them into the design.

As for teaching students to think in a more three-dimensional fashion, I think that I was only moderately successful. Some students did accomplish very skillful projects and clearly understood the principles of dovetail joinery. But a few were overwhelmed by their project. In fact, each year two students actually dropped the course three-quarters of the way through it. One apologized to his peers at the final session and admitted that he had done battle with a difficult concept and lost.

The fact that this student recognized that he had little talent in working with his hands in a three-dimensional way was itself, to my mind, a reasonable outcome. It reminded me of a comment once made by Cary Carson, the director of research at Colonial Williamsburg and himself an astute scholar of material culture studies. that "college courses teach us what we do well and what we should avoid. They teach us where our talents lie and those subjects which may remain forever difficult."[4]

One final comment about the course deserves to be made. Teaching a course like this one involves taking risks in several different ways. It tests, for instance, the departmental conception of appropriate fields of study and methodology. One member of my department understandably expressed skepticism that I should be teaching a "studio arts furniture course in the History Department." (I had made it clear to the Studio Art Department when they graciously allowed me to use their woodshop that my course was a history course, with a "woodshop laboratory experience," and not a studio art course.[5]) And I explained to my colleague that the goal of a studio class was to produce a work of art while the goal of my course was to understand the history of furniture.

The class was also risky because it pushed me beyond my background in the woodshop in some areas. Knowing this, before starting this course, I had enrolled in a woodworking course myself with Yeung Chan, a noted Chinese-American woodworker, to brush up on my own skills. But it wasn't enough. While I was eager to add the workshop component because of my own interest and considerable background in woodworking, I had intended—naïvely, it seems, in hindsight—to work entirely with hand tools. But we needed to dimension the wood on the table saw and run other machines like the bandsaws where my own background was limited.

I responded to this deficiency by asking for help from some of the staff in the woodshop and from some of the visiting furniture makers who spoke to the class. Students who were versed on these tools also helped me out. I learned a lot in the process even though, at times, the student refrain—"in our studio arts class we did it this way" was humbling.

Most risky of all was doing an actual demonstration of cutting dovetails by hand in front of the class and then passing them around for student appraisal. While I approached this task with trepidation and a lot of practice, it worked out well. I was gratified when one physics major, who had been skeptical about the whole course, came up after the demonstration to say how useful the demonstration had been.

When I teach this course again, I will also need to develop a better sense of the timing of demonstrations in the woodshop, a better knowledge of some of the machines themselves, and a more collaborative structure where students can work on their skills in groups and help each other more efficiently. I will also have to explore how to manage the extra time that is entailed in the monitoring of students in my woodshop laboratory. Teaching this course involved a risky venture into uncharted territory, but it has proven to be energizing and rewarding.

ENDNOTES

[1] I designed this course as part of my participation in the Senior Faculty Development Program in 1998. Dean Elizabeth McKinsey explained that "the goal of the program is to provide an opportunity to reflect on your teaching, scholarly or creative work, and professional progress in a supportive and collegial context" (letter to author, June 4, 1998). As part of this program I took a course with Yeung Chan at the Marc Adams School of Woodworking in Indiana in the fall of 1998. A Rockefeller Brothers Grant supported additional hours for the technician who kept the woodworking equipment up and running and for the two visitors to the class, Yeung Chan and Arthur Gropen.

[2] I picked this quote from James Axtell, whose own footnote says that neither he nor Geertz can find where Geertz used this phrase. See Axtell (2002), footnote 4.

[3] Will Hollingsworth made the comment in a meeting in May, 2001.

[4] Dr. Cary Carlson, comment to the author, sometime during 1982-83 when he was the visiting professor of American Studies at Carleton.

[5] I am indebted to Fred Hagstrom, Stephen Mohring, and Tim Lloyd in the Studio Art Department for allowing me to use their facilities, helping me with details of the course, and in general supporting my exploration.

REFERENCES

Axtell, J. (2001, August). The pleasures of teaching history. *The History Teacher, 34*, 4, footnote 4, from http://www.historycooperative.org/journals/ht/34.4/axtell.html

Dewey, J. (1902/1974) *The child and the curriculum* and *The school and society.* Chicago: University of Chicago.

Holbrook, D. (2002, January). A case against teaching? [Review of article by L.D. Spence (2001, November/December). The case against teaching. *Change*, 11-19]. *The Teaching Professor, 16,* 1, 2.

Teaching and Advising Exceptional Students

Robert Tisdale

DEFINITIONS AND PERSONS

This essay might be said to focus on "non-traditional students"—not older students, but rather those who have not enrolled in selective liberal arts colleges in significant numbers until very recently. Identifying traditional students itself presents a problem: Many undergraduates who seem part of the usual demographics are not so in actuality. They may be white and smart, but they may also be first generation college students, first or second generation immigrants; they may have lived in poor or distressed families on a ranch or farm rather than in a city or suburb, they may come burdened with personal issues as well as misapprehensions about college. If they have high grade point averages (GPAs) and high SAT scores, however, then they are usually considered part of the norm—i.e., admissible without dispute about "fit." Contrariwise, many students of color arrive with top-of-the-line computers and academic credentials. They are children of families who have been in the U.S. for centuries and who have the status and earnings of professionals; they live in wealthy suburbs where their children have attended excellent schools. In this essay, in fact, the identification of the students termed "exceptional" probably depends largely on expectations of their college performance

> The students discussed in this essay ... are exceptional because they display many qualities that lead to success in life but can actually cause trouble in college.

ROBERT TISDALE is the Marjorie Crabb Garbisch Professor of English and the Liberal Arts. A member of the Carleton faculty since 1966, he earned his B.A. degree at Princeton University, an M.A.T. degree at Wesleyan University, and M.A. and Ph.D. degrees at Yale University.

from information submitted to the Admissions Office—information that suggests formidable challenges ahead.

These students who merit extended discussion around the admissions conference table are those who have something really special going for them, who present special opportunities for the college or university, but who don't meet some of the usual admissions criteria. They may be children of alumni or athletes, artists, musicians, or class leaders; but the question arises early on, "Can they make it here academically? Will they survive, thrive, enjoy their four years, and graduate?" Let me offer two slightly fictionalized examples to illustrate the sort of student this essay discusses.

The first student, whom I will call Lin, was born in Laos, grew up in a relocation camp speaking Hmong and Lao, and came to this country at age seven. Her family lives in Minneapolis and speaks Hmong at home. She herself has attended American schools since first grade and has spoken English fluently for 10 years, has taken care of her siblings for dozens of hours weekly, compiled a solid record at school, exhibited extraordinary resilience and leadership qualities as a teenager, and entered college intending to be a scientist. Her family's structure and tone has changed radically as a result of their many losses and moves, and her father's status and authority have suffered.

The second student, Luis, did well in a very poor and badly staffed inner city high school. His parents are separated, and he has been contributing the income of his 30-hour a week job to help support his family (mother and three siblings). Luis spoke Spanish at home, but, like Lin, is utterly fluent in English. He really would like to become an artist, but because of his mother's conviction that he would never be able to earn a living that way, he is considering majoring in economics. Luis is very charming and outgoing and gained political office in college the first chance he had.

Both students will be peer leaders next year. They were admitted with decent GPAs but rather low SAT scores, and the admissions staff worried that Carleton might prove too academically demanding for them in their first two or three terms. Their extraordinary record of personal initiative, stamina, motivation, and achievement out of class indicated that they would contribute significantly to other students and the life of the institution. But would they survive and eventually flourish academically?

CHARACTER COUNTS

Predicting success challenges the experts, but for those who must make such predictions regularly, character and leadership count. If a student with a low SAT or GPA has met and conquered tough challenges, demonstrates motivation and initiative, and has the strong backing of adults whose judgment may be trusted, then many of the most serious questions have been answered. Those students who look as if they will contribute the most to others and the institution and who have grit and mother-wit will be admitted. The faculty is privileged to advise, counsel, and teach them.

The students discussed in this essay, like Lin and Luis, are exceptional because they display many qualities that lead to success in life but can actually cause trouble in college: They have extraordinary social skills, strong religious upbringing, or spiritual values derived from struggling and overcoming obstacles. Many are bicultural, having undergone migration or immigration and adapted to a different culture while maintaining a connection to their families' own traditions. They display the ability to think on their feet and are ingenious and imaginative in solving practical problems. They are articulate, cooperative, personally charming, with a good sense of humor, and great stamina. If given an opportunity, they are often exceptional leaders.

> Predicting success challenges the experts, but for those who must make such predictions regularly, character and leadership count. If a student with a low SAT or GPA has met and conquered tough challenges, demonstrates motivation and initiative, and has the strong backing of adults whose judgment may be trusted, then many of the most serious questions have been answered.

However, if they are also first generation college students from families struggling to survive day to day, they may at first think of college as a rather exotic, arcane experience rather than a practical one. Carleton looks like a different sort of place altogether from their previous neighborhoods and schools, and to the degree that we reinforce that impression and fail to demystify higher learning and emphasize its relation to adult reality, we contribute to their difficulties.

BRONZE ISN'T GOOD ENOUGH

In completing their very first essays, problem sets, or quizzes, the undergraduates I am concerned with demonstrate that, for whatever reason, they have not learned the games we play. As much as being "taught," they must be "socialized" into academia. They may have been resisting schooling all along for a dozen reasons; but at Carleton, where they can concentrate on three subjects at a time, truly learn from and respect their teachers, have a choice of courses, and access to support systems for health, math, writing, speaking, and even social or folk dancing, the problem more often than not is getting students to admit the need for help and use it.

These students may be as proud as Olympic gold medalists and with equal reason—so proud that admitting any deficiency or achieving less than the gold is unthinkable. But denying the need for help may quickly become a matter of academic life and death. Because such independence is sanctioned and reinforced by American society, however, students who have survived through self-reliance will have trouble using resources the college provides and abandoning their formerly successful strategies of independence. They have been working long hours at home or in the local garage, but many have not spent equally long hours at a desk studying highly technical subjects. Heretofore they have not needed a conference with a teacher to help them understand an assignment; in fact, many such strategies that other students have learned will strike them as childish or even humiliating.

College teachers and successful students know, for example, that an excellent way to prepare for an exam is to anticipate questions the instructor will ask. But the very idea that one would have to think like a teacher in order to prepare for an exam, or proofread an essay *aloud* in order to hear its deficiencies and *revise* what has been labored over for hours strikes students as acting the nerd. One should, of course, *be bright enough* to understand and excel in the system; if you have to *learn* how to work it, something must be wrong. After all, *you are here to show them you belong here.*[1] And when an instructor says, "Your exam should reflect your study and your own best thinking on the subject," surely that means that you speak *your* mind; you don't try to figure out what the instructor will deem discussible and then pitch your preparation to that agenda.

The dangers outlined here may be compounded by a further difficulty inherent in the change from a secondary school to college schedule. The trouble is, as one bright advisee said, "students here have too much time," and their unstructured time just melts away. Luis, with lots of apparently "free" time, found himself spending far too much of it socializing, largely as a distraction from work more challenging than he had ever encountered before. He might have been better off in a sport, profiting from the structure it provides. Our athletes, who have to squeeze studying into their schedule, read assignments on a bus, and arrange for absences to be excused and friends to take notes for them, are often the ones who get the work done—not always done well, mind you, but *done*.

Another problem is that students who embody their family's highest hopes often enroll in the most difficult courses and majors, especially pre-med science and math. In Calculus II, Equilibrium and Analysis, or Energetics and Genetics, freshmen encounter masses of new material presented at a pace much faster than any Advanced Placement course, if they were lucky enough to take one. They attend only three classes a week; labs last a whole afternoon; a lecture hall may hold 60 students; help sessions are sometimes convened by undergraduates who are able and helpful but do not have their professors' deep understanding of principles. Our terms of 10 weeks are too short to allow much maturation in the understanding of crucial concepts, so if you catch a cold, miss a lab, or cannot attend a help session because of a conflict, you lose crucial time to ask questions and apply concepts. Our unforgiving schedule tests even the best prepared and most savvy students, and it punishes those who are just learning how to schedule free time and are not accustomed to seeking additional help. Carrying the burden of unrealistic expectations and weak preparation, students like Luis can go under. In fact, his ever deeper immersion in social life became, as Stevie Smith's famous poem puts it, "not waving but drowning."

Furthermore, as some genius once said, "the perfect is ever the enemy of the good." For many students with very high personal standards and fine records from secondary school, merely good performance on an essay or exam is unacceptable; they are used to excelling among their peers and will tolerate nothing less. Others may have so much to prove that they may believe that their work must always be first rate. In either case, the imperative to excel can lead to procrastination, growing anxiety, and finally work missed or done so late that it interferes with subsequent assignments and earns less than full credit. Strong students from weak schools may also arrive with a different kind of "standards" problem. Some who are not perfectionists have been praised for showing up, being courteous, doing the assigned work, or most of it. This may have been good enough in high school, but it is potentially fatal in college, where students must not only do all the work but do it well and on time.

ANXIETY: SOME CAUSES AND EFFECTS

Anxiety turns out to be particularly subversive of good performance. Joseph Williams, the wonderfully sensible University of Chicago teacher of rhetoric to undergraduates, lawyers, and bureaucrats, has identified "performance errors" (misspellings, solecisms, etc.) as the fruits of anxiety or boredom. If a writing task is too easy, the bored student lacks the alertness to see what the page really says; one who has often been "Mickey-Moused" lacks a long attention span. On the other hand, if the task is too difficult, the threat of defeat keeps the writer from paying attention; it clouds thinking, prevents development of ideas, hastens conclusions, and makes careful revision and proofreading almost impossible.[2]

The exceptional students I am writing about also confront an amazing variety of anxieties not apparently related to the classroom. Some have gained extraordinary maturity by taking care of their siblings or even their parents. When these young people leave home, their parents' tears of pride mingle with tears of separation and loss. When the son or daughter who has been a family's chief negotiator, translator, or living proof that all the sacrifice and pain were worth it, goes off to college, the parents cannot be sure that he or she will return except as a visitor. In fact, for some undergraduates, success depends on **not** returning permanently, since their neighborhood and childhood friends may not be where success—or perhaps even survival—resides.[3]

Of course, exceptional students selected for their extraordinary character are often those who help hold a family together. When they arrive at college, they must overcome intense feelings of separation and guilt. Lin's crucial role in her family became evident when her sister started rebelling against her parents. Suddenly they were calling Lin every day. At Carleton, she could not shed the burden of responsibility she carried within her family. Her new freedom not only seemed unfair or unearned, but it was virtual, not real. In general with these hyper-responsible students, the pressure to stay intimate with the family is intense, and the pressure to excel for the family increases. Telephone cards or cell phone contracts now enable daily communication, preventing students from remaining untroubled by the family's struggles long enough to study effectively. Paradoxically, the more interconnected the family and the more responsible the student, the more stress such troubles cause.

MOTIVATION

An instructor may thus observe in a student weak motivation or lack of focus that in reality stems not from academic irresponsibility but rather from heightened family responsibility and fidelity to cultural tradition.[4] Without a student's trust and extraordinary openness in sharing personal issues, however, an instructor or advisor may not be able to identify the real problem among various possible causes of weak performance.

Regrettably, among these exceptional students, family pain and struggles are all too prevalent. In one year my students and advisees had to deal with everything from parental separation and divorce and another parent's loss of employment to one mother's uterine cancer, a sister's brain cancer, a brother's rebelliousness that led the parents to anger and accusations of abandonment directed at my advisee, a boyfriend's depression and failure at a distant university, a brother's mortal illness, a brother's sudden death, and worry about friends working at the World Trade Center on 9/11.

> An instructor may ... observe in a student weak motivation or lack of focus that in reality stems not from academic irresponsibility but rather from heightened family responsibility and fidelity to cultural tradition.

The student whose friend worked in the Twin Towers found out he was okay; she had been badly shaken but was okay. However, the student whose brother was accidentally killed the day school began would occasionally find herself walking across campus with tears in her eyes, wondering where she was going and what she was doing here. Another student whose younger brother left home spent hours each week on the telephone trying to calm and reassure her parents that she still loved and honored them; she had to convince them that they could rely on her not to abandon them in spite of her being 400 miles away. These calamities (and these are only the ones I was told about) happen to many, but some students carry more than their fair share. And they deal with such burdens in addition, of course, to the common shock of separating from pets, home, friends, school, and neighborhood and having to learn a whole new physical, bureaucratic, and social environment.

How do we know when students are distracted by genuine problems and when they are just lazy, lack motivation, or have the wrong priorities? It could be all three or none of the above. In helping such students help themselves, whether it be overcoming their inertia or pride—whatever their resistance is—we can't assume the worst and give up. With such a student in the office, we can call the Academic Support Center or the ESL (English as a Second Language) instructor and have the student make an appointment on the spot. We can

> My own experience convinces me that knowing about students' lives helps me and, sometimes, even the students. The primary issue for me has been how to acquire relevant but personal information without violating appropriate personal and professional boundaries.

later send an e-mail or even phone the student to find out if he has kept the appointment. If not, we can talk again, and this time it can be made very clear what consequences will ensue if he doesn't get what help he needs. Our Academic Standing Committee makes those consequences abundantly clear with its message, "Take and pass 18 credits." The "or else" is an enforced leave of absence from the college.

If the student's issue is priorities (like family problems or a romantic break-up), then perhaps it is best dealt with away from campus. If the issue is lack of motivation, time spent in "the work force" may provoke a re-evaluation. If the problem is too little study and too much socializing, the threat of separation from the college should be a genuine deterrent. In addition to having students tell me in conversation or journals not only what they are studying but also how they are studying and what is helping or impeding them, I can call a class dean, a dean responsible for advising, or one responsible for residential life. These administrators (many are former teachers) sometimes have far more insight than I do. And they know that students learn from consequences, not preachments or endless extensions and a groundless softening of standards.

LEARNING WHY STUDENTS DON'T LEARN

A faculty member may understandably prefer not to know about students' extracurricular lives, believing that he will only meddle and wanting not to get involved in counseling situations for which he is ill prepared. My own experience convinces me that knowing about students' lives helps me and, sometimes, even the students. The primary issue for me has been how to acquire relevant but personal information without violating appropriate personal and professional boundaries.

One way to learn about life out of class is to have students keep journals related to their study, jottings that include mention of obstacles encountered in doing the work of the course. Students will share what they feel comfortable letting us know about, and we can respond by asking how serious the hurdles are or suggesting resources to overcome them. At least their journals will remind us that our students have lives sometimes as complex and challenging as our own.

Sometimes, however, regular conferences are the only strategy needed. When Lin came into my office and said it wasn't a good day to talk, I simply asked why. She began crying and I considered myself entitled to inquire about the problem. Luis, on the other hand, has never responded to opportunities to discuss the troubles he is having with his studies. I suspect that pride is the culprit, but he may also refuse to acknowledge to himself that his parents' hopes are not his and that he would rather play music than study economics. In any case, we need not be more intrusive than we believe is appropriate.

What other teaching and advising strategies or tactics will work for the students I have described? As one of my favorite deans reminds me and my colleagues, very few students really want to fail. We can and must believe in our students and help them learn how to succeed. Some arrive suffering from what Claude Steele calls "stereotype threat" (their own expectation of underperformance or failure)[5] and do not demonstrate their true ability even if their families are healthy and stable. This may be as true for white children of working class parents as for students of color. If we enter a classroom with preconceived notions about who will excel and who will do poorly, we reinforce internalized stereotypes.[6] Ideally, we would find out what the students know and teach them, in ways appropriate to their learning styles, as much as possible in the allotted time and topic. Unfortunately, such teaching often runs afoul of predetermined syllabi, and we often cannot adjust our teaching to how they learn most effectively. But those students who have not already experienced the best give us a chance to make a significant difference.

If we adopt an individualized learning strategy, how do we find out where students are within the parameters we have imagined for a course? If we assume that students do not want to fail and that they will do their best if they can, then we gain the best chance of seeing their best, if the course is designed to truly motivate them. In the case, for example, of a composition course, we may have to let them choose their own essay topics rather than assign topics that some will find interesting and others boring or intimidating. They may have to write several essays on the same topic to learn what "depth" and "development of an idea" feel like. For other courses in which students cannot choose their topics of study, we have to demonstrate relevance and significance.

As I suggested above, most students need to learn how to learn and perform in this new environment: how to craft discussible questions, how to imagine a reader's questions and objections, how to understand general rules through simple application, how to devise controls and verify experimental results, how to use relevant evidence to advantage, how to use writing in order to think clearly, how to investigate and articulate matters crucial to themselves and others. They must get right to the point, not rely on mechanical correctness or an impressive style. They often have to learn to delete the first and last paragraphs or even pages of an essay because they have docilely followed the format of the "five paragraph theme," or they have been taught to write as if giving an after-dinner speech: "Tell them what you are going to tell them; tell them; tell them what you have told them." In a four-to-six page college essay such repetition may earn a C- at best.

Students who have been getting Bs for good attendance and As for turning in mediocre work now have to learn how to write economically, moving back and forth as necessary between generalizations and specific, supporting details to develop their ideas. They must read hundreds of pages of often dense, technical prose every week and remember the salient facts. All of a sudden the game is being played faster, with a smaller, harder ball. And the crucial question arises, do these students really want to be where intellectual work is done?

Alumni, teachers, and friends who know the student and are familiar with a variety of institutions will have helped the traditional student find a suitable college. But first generation students with few college-educated friends will lack critical information because they haven't heard the instructive anecdotes. Luis, for example, has had trouble imagining how truly serious we are, with our distribution and language requirements, numerous essay assignments, and sustained research projects. Yet he is not one of the sort of students that John McWhorter describes in *Losing the Race*, none of whom would last long at Carleton. Here it is not cool to be anti-intellectual, to lack curiosity, to do the least to get by. For Luis, the problem may be suggested by the metaphor a colleague uses to describe Carleton. He says that it has "a very short on-ramp," requiring quick acceleration and total attention. Some students enjoy this, routinely playing the "I'm more stressed than you are" game, citing the number of pages they must read or write before dawn breaks, the difficulty of optional microeconomics problems, how many *kanji* they must learn for each Japanese class. Even extracurricular activities are taken seriously. Those who arrive nonchalant about pollution, world hunger, or the plight of the homeless quickly learn that engagement is not optional. You must care deeply about something or appear to be a fugitive from a country club. That makes it lots more fun to teach here but no easier, especially in helping those who must learn how to survive our pressure cooker in 10 weeks.

Let me venture another huge generalization: I see students stressed less by learning the material than by how we test that learning. We want them to understand concepts well enough to apply them, not just reiterate and explain them back to us, so we ask them to use the concepts in new contexts. It's not just "What are the most compelling push and pull factors in immigration?" Rather the challenge is "Let's apply these ideas about immigration to the Native Americans whose memoirs you have just read."

Learning to ask questions of the sort we find useful may be the highest hurdle. A weak secondary school may even have discouraged asking fundamental questions because such behavior can (or seem to) evidence inattention or disrespect for a lecture, assignment, or even the teacher. Many students are surprised to have their preconceptions and cherished values questioned, often most effectively in late night bull-sessions that challenge their faith or at least their piety.[7] Some wonderful homes, especially of recent immigrants or families under extraordinary pressure, discourage youthful questioning of an elder's experience or opinions. But at Carleton, in classrooms and dorms, such piety is dysfunctional rather than respectful. We believe that a truly liberal education requires that one identify and test the assumptions that our culture inculcates. We study phenomena historically, trying to discover what really happened, knowing at the same time that we will never know for certain; that we will only be able to collect and assess different versions and interpretations of events.

Unfortunately, our epistemological sophistication may be taken by students as complete relativism or sanction for it. Writing about the intellectual and ethical development of college students, William Perry (1970) points out that different students entering college may arrive with very different attitudes towards learning. Some are still at the absolutist stage, expecting indisputable answers. Others are relativists, believing that each person has his or her own "Truth" and that all are equally valid. The most mature acknowledge that different perspectives yield different views, while at the same time knowing that they must commit themselves to act on what they believe to be the most reasonable view they can achieve. Many of our students lack that maturity and are badly shaken when their unexamined faith begins to come under attack. They may retreat to relativism or reject intellectual inquiry altogether. The problem is that we may never recognize the presence and consequences of such diverse learning styles and stages, even if we are teaching a course where such issues are crucial. Some of the exceptional students I am discussing do not have such problems, but those whose strength derives from an unquestioned creed may find intellectual inquiry uncomfortable and even threatening.

> Historically, [college academic support] resources have been used more often by students trying to raise a B to an A than by students trying to raise a C- to a B-. Something is wrong with this picture ...

EXPLOITING OUR RESOURCES

My most intractable problem as a teacher and advisor has been to enable students to recognize that it is easy and laudable to use the college's resources and that it may be self-destructive not to. Historically, these resources have been used more often by students trying to raise a B to an A than by students trying to raise a C- to a B-. Something is wrong with this picture, but I have learned that just talking about the situation does not usually overcome a student's resistance. Students resist because of their pride, but also, I fear, because they do not really trust that we can teach them much. They have been reading since first grade, so how can some administrator teach them to read more effectively or efficiently? They have been writing since second grade, so how can an undergraduate writing tutor help them write better? For a 19-year-old to be told that she doesn't write well and could profit from meeting with a tutor could be humiliating, especially if she has been told otherwise by secondary school teachers. Students also resent having to add extra meetings to their already full schedules, especially they interfere with social engagements.

Quoting Steven Davis, the director of our academic support services, I continually repeat to my advisees and students the following statistics: For all TRIO students[8] who are advised to get some academic help, over 90% of those who sought and used help have graduated; less than 70% graduated of those who did not use appropriate college resources. Of course, the student who most needs help is the one least likely to see the instructor after class, ask for clarification, show up for tutoring sessions, or use the strategies suggested to learn vocabulary, understand and remember the reading, or organize and clarify his writing.

We will not always be able to figure out what a student's resistance to getting help is, but I suspect it's usually more like the resistance to informing the bank your loan payment will be late than to making that trip to the dentist. Shame is involved; you didn't meet expectations, especially yours, and you don't want to confront that ugly situation, because "God don't love ugly."

One of these days, I may find some games to play with new students in their first weeks here that focus on admitting a need for help and getting it. Some day I may find a magic formula to provoke students to open up, the way the words "Tell me about your high school" did last year during first conferences with advisees. So far, my most effective resources have been the telephone, e-mail, a soft chair for students, my thoughtful and generous colleagues, lots of patience, as few assumptions as possible, and a wonderful student support staff without whom the college would lose many exceptional students.

FURTHER ISSUES FOR RESEARCH AND REFLECTION

The two young people I have described above to illustrate the meaning of "exceptional students" may also help me pose two topics for consideration.

First, I have noted that some students who have perfect command of oral English have difficulty reading and writing "textbook" English. This seems especially true for ESL students. My observation is that they can learn scientific English but have difficulty with the discourse of humanistic studies. This may be because a scientific term, once learned, may be relied on to have a stable meaning and usage. However, humanistic study prizes subtle, nuanced, and innovative discourse heavily reliant on allusion and departure from convention. This language will present difficulties for all students, but, my hypothesis goes, especially for those like Lin, whose native language is not derived from Latinate or Germanic roots. Her native language supplies no cognates for her, and her family's culture, though rich, limits her means for decoding Western academic writing. One of my colleagues tells the story of holding a discussion about character and fate, during which he referred often to Homer's epics. At the end of the conversation one of his Chinese American students inquired quite understandably, "Who is Homer?"

> One of these days, I may find some games to play with new students in their first weeks here that focus on admitting a need for help and getting it. Some day I may find a magic formula to provoke students to open up, the way the words "Tell me about your high school" did last year during first conferences with advisees.

Second, I have noted that some undergraduates react to academic difficulty with renewed effort and others seem dispirited or paralyzed. In this connection, Kathie Galotti, a colleague who also has an essay in this volume, has recently made me aware of the work of Carol S. Dweck (1999) whose *Self–Theories* discusses the relationship of theories of intelligence to motivation and academic performance.

There is some evidence that in addition to his imperative to excel (a distinguishing characteristic of Luis, for example), a person's conception of his own intelligence may affect his performance quite powerfully. Dweck claims that students who believe intelligence is an entity unable to be changed and who want to prove that they possess intelligence by demonstrating mastery can be stymied by an early lack of success; they may come to view academic challenges as problems to avoid rather than opportunities to develop intellectual skills. They tend to see weak academic performance as confirmation of low intelligence rather than as a stage in the learning process. Thus, exceptional students who believe that they must prove that they belong may be devastated if they perform poorly. Dweck's work suggests that such students will be more easily defeated than others, especially if they have entered college with a weak academic background as well as a dysfunctional theory of intelligence. ■

ENDNOTES

[1] A paradigmatic example of this phenomenon may be seen in Ron Suskind's *A Hope in the Unseen* (1998).

[2] Joseph M. Williams (1990) has also published the best text I know for well prepared college students of composition.

[3] John McWhorter's *Losing the Race* (2000) focuses on students who have a learned antipathy to intellectual effort and achievement and who collectively create an anti-academic ethos hard to deviate from. For my reflections on this discussion, see below.

[4] Cf. The Challenge of First-Generation Students by Roland Merullo (2002).

[5] Claude Steele's ideas (1999) are cited and discussed in McWhorter (2000, p.116).

[6] On the issue of stereotyping and its results, see also Stephen Carter (1991).

[7] See Richard J. Light (2001), who bases his discussion of advising and teaching undergraduates on interviews with undergraduates at Harvard.

[8] TRIO is a program funded by the federal government that provides tutoring, books, and other resources for students who meet certain criteria, such as low parental income, first-generation status, etc.

REFERENCES

Carter, S. (1991). *Reflections of an affirmative action baby.* New York: Basic Books.

Dweck, C. S. (1999). *Self-theories: Their role in motivation, personality, and development.* Philadelphia: Psychology Press.

Light, R. J. (2001). *Making the most of college: Students speak their minds.* Cambridge, MA: Harvard University Press.

Merullo, R. (2002, June 14). The challenge of first-generation students. *The Chronicle of Higher Education*, B10-11.

McWhorter, J. (2000). *Losing the race.* New York: The Free Press.

Perry, W. G., Jr. (1970). *Forms of intellectual and ethical development in the college years.* New York: Holt, Rinehart & Winston.

Steele, C. (1999a, August). Thin ice: "Stereotype threat" and black college students. *Atlantic Monthly, 282,* 2, 44-54.

Steele, C. (1999b). Stereotype threat and the intellectual performance of African Americans. *Journal of Personality and Social Psychology, 69,* 797-811.

Suskind, R. (1998). *A hope in the unseen.* New York: Broadway Books.

Williams, J. M. (1990). *Style: Toward clarity and grace.* Chicago: University of Chicago Press.

106 — REFLECTIONS ON LEARNING AS TEACHERS

Teaching Yesterday, Today, and Tomorrow

Linking Course to Dramatic Production: The Euripides Project

Clara Shaw Hardy and Ruth Weiner

[WEINER AND HARDY] INTRODUCTION

Northfield, Minnesota, like many towns these days, has a great coffee shop. It has become a meeting-place for late-night students, early-morning lawyers, town radicals, and faculty like us from two colleges and all disciplines. It was there that we, Ruth Weiner, director of the Studies in Theater Arts Program, and Clara Shaw Hardy, chair of the Classics Department, hatched the scheme that became the Euripides Project.

Each of us had reasons for entering into the collaboration, and we'll outline those in more detail below. Weiner had never directed a Greek tragedy and now, for reasons that she will explain, was eager to attempt one. But the production she was starting to imagine relied on skills and resources she couldn't provide alone. Hardy had been teaching Greek drama for some time and was becoming increasingly interested in aspects of performance, both ancient and modern. Thinking about the plays as dramatic performances rather than texts was influencing her interpretations of them, while having students confront modern productions looked like a powerful way of engaging them in the material. But she had no experience with coaching students to help create a production themselves.[1]

The system we settled on was one that Ruth Weiner had already developed with a team-taught course and production of *Hamlet* in the fall of 1997. Our project involved an even larger cast of collaborators to deal with the differ-

CLARA SHAW HARDY, associate professor of classical languages and women's and gender studies, joined the Carleton faculty in 1990. She earned her B.A. at Oberlin and her Ph.D. at Brown University. RUTH WEINER, professor of theater arts and English, joined the Carleton faculty in 1969. She earned her B.S. and M.A. degrees at the University of Wisconsin.

ent issues presented by Greek tragedy. With the aid of the college, Weiner hired a choreographer, Devin Carey, and commissioned a translation of the play we had chosen from classicist and poet Robert Hardy. In the winter term of 2000, Carey worked with Weiner and a dance class to choreograph the choral dance pieces that would later be part of the play. In the spring term, we offered a new course cross-listed in classics and theater arts called "Euripides: Project Course." We taught the course together, each attending all classes and running most of them as a conversation among the two of us and the students who enrolled. We'll describe the course more fully below, but its central feature was that it required all 28 students to participate in that term's Carleton Players' production of Euripides' *Iphigeneia at Aulis*, directed by Weiner.

We chose the *Iphigeneia at Aulis* (*IA*) after a great deal of discussion. Euripides has a modern feel that makes his tragedies more accessible than those of Aeschylus or even Sophocles. The story of the *IA* takes place immediately before the Trojan War. Agamemnon, the Greek general leading the expedition against Troy, has been told that the ships cannot sail from the port of Aulis until he offers his daughter, Iphigeneia, as a human sacrifice to raise the winds. Agamemnon pretends that he wants to marry her to Achilles and sends for her on this pretext. But at the beginning of the play Euripides has him change his mind about the sacrifice. Before he can stop her, Iphigeneia arrives at the camp accompanied by her mother, Clytemnestra. As the play unfolds, in fact, each of the major figures in the Trojan War legend (Agamemnon, Menelaus, and Achilles) decides that pursuing the war is not worth the cost of the life of this young woman, and we teeter on the edge of radically changing myth and history as we know it. At the end of the play, however, Iphigeneia herself decides that she must die and goes willingly to the sacrifice.

As we relate our experiences individually below, it will be evident that the relationship between the course and the production was not as symmetrical or reciprocal as the term "linking" implies. Because Players' productions are open to all Carleton students, some students in the production (including the young woman who played Iphigeneia) were not in the class.[2] While both of us taught the class, only Weiner directed the play. Ideally, both Hardy and Weiner would have been at every rehearsal as well as every class. But the happy accident that it was Clara's husband, Robert Hardy, who wrote the translation (along with the fact that the Hardys have two young children) meant that

Clara could not always attend rehearsals when Rob did. And many of the production design decisions had to be made by Weiner before the course even started. Nonetheless, we both feel that the combination of course and production generated mutual benefits for us as well as for our students. In the next sections each of us in turn recounts her experience with the whole.

[WEINER] THROUGH A DIRECTOR'S EYES

Every modern production of a Greek tragedy tries, on some level, to recreate for a contemporary audience the quality of the experience of the Greek public.[3] In addition, we who teach theater at the college level face the added challenge of crafting an experience that will broaden the horizons and enrich the lives of the participants, our students. For Carleton's production of Euripides' *IA,* we believed that our best chance of achieving this synergy was to try to understand the ancient context and to apply this understanding to the problem of how to make an ancient Greek play compelling to our audience. It was to accomplish this that we set up the project course in Euripidean tragedy.

> Every modern production of a Greek tragedy tries, on some level, to recreate for a contemporary audience the quality of the experience of the Greek public. In addition, we who teach theater at the college level face the added challenge of crafting an experience that will broaden the horizons and enrich the lives of the participants, our students.

All theatrical production relies on collaboration between a range of artists and technicians. For example, in addition to our translator and choreographer, we worked with our staff designer/technical director and our staff costumer. Hardy and I, however, took the idea of collaboration further, bringing it into the organization of the course and into our own practice. Through the conjunction of course and production we combined normal theatrical practice with a new kind of pedagogy based on the idea that actually participating in a theatrical production would give students new insights and skills in textual analysis. We worked closely with each other and with colleagues in other disciplines with the ultimate goal of creating a unified, vital, exciting production and a comprehensive educational experience.

Regardless of the context—professional, educational, community-based—the first goal of anyone putting on a play is to do the best possible job. I came into the project course with a limited experience of producing Greek drama. In over 30 years of directing, I have only directed one Greek play—and that one three times—a comedy, Aristophanes' *The Birds*. Of course it wasn't easy; anything with a large dancing chorus is an automatic logistical headache, but the *story* of *The Birds* is relatively accessible, and *The Birds* is a crowd-pleaser and probably always was. Most important, the chorus didn't present any real problem that couldn't be fixed with sequins, feathers, lurid makeup, and lively, contemporary world music. In *The Birds*, the chorus could work the way a chorus in a musical works, lending its collective power to points of transformation in the plot and underlining thematically significant moments. But the tragic chorus seemed different to me: the linkage with the plot felt elusive; it was less malleable, and had more *gravitas*.[4]

I have studied Greek tragedy and teach the plays in my drama courses but have never felt able to produce one, mainly because I didn't know what to do *theatrically* about the chorus. I had seen and read about enough productions of Greek tragedies, some of them highly regarded, with what I considered to be deadly choruses, that I never wanted to attempt one. The idea of a static group of masked people, chanting in unison, *felt* intrinsically un-dramatic. Solutions, such as using a single person as chorus or cutting the chorus entirely, seemed to side-step rather than confront the problem. The chorus is the origin/source of all drama and could not be ignored. It didn't seem fair to eliminate the chorus and just do the story.

It wasn't until I saw Ariane Mnouchkine's *Les Atrides* comprising *Iphigeneia at Aulis* and *The Oresteia* at the Cartoucherie de Vincennes outside of Paris in 1990, and later, again, at the Brooklyn Academy of Music in October 1992 that I had some notion of the theatrical power the tragic chorus could command. Mnouchkine's masked chorus looked more South Asian than European, and danced to music which was more East Indian than European in feel. The athletic and exciting dances along with the exotic music had the effect of distancing the chorus, underlining its Asiatic foreignness, which made it very intriguing, as if the distance in space could represent the distance in time. This production, along with others such as Garland Wright's 1992 *Clytemnestra Project* that opened the 25th anniversary season at the Guthrie Theater in Minneapolis, demonstrated to me that the tragic chorus could be theatrically exciting on the most elemental level.

At the same time I still needed the course to ground the Carleton production in enough of a theatrical and historical context so that I had the courage to undertake translating an entire play into theater. Studying Greek drama in class gave me a sense of security about what I was doing as well. It also lent the performances of 18-year-old college students the authority that comes from an understanding of the dramatic text as the tip of the iceberg, the visible expression of an accretion of cultural and artistic belief and practice 2,500 years old. Simply knowing more about practices such as sacrifice, particularly ancient Greek attitudes toward human sacrifice (the crux of the plot of the *IA*), was enormously valuable. The Thucydides readings we assigned helped those of us working on the production to see Euripides' version of the beginning of the Trojan War as a template for the contemporary Peloponnesian War.

> The great personal advantage of working on the play in both the course and production was the coherence it gave to my work. Suddenly, the separation between the academic and the theater part of my job was gone.

The great personal advantage of working on the play in both the course and production was the coherence it gave to my work. Suddenly, the separation between the academic and the theater part of my job was gone. I could immerse myself in the text (which would yield a better, more thoughtful production) and use questions that arose in rehearsal to make for livelier classes.

Before rehearsals started, Rob Hardy and I went through the text, comparing his translation to others and trying to settle on both the closest to the original Greek and the most expressive English text that we could devise.[5] The actors and I continued to work with Rob Hardy on the spoken text, listening for what we wanted. There are many joys in working with an on-site translator, but one of the best is that if there were bits of dialogue that felt either awkward or stilted, Rob could work with us instantly to adjust them. This happened not only in early rehearsals but right through the rehearsal process. This also highlighted for students the constructed nature of any translation.

My goal, as director, in these early rehearsals was to ensure a clear understanding not only of what was being said, but of *how* it was said and of what was going on—what the stakes were in each scene. At the same time, each actor was struggling to understand his or her character and working on that character's key relationships. This also referred us back to the class, for we met these same characters in other works we read. I saw the play as progressing in three separate modes: (1) plot/scenes, (2) choral interludes/music, and (3) dance, only coming together at the end of the play when Iphigeneia accepts the necessity of her sacrifice. She becomes, in a sense, the creature of the chorus. Her lines shift from prose to poetry and she joins in the final choral dance.

From the beginning, we held separate chorus rehearsals. The choral dancers worked with the choreographer, separately from both actors and the speaking chorus who worked with me outside of regular rehearsals. The speaking chorus rehearsals were concerned, first, with determining the purpose, mood, relation of each of the choral intervals to the story being told (how each was unique), second, finding the most effective way of allocating the lines among the four chorus members, and, third, connecting each choral interlude to the correct dance and music.

As students became more familiar with the myths and variations referred to in the works we studied in class, the quality of the choral readings grew exponentially. For example, Cassandra's lament embedded in the third choral ode grew in resonance and meaning as the actress studied the events of the Trojan War, as well as those of the Peloponnesian War which it so often symbolized.

Of course everything wasn't smooth sailing. Ironically, what I *didn't* see as a problem when I undertook to direct the *IA* was the fragmented structure of the play itself. The *IA* tells a story—to all appearances it has a clear dramatic arc—but the structure is deceptive. In discussing his Guthrie production of *The Clytemnestra Project,* Garland Wright characterized the three Clytemnestra plays as "vaudevilles" with a scene-song-scene structure "with each scene ... becoming its own tiny play. ... The overall work is not held together by a story or an arch, but rather by a series of images, ... like a scrapbook of family photos" (Lewis, 1996, p. 42).

This is an important insight about the structure of Greek tragedy. It is as if we are given a glimpse of each character who makes his or her argument, then cedes the stage to other characters who do the same thing. These individual scenes are loosely linked by the choral interludes which both belong and do not belong to the story. At the beginning, the chorus are spectators, groupies, and tourists from Chalcis come to see the Greek heroes. They arrive after the long-ish prologue in which Agamemnon tries to forestall Clytemnestra's arrival. In contrast to the dark opening scene, the chorus mood is festive, bringing the perspective of the outside world to bear on the world of the army. Only in later odes does the chorus step back to speak directly to the audience about the background of important characters or tell us stories relevant to the play's plot.

Early rehearsals suffered through major upheavals: dancers dropped out, students couldn't come to rehearsal because they had choir or track. Those unused to doing theater had no idea of the amount of time, energy, and stamina a production as ambitious as the *IA* would demand. Still, the production would be the primary focus of our course, and those who wanted to do well in the course had to make it their primary focus as well.

For our music, we combined different genres with live, on-stage percussion. We found what we believed were the correct sounds in Japanese music like Ondekoza and taiko and kodo drums, in Gabrielle Roth's "Bones," and in Finnish pop. All of the dances and choral odes were set to music, as well as the end movement of the play, when Iphigeneia agrees to her sacrifice and is taken from Clytemnestra by the chorus.

Our total rehearsal period was eight weeks with a possibility of rehearsing about three hours a night four nights a week. I could schedule weekend afternoon rehearsals during the last four weeks. After about two weeks of text work I began to block, mostly large movements, including how the chorus would move in relation to the actors. Our set, designed by our staff designer/technical director Walter Wojciechowski, was an arrangement of angular platforms and scaffolding made of iron and steel. I wanted a genderized space, an environment that was harsh and uninviting, both to the chorus of young women and to Clytemnestra and Iphigeneia when they arrive. I wanted the other elements of production as well as the set to emphasize this lack of accommodation. Neither Clytemnestra nor Iphigeneia ever looked comfortable in the space as the men all did. Clytemnestra, for example, wore fragile shoes with very high heels, which meant that she had to be helped whenever she moved across the platforms. Iphigeneia wore a gauzy white dress.

Also, the set was divided at its highest point (about 11 feet up) so that the actors could not move across the platform system from stage left to stage right or right to left. This made the set look unfinished, so that when the bridge between the two halves of the set closed for the sacrifice at the end of the play, it signified, with a certain amount of irony, a repairing of the rift between men and women, the play's two factions. The final image of the play, after the sacrifice, was, in sequence, (1) the wind rising (depicted by the movements of the chorus down on the stage floor), (2) the army leaving for the ships over the back of the high platform unit (Agamemnon last), and (3) Achilles, before he leaves, lifting the body of Iphigeneia and laying her across Clytemnestra's lap. As the lights dimmed on everything else on stage the sound rose in volume and Clytemnestra, on the bridge which we had lowered between the two platform units, was left holding the body of Iphigeneia, pinned in a harsh white spotlight.[6]

> The moments that *resisted* integration taught me the most about this play. Confronting the problems posed by the chorus helped me understand the chorus' *raison d'être.*

With the integration of the dance and speaking choruses with the body of the play we were ready for performance. But, in an odd way, the moments that *resisted* integration taught me the most about this play. Confronting the problems posed by the chorus helped me understand the chorus' *raison d'être*. The story of the sacrifice of Iphigeneia can be easily told without a chorus. What the chorus does, apart from supplying some history and a public forum for the events of the play, is speak to us directly about the theater.

This is perhaps the most important way the course influenced production. Arnott and other readings supplied a historical and religious context not so much for the story of the play, but for the form itself and its role in ritual. Students became fascinated with alternate manners of dealing with the chorus on stage, and the chorus began to feel like our direct link to an ancient need to create rituals of worship, celebration, and mourning. This may not be much of a discovery for classical scholars, but for me and the students it utterly changed the way we look at Greek tragedy. For me, the chorus is about the theater itself and it celebrates theatricality independent of the particular story of the play.

[HARDY] A CLASSICIST'S PERSPECTIVE

I think that most classicists, perhaps especially those who teach in small colleges, consider themselves evangelists of the field. We want to bring the texts and culture we love to life for students who find them alien and remote in almost every way. The theater is a particularly effective place to do this; any production of an ancient play makes the text live, literally, in real time. When such productions are available in our area, I always take students, and whether the productions are good or bad the experience of attending and discussing one never fails to enhance students' understanding of the material; repeatedly, students have told me how different their response is to a live person on a stage than it was to that character's speeches on the page. The prospect of teaching a course in which students could not just attend, but would actually help create such a production was thus an enticing one for me; I jumped at the opportunity.

I was also attracted by the format of a team-taught course and the prospect of working with Weiner. Classics prides itself on its interdisciplinarity; the field comprises history, literary studies, anthropology, archaeology, and numerous sub-fields which take the engaged practitioner from humanistic to scientific and social scientific areas. Practically speaking, however, this makes many of us as teachers of classics into dilettantes in other specialties. I was used to introducing issues of production to students of ancient drama (and particularly the circumstances of ancient production). But I lack expertise, and in particular practical experience, with reading a dramatic text as a script for performance. This, of course, is exactly the way in which Weiner is trained to approach the texts, and it was clear from our first conversations and the first day in the classroom that her approach was productively

> I saw the link between course and production as a method of assuaging what I have come to think of as my lab science envy ...

complementary to mine. Each class we taught together enacted for our students the possibilities that open up when one discipline engages another.

Finally, I saw the link between course and production as a method of assuaging what I have come to think of as my lab science envy. Labs give students hands-on experience with the processes they study and thus cement their theoretical knowledge in a concrete, practical way that had seemed to me unavailable in the humanities. Lab assignments also foster a close and productive group dynamic among students who are working together intensively and at all hours. By contrast, students tend to do the traditional reading and writing of classics courses in isolation from each other. But theater students gain plenty of hands-on experience along with group solidarity in late-night rehearsals and in the struggles to make a text come alive.[7]

Our primary goal for the course, then, was to arrive at both a theoretical and a practical understanding of the *IA* and, by extension, other Greek tragedies. As we read and discussed the plays in class, my role was to teach students about their ancient contexts. This included the physical aspects of ancient theater as well as its ritual context (the plays as parts of a religious festival in honor of Dionysus and the ritual of sacrifice central both to that context and to the *IA* in particular). It also included the political context (for example the way in which the Trojan War stood in for the Persian Wars early in the 5th century and the Peloponnesian War in Euripides' later plays).

In these respects the course was exactly like any other course in translation that I teach. But because Weiner was teaching it with me, the ancient context was not our only focus. Throughout the term while discussing the ancient context we also examined issues of modern production. We discussed in detail those features of Attic tragedy that are most challenging for modern directors and audiences: the lack of action; the long, rhetorical speeches; the alien phenomenon of the chorus. And more and more as the course progressed students developed ways of seeing how the themes central to the tragedies (family relationships, conflicting public and private obligations, the limits of human autonomy, etc.) had resonances for their own lives.

Above all, because all of the students were involved in the production, the *IA* became something of a touchstone for us, a testing ground for these issues and a point of comparison to the ways they operated in other plays. The privilege of having the production linked to the course had multiple consequences for the learning of the students and for my own understanding of the plays: both tragedy in general and this tragedy in particular.

First of all, the production solved a pedagogical dilemma I have felt ever since I began teaching classics. Most of us in this field teach two quite different types of courses to undergraduate students: either the painstakingly slow readings of texts in their original language or much quicker romps through them in English translation. The language students, who might spend an entire 10-

week term reading only one play, can get to a very full appreciation of its themes, structure, diction, and imagery. On the other hand, their experience of the text slowed to this rate is highly artificial and utterly split from the text's intended context of performance in real time. In the translation courses students can cover a much larger amount of material and get a better idea of large trends in literary genres, but will seldom spend more than a class or two on each text. Unless they write a paper on a particular text, they rarely get to know it very thoroughly.

> Of course the students' involvement in the production of the *IA* entirely changed their experience of that play .... For eight weeks they lived and breathed that text; they engaged the issues it raises and its dramatic difficulties at a level I have never seen in courses of this type.

Of course the students' involvement in the production of the *IA* entirely changed their experience of that play. For the first time in my career, I was able to help students who had no Greek gain a deep and intimate knowledge of an ancient text. For eight weeks they lived and breathed that text; they engaged the issues it raises and its dramatic difficulties at a level I have never seen in courses of this type. Linking the production to the course made me realize just what is possible in the context of a course in translation.

In addition to this bridge that the course constructed between detailed and general levels of student learning, watching the production develop through rehearsal to performance taught all of us (and I include myself here) some vivid lessons about reading ancient tragedy. These are lessons that may be obvious to theater practitioners, and I had always paid lip service to them in the past, but watching our *IA* on stage brought them home to me in unforgettable ways.

I'll start with the aspect of sound in the play. Euripides' use of music was noteworthy in the ancient world. We know that in his later plays (and the *IA* is his last extant) he gave increasingly elaborate sung roles to his actors, but it is difficult to imagine just how this would have affected the tragedies in performance. In Weiner's production music, percussion, and other non-verbal sounds were essential elements, and their emotive effects were striking. I'll give just a couple of examples. The third choral interlude directly follows the scene in which Iphigeneia's mother Clytemnestra discovers that the wedding to Achilles is only a ruse to lure the girl to her sacrifice. The ode starts out as a festive and excited narrative of the wedding of Pelius and Thetis, Achilles' parents, then shifts into a lament for Iphigeneia, whose marriage will be to Death. The shift in mood effected by the music within this chorus was extremely moving. At the end of the play the beautiful and wrenching lyric lines of Iphigeneia as she was led off to sacrifice were accompanied by choral singing, and again the emotional effect was stunning.

In addition to the sound, the presence of bodies on a stage meant that we were constantly reminded of the visual element of drama. When you read, your attention will inevitably be focused on the words, and I for one don't always succeed in reminding myself that an audience is watching actors, not just listening to them. Perhaps the most vivid example of how the visible element came to affect my response to the plays is with the non-speaking characters. The stage is rarely inhabited by the speaking character alone, although this is the impression you will have as you read through a given speech and focus on the text. There are also the other central characters, who are responding to the speech, as well as (sometimes) non-speaking characters and almost always the chorus. While I have always found Iphigeneia's plea to her father to spare her life quite moving, I realized in watching the play that the effect of her words was greatly intensified by the sight of her helpless and devastated father who must listen to them with us.

Perhaps the most unexpected element that we discovered in putting the play on the stage was the presence of the audience. The 30,000 bodies who watched the plays in their first performances are even easier to forget about than the bodies on stage when you're reading these texts. But on opening night of the show, suddenly there were audible responses to the events unfolding on stage; the audience became part of the drama. We discovered things we had not anticipated in rehearsal: most disconcertingly, that some scenes turned out to have comic elements we had been unaware of. Clytemnestra's scene with Achilles, for example, got some laughs, and we hadn't been thinking of Achilles as a particularly laughable character. Yet once it had happened, it opened up all sorts of new areas for discussion: the highly complex range of emotions the audience must go through as it watches this tragedy; the function of laughter as a way to release unbearable tension; and the aspects of Achilles that Euripides is certainly critiquing, especially his solipsistic response to the mother's anguish.

Above all, the unexpected reactions demonstrated for the students what I believe is the single most important lesson about the ancient world available from modern productions: no audience is monolithic. Audience response will be as complex and varied as the audience itself; while we can identify tendencies and rule out crude anachronisms, the business of defining how "the Athenians" reacted to a given play in its initial performance is highly complex, and students, through their lived experience, gained a practical understanding of this complexity.

[WEINER AND HARDY] CONCLUSIONS

Assessing the value of the project course and performance two years later, we think it accomplished even more than we imagined it could. It introduced student audiences to a form with which they had little familiarity through an engaging and exciting production. More important, it gave participants a sense of mastery over complex, difficult material. It involved us all theatrically with music and dance as well as language. Because we felt drawn in to the production, we experienced empathy with the characters. This, in turn, enhanced our understanding of the harshness of the choices forced on *all* the principals.

Designing a class based primarily on the work of one playwright allows for extraordinary focus. We believe that the combination of the class and the production provided an integrated and intense experience for the students. The production functioned as an extended lab experiment for our students that term. From it they gained practical, hands-on experience of the way a dramatic text works that no reading or discussion could have replicated. They also achieved a group dynamic and solidarity that we have seldom seen.

Combining the course and production left Clara Hardy with the resolve to make the production experience more central to the teaching of classical drama in the future. She is currently studying production technique with Ruth Weiner with the aid of a grant from the Andrew Mellon Foundation. It also confirmed Ruth Weiner's belief in the educational value of connecting the production of a suitable play with a course.[8] The opportunities for multiple collaborations, the incentives to try new areas of activity, and the discoveries that may arise from a close study of both the text to be performed and related texts are too good to miss. ▪

ENDNOTES

[1] Hardy was already aware of classicists such as Mary Kay Gamel (University of California, Santa Cruz), John Gruber-Miller (Cornell College), and Anne Groton (St. Olaf College) at other institutions who regularly and successfully had students produce ancient plays. To Hardy it was a tantalizing yet daunting proposition.

[2] A total of 57 students were involved in the *IA*, with a cast of 33 (including the chorus, 4 separate speakers and 18 dancers, and 10 named roles, 8 of them speaking), student dramaturgs, musicians, designers, and crews.

[3] For a detailed reconstruction of this experience, see Arnott (1991), pp. 5-43.

[4] Greek tragedy is structured around the alternation of scenes between two or three actors and choral interludes. In the original productions, a group of 12 men danced and sang the choral odes; these odes are in a very different register from the dialogues, and their lyrics can feel tangential or even unrelated to the plots.

[5] We decided to cut the fragmentary and problematic messenger speech that ends the play in the manuscripts and end with an enactment of the sacrifice itself after Iphigeneia's lyric farewell.

[6] Photographs of the production may be found at http://www.acad.carleton.edu/curricular/THEA/photo/iphigeneia/index.html.

[7] There is a review of the literature on "active learning" in Bonwell and Eison (1991); also interesting is Lesgold (2001). Our project (on the lab analogy) emphasized not only active, but also cooperative, learning: see Johnson, Johnson and Smith (1991).

[8] Suitable plays, plays with a curricular tie-in, might be plays centrally concerned with alien cultures, specific literary genres, or plays that draw from a variety of disciplines, such as Tom Stoppard's *Arcadia*.

REFERENCES

Arnott, P. D. (1989). *Public and performance in the Greek theater.* New York: Routledge.

Bonwell, C. C., & Eison, J. A. (1991). Active learning: Creating excitement in the classroom. *ASHE-ERIC Higher Education Report, 1.* Washington, DC: The George Washington University.

Johnson, D., Johnson, R., & Smith, K. (1991). *Active learning: Cooperation in the college classroom.* Edina, MN: Interaction Book Company.

Lesgold, A. (2001). The nature and method of learning by doing. *American Psychologist, 56,* 11, 964-73.

Lewis, J. (1996). "The Clytemnestra project": The Guthrie Theater. In Mark Bly (Ed.), *The production notebooks: Theater in process: Vol. 1* (pp. 1-62). New York: Theater Communications Group, Inc.

Doing Ethnography: Learning Ways of Thinking and Writing Anthropologically

Pamela Feldman-Savelsberg

Through experiencing the process of doing ethnographic field research, beginning anthropology students learn how we know what we know in anthropology. By trying out various genres of anthropological writing throughout the research process, introductory students also experiment with different ways of thinking anthropologically. In addition to the cross-cultural encounter with multiple perceptions of reality, students directly experience multiple ways of perceiving and representing the realities of their own college community.

CREATING ANTHROPOLOGICAL KNOWLEDGE

Since my first undergraduate ventures into the world of cultural anthropology, I have found its subject matter absolutely riveting. The films I saw, the books about life in far-away places, and the stories of my professors revealed new worlds. They also raised fascinating questions about the ways very different societies work, acting as a mirror to reflect (or refract) how my own society works. I delighted that these questions were esoteric (making the knowledge seem special) while simultaneously dealing with the fundamentals of how people live together in groups. Did Iteso men in East Africa really replicate so-

> I wanted to invite my students to question how we anthropologists know what we know, as I had done in my youth. At the same time, I wanted that questioning to be grounded in the experience of *doing* anthropology ...

PAMELA FELDMAN-SAVELSBERG, an associate professor of sociology and anthropology, joined the Carleton faculty in 1993. She earned her B.A. degree at Indiana University, Bloomington, and her M.A. and Ph.D. degrees at The Johns Hopkins University.

cial hierarchies in the way they sat and joked at millet-beer parties? Did the color symbolism of Ndembu art really reflect tension and mediation among different stages of the ritual process? If Beng babies are "wiser" because they are closer to the realm of the ancestors (having just journeyed from that realm to ours), are we fools to coo at our babies, repeatedly telling them, "here is your nose, here is your cute little nose?"[1] I depended on the ability of the subject matter to captivate my students when I first began teaching, as a graduate teaching assistant and in my temporary appointments before landing my "real" (i.e., tenure track) job at Carleton. But somehow, it didn't seem enough.

I had "grown up" in anthropology during the 1970s and 1980s, a period of self-doubt and reflection in the discipline. We questioned not only the historical relation of the field to colonialism but also our ability to know and represent the "other." We debated these epistemological questions before we had ever been "in the field," before we had experienced the "dirt and despair of fieldwork" and its transformation into the "spit and polish" of published articles and monographs.[2] When I arrived at Carleton, I wanted to invite my students to question how we anthropologists know what we know, as I had done in my youth. At the same time, I wanted that questioning to be grounded in the experience of *doing* anthropology, something I had come to only at the end of graduate school. So, I tried to conceptualize a new way to introduce a discipline, my discipline, to introductory students.

My primary goal is to get students to understand—and to question—how knowledge is produced (how we know what we know) in anthropology. One way to approach this goal is to have students produce their own ethnographies of their immediate life-worlds. This experiential learning allows students to DO the subject matter of anthropology rather than merely read about it. It gives students a sense of what it feels like to do science.[3] Reading and writing remain important, giving students the background information to understand better the doing of science. Reading is also important as mode of discovery, opening up a world of "findings" *and* of modes of analysis that anthropology students cannot learn through close observation of their immediate environment. Writing is likewise a mode of discovery and expression. Field research, reading, and writing are *all* central parts of the scientific enterprise. They constitute data collection, data analysis, and critical engagement with a community of scholars. Thus, in my teaching I combine doing ethnographic fieldwork with reading and writing to give a multifaceted introduction to my discipline. To provide introductory students the opportunity to think and act like anthropologists (in other words to experience anthropology's unique methods of data collection and analysis), I developed an extensive ethnographic fieldwork assignment, the Ethnography Project.

TEACHING ETHNOGRAPHY TO INTRODUCTORY STUDENTS

Anthropology is the study of human beings in all their diversity. As with many liberal arts disciplines, students generally are introduced to anthropology by reading the intellectual products that anthropologists create—ethnographies and journal articles. These are polished, published descriptions and analyses of the ways of life, the culture and social organization, of particular peoples in specific times and places. Reading ethnographies, learning the "facts" within them, and even ferreting out their key concepts and theoretical framework are familiar activities for liberal arts college students. Understanding the ways that anthropologists produce these ethnographies, however, is harder for students to grasp.

Sociocultural anthropology is unique because anthropologists actually go and live with the people they are studying. Methods of data collection involve participating in everyday life while simultaneously observing it. In professional parlance, this messy, theoretically informed immersion experience is referred to as "ethnographic fieldwork." Anthropological theory-building is often "grounded"—that is, anthropologists often proceed inductively, developing concepts and explanations from patterns that emerge through observing the flow of life. While our research questions grow out of comparison and prior theory building, we rarely proceed deductively (starting with an explanatory theory and finding data that either illustrate or disprove that theory).

The Ethnography Project runs parallel to the more familiar reading, discussion, and analysis approach to learning anthropology in my Introduction to Anthropology course. Students spend the 10-week term conducting original ethnographic fieldwork on an aspect of Carleton culture. Students choose their own topics, often with great thoughtfulness and creativity. Frequent themes are studies of formal vs. informal leadership in campus activities (athletic teams, musical groups, special interest houses), and gendered patterns of dominance and subordination in communication. Role and boundary maintenance on the geology overnight fieldtrip, ways that shoppers hesitate and seek approval, enforcement of unspoken rules of etiquette in an art gallery, and speech patterns in relations among a group of lesbian and straight friends are some of the more unique topics of recent years. Students have found out, for example, that shared memories of experiences on the cross-country team and the conversations they engender help long-distance runners develop a distinctive sub-culture within the track team (Margoles, 2002). Decision-making in an *a cappella* singing group "involves not only those decisions and their practical results, but rests within a framework of social ties … [Decisions are shaped by these social ties because of] the need to be efficient and the desire to be liked" (Busiek, 2002, p. 1).[4] And, straight friends of a lesbian couple explore tensions between comfort and correctness by developing distinctive speech genres including slang, double standards, and insurance (Moreno, 2002).

The project is divided into distinct steps, with each step featuring both a stage in the research process and a distinct genre of ethnographic writing. These steps include writing up the research question in proposal form (the first and hardest of all assignments), writing fieldnotes (which involves sharpening observational skills and the ability to translate observation into text), describing methods in practical detail, preliminary analysis and in-text memoing (including the creation of analytic categories from data at hand, i.e., inductive reasoning), ethnographic description, ethnographic analysis, and a final reflection on the fieldwork process. The steps allow students to role-play being a professional anthropologist. Each step involves a short written assignment, often only one page long.

The project focuses on designing an ethnographic question, practicing methods of observation and participant observation, and working toward a multiperspectival form of ethnographic description called "thick description" (Geertz, 1973). Almost every written assignment goes through two drafts, receiving comments and suggestions from peer writing assistants as well as from me. All drafts are collected into a portfolio, providing students with a record of the development of their thought throughout the research process. At the end of the term, students hand in this portfolio along with a two-part "research report." The first part is a mini-ethnography, which allows students to describe and analyze what they have observed over a 10-week term. The second part is the student's written reflection upon his or her experience doing "hands-on" field research about culture and how this experience relates to those of professional, published anthropologists.

WRITING TO THINK AND THINKING TO WRITE

Doing ethnography is more than doing fieldwork. Since the end result of the anthropological discovery process is producing polished, written ethnographies, writing is an essential part of the ethnographic experience. The Ethnography Project focuses on developing writing skills for a variety of anthropological writing genres, with each writing genre corresponding to a stage in the research process. Through this structured series of assignments, I aim to teach research and writing skills as a repertoire of modes of thought which, taken together, lead toward a new, holistic understanding.

I approach different writing genres as different ways of "thinking across the page." Experimenting with genres of ethnographic writing is akin to role playing with different anthropological perspectives. An analogy from our anthropological readings helps students to understand my pedagogical goals. We explore the meaning of *keneh*, or thinking-feeling, an important concept in Balinese notions of the role of emotions in health and illness (Wikan, 1989). Our experiments with ways of writing fieldnotes and turning them into ethnographic description and analysis are experiments with thinking-writing, an interactive process that uses writing and re-writing as tools of discovery.[5]

> Learning a new discipline, and learning to write in a new discipline, is analogous to learning a new language—a language in which one must speak, read, and write. Anthropological terms and concepts constitute the vocabulary of my language. These concepts relate to each other and make sense in a particular order, my discipline's grammar.

I pay so much attention to writing and writing-thinking in this project because students' writing is so intimately tied to their reading. Learning a new discipline, and learning to write in a new discipline, is analogous to learning a new language—a language in which one must speak, read, and write. Anthropological terms and concepts constitute the vocabulary of my language. These concepts relate to each other and make sense in a particular order, my discipline's grammar.

As in language, conventions of use allow the anthropologist to deploy vocabulary and grammar in eloquent ways, evoking past conversations (perhaps debates in the field about the relative importance of symbols vs. social structure) to frame present ones. Students of anthropology can learn vocabulary and grammar by reading anthropological texts, but they internalize them and gain fluency by putting them into practice through the Ethnography Project. Likewise, they learn conventions of use by reading and discussing the works of professional anthropologists. But by tacking back and forth between their own field research and the published ethnographies on our syllabus, students learn about past anthropological conversations and are enabled to participate in current conversations more fully. This participation involves critical reading as well as writing (Fabian, 2001).

LEARNING CONCEPTS THROUGH PROCESS

One of the most obvious goals of an experiential project such as this one is putting anthropological terms, concepts, and methods into practice. Practice is more than a trick to internalize concepts. *Doing* ethnography enables students to gain deep insight into the process of anthropology and the challenges that went into producing the polished ethnographies they read for class. I present three brief, related examples.

Through experience, students learn about the method of **participant observation**. Choosing a social venue with which they are already familiar, students participate in some aspect of social life (e.g., as an occupant of a dorm room, as a member of a sports club). While participating, they simultaneously observe the social scene of which they are a part, seeking clues and patterns that will answer their research question (e.g., what ritualized social actions serve to create and maintain personal boundaries in a crowded dormitory). Student anthropologists experience the role conflict between being a participant and being a scientific observer.

Experiencing participant observation introduces students to the concept of the **collaborative nature** of anthropological fieldwork. Social and cultural anthropologists are generally lone wolves in the academic community; they most frequently do their research far away from colleagues, instead immersing themselves in the cultures they study. Despite this adamantly independent spirit of striking out on one's own, one of the characteristics of anthropological research is its collaborative nature. The collaboration, however, is with the people one is studying. What kinds of questions get asked and answered and what kinds of social actions get revealed and observed depend upon the interaction between the researcher and the researched.[6]

Students begin to question the quality of data whose collection is so dependent upon the unique personal interaction among a researcher and his or her research subjects, and learn that this type of data collection is best suited to exploring how participants give meaning to their actions. Some students thrive on the **ambiguous nature** of fieldwork, while others are disturbed by the unpredictability of the process. Part of students' appreciation of how anthropological knowledge is created includes letting the frustrations of mid-project lead to an understanding of just how much "grit work" goes into ethnographic fieldwork.

Students' new-gained practical knowledge (based on learning by doing) and insights into the process of anthropological research enables them to read ethnographies with a deeper, critical understanding. They may even become bold enough to consider critiquing, with sensitivity, the methods of published authors. No longer are anthropological texts "just the facts, ma'am," but rather products of a process of research, thinking, and presentation.

AMBIVALENCE AND LEARNING FOR STUDENTS: CHALLENGES OF EXPERIENTIAL LEARNING

Introductory students confront several challenges in pursuing this ethnographic research project. In addition to the most obvious challenges of maintaining interest and staying organized throughout an entire term, students confront many of the difficulties that plague professional anthropologists. They lack the confidence of feeling that they already "know" the field, however, and this can make the process uncomfortable for some (particularly for Carleton students who want to do things well and "right"). While a few students remain uncomfortable throughout the term, resenting the risky and time consuming nature of experiential learning, most overcome their discomfort to arrive at a new level of anthropological understanding and a sense of personal accomplishment.

Choosing a topic that is anthropologically interesting from familiar situations is difficult, especially if one approaches anthropology with the [now greatly outdated] assumption that anthropologists study only the exotic other.

When I first began this project I was nervous. I thought that anthropology was the study of other cultures. How would I conduct an anthropological study in my own society, especially as a novice to the field? I wanted my project to be interesting, to have an edge, and I thought for that to be possible I would have to go out looking for an exceptionally interesting group around Carleton to create a more exotic feel for my fieldwork… [Eventually] I came to my research question through my own experience of shopping…. (Speigner, 2002, p.1)

What could be anthropologically interesting about something so mundane as shopping for clothes at Ragstock? I was frankly doubtful at the onset of this student's project, no doubt (unanthropologically) blinded by my own prejudices that shopping is a distasteful necessity, a distraction from the life of the mind. But the ways in which shoppers express hesitation and seek approval for their choices and the effect of group size and gender on this approval seeking revealed an important social aspect of shopping, worthy of scientific analysis.

The challenge of finding interesting anthropological questions in the mundane particulars of everyday life at college is compounded by our familiar models of doing science. Most introductory students enter the classroom with a model of scientific inquiry based on deductive thinking, starting with an explanatory theory or hypothesis about how some aspect of the world works, and then finding evidence that either supports or refutes the theory. When the setting is very familiar (one's own culture) what seems like an explanatory social theory is often a participant's culturally specific way of explaining the world. For junior anthropologists, what seems like deductive thinking is often working on *a priori* assumptions. Eventually students recognize that they (or "we") think and act using deeply internalized folk or cultural categories that powerfully shape perception, just as the Trobriand Islanders and other famous "others" do. Including themselves in a global rainbow of otherness helps students to distinguish between *a priori* assumptions and scientific theory.

But, ethnography's emphasis on inductive reasoning also requires a reorientation for students. They need to throw out those *a priori* assumptions and work from the bottom up, approaching culture as a language learner. This reorientation is compounded by the challenges of doing research in a familiar setting and asks students to imagine themselves as strangers. One student described this challenge as coming to grips with the "distinction between doing and knowing culture" (Olson, 2002:1).

No matter how well students can do culture (i.e., participate), getting to know culture (i.e., learning about the meaning of an abstract principle, culture, by analyzing a specific example of a culture) is fraught with unexpected challenges. Even the best conceived research plans need to be adjusted midstream. The fieldwork process is ambiguous, with fluid boundaries and unpredictable events. Students prepare for doing ethnography and get a sense of "real" anthropologists' experience by reading their completed ethnographies and by reading their published reflections on fieldwork. These polished, professional accounts can give a false sense of security, a sense of "recipe" when real fieldwork requires constant innovation.

> It sounded simple enough. After all, I head read accounts of *real* anthropologists' experiences in the field and all *they* did was go and observe some people. As near as I could tell everything was really obvious and their analysis came to them right away. I thought that all I had to do was follow their methods and certainly everything would fall into place as well. (Moreno, 2002, p. 1)

Once students actually conduct an ethnographic research project, they are confronted with surprises. Most of these surprises are instructive, although some at first appear merely frustrating. People in "the field" don't act in expected ways. Well formulated research questions prove unmanageable. Events and examples do not emerge discretely from the observed flow of life.

AMBIVALENCE AND LEARNING FOR PROFESSORS: MY ONGOING STRUGGLES WITH THE PROJECT

The Ethnography Project is my developing attempt to structure a unique process that includes the advantages of experiential learning (*doing* social science) without denigrating learning by reading, listening, discussing, and writing. After all, it was through these latter modes of learning that I developed my interest in anthropology.

Reading and discussion remain important to me as a teacher because they are a central part of professional anthropological practice. If I seriously want to give students the full experience of doing anthropology, then I need to integrate the fieldwork process with the readings on the syllabus. Making a connection between the Ethnography Project and other class content in a sustained fashion is an ongoing challenge. Readings on fieldwork (Lee, 1984; Bohannon, 2001; Berreman, 1962) and an ethnography of college life (Moffat 1989) at the beginning of the class work well. But concepts, e.g., on culture and language, on exchange systems, on leadership and politics, that would be helpful as students develop their research topics need to be introduced, through ethnographies, throughout the term. At times teaching anthropology through ethnographic *fieldwork* and teaching anthropology through *ethnographies* seem like teaching two parallel classes. With every term I find new opportunities to bridge the two endeavors. For example, when teaching about the advantages and limitations to using language as an analogy for culture, I also discuss how the writing genres we practice are analogous to different modes of thought or different cultures of communicating within the anthropological universe. When discussing particular principles of social organization, I draw on past student ethnography projects as well as on our classroom readings to illustrate concepts.

The other major challenge I face in teaching this project is making clear the relation between ethnographic field research, anthropological thinking, and anthropological writing. Although learning "good writing" is highly valued among Carleton students, many assume that they either already are good writers or that they should learn good writing in another venue.

> Doing science, even a "soft" science, is a very deliberate, self-conscious, and in the end reflective exercise.

Many of our students are good writers. It is challenging to convince stronger and weaker writers alike that our emphasis on anthropological writing genres means that there are many modes of good writing, corresponding to modes of good thinking. A few students each term resent meeting with writing assistants, because they "already know how to write." These students would be more comfortable using "teaching assistants," a position that we don't have in the social sciences. I try to deflect student resistance to "help with writing" by explaining that the writing we are doing is trying out different modes of thought. A complete ethnographic experience involves frequent switching of gears among different ways of thinking about data, as well as different ways of writing about data.

LEARNING WHILE AWAKE, AND WAKING UP TO DIFFERENCE

> ...I enjoyed the fluidity of the field experience. As an anthropologist you have to be willing to adapt and modify your research in the field; this exercises a certain present mindedness. (Erickson, 2002, p. 8)

For all its challenges, the Ethnography Project continues to be a satisfying way to introduce students to my discipline. It invites them to wake up, to actively engage in creating the same kind of knowledge that they read about in class. They discover patterns in the flow of social life but only if they are willing to risk going with the flow during the participatory phase of ethnographic research. Students learn that, while going with the flow, they need to sharpen their powers of observation and constantly question what they are observing. Doing science, even a "soft" science, is a very deliberate, self-conscious, and in the end reflective exercise. The experience of doing ethnography, including the reading and writing as well as the field research that involves, helps students understand how we know what we know in anthropology and thus better understand how we know what we know about human and cultural diversity.

In this way, the Ethnography Project is more than a teaching tool. It addresses the values and academic mission of Carleton College as well as an ethos underlying most anthropological work. Recognizing identity (culture is learned and shared, part of being a member of a group) and difference (cultures are distinct from one another, specific to particular times and places) are central to the anthropological project.[7] Doing anthropology through the Ethnography Project aims to help students critically examine cultural differences. Part of this involves recognizing themselves and their everyday environment as part of the range of cultural differences found worldwide.[8] Students suspend everyday assumptions of the ordinary to make the familiar strange, to treat themselves or their familiar surroundings as if it were part of a different culture. By experiencing and reflecting upon how anthropological knowledge is generated and presented, students learn about one way (social scientific scholarship) that we construct knowledge about cultural differences. My hope is that they continue to add the sharpened perspective of the astonished observer to their lives. ▪

ENDNOTES

[1] I draw these examples from the work of one of my most inspiring undergraduate teachers (Karp, 1980), from one of my most inspiring undergraduate readings (Turner, 1967), and from one of my most inspiring colleagues (Gottlieb, 1998).

[2] I am grateful to my colleague James F. Fisher for this felicitous phrasing.

[3] Modules in experiential learning are becoming ever more common in many disciplines; for an example from chemistry, see Trish Ferrett's contribution to this volume. James Spradley and David McCurdy were pioneers in introducing introductory anthropology students to ethnographic fieldwork (Rice and McCurdy, Eds., 2000). Shorter versions have been adapted to different teaching venues (e.g., Goodman, 2000). These projects connect disciplinary knowledge to the "real world" (Newman, 1999).

[4] This and other excerpts from student papers are quoted with written permission of the authors.

[5] I am lucky to collaborate with three peer writing assistants (usually anthropology majors) to teach anthropological thinking-writing by working individually with students on multiple drafts in each writing genre.

[6] In class, we discuss ways that this collaboration between the researcher and the researched places two types of responsibility on the researcher: 1) the ethical treatment of human subjects; 2) the ethics of representing others to a broader public.

[7] At Carleton, this is formalized through the "Recognition and Affirmation of Difference" requirement. Introduction to Anthropology and the Ethnography Project, especially its final, reflective field report, play an important role for students in fulfilling this requirement. For further commentary on the RAD requirement, see Cathy Yandell's essay in this volume.

[8] Hill (1999) identifies anthropology's ability to challenge students' assumptions regarding human diversity as an important contribution to civic understanding and global coexistence.

REFERENCES

Berreman, G. (1962). Behind many masks: Ethnography and impression management in a Himalayan village. *Society for Applied Anthropology, Monograph No. 4.* Washington, DC: American Anthropological Association.

Bohannon, L. (1994). Shakespeare in the bush. In A. Podolefsky and P.J. Brown (Eds.), *Applying anthropology: An introductory reader* (6th ed., pp. 150-155). Mountain View, CA: Mayfield.

Busiek, A. (2002, June). *(Carleton) Knights of the round table: Exit 69 and its decision-making processes.* Unpublished term paper for Sociology/Anthropology 110, Carleton College.

Erickson, R. (2002, June). *Power construction and etiquette behavior: Field research in an art gallery setting.* Unpublished term paper for Sociology/Anthropology 110, Carleton College, June 2002.

Fabian, J. (2001). Keep listening: Ethnography and reading. In J. Fabian, *Anthropology with an attitude: Critical essays* (pp. 53-69). Stanford, CA: Stanford University Press.

Geertz, C. (1973). *The interpretation of culture.* New York: Basic Books.

Goodman, B. (2000). Cultural anthropology 101: Teaching cultural anthropology scientifically. In P.C. Rice and D.W. McCurdy (Eds.), *Strategies in teaching anthropology* (pp. 63-70). Upper Saddle River, NJ: Prentice Hall.

Gottlieb, A.J. (1998). Do infants have religion? The spiritual lives of Beng babies. *American Anthropologist, 100(1)*, 122-135.

Hill, C.E. (1999). Challenging assumptions of human diversity: The teaching imagination in anthropology. In B.A. Pescosolido and R. Aminzade (Eds.), *The social worlds of higher education: Handbook for teaching in a new century* (pp. 271-279). Thousand Oaks, CA: Pine Forge Press.

Karp, I. (1980). Beer drinking and social experience in an African society: An essay in formal sociology. In I. Karp and C.S. Bird (Eds.), *Explorations in African systems of thought* (pp. 83-119). Bloomington, IN: Indiana University Press.

Lee, R. (1984). Eating Christmas in the Kalahari. In R. Lee, *The Dobe !Kung* (pp. 151-157). Fort Worth, TX: Holt, Rinehart and Winston.

Margoles, S. (2002, June). *Separate subcultures.* Unpublished term paper for Sociology/Anthropology 110, Carleton College.

Moffat, M. (1989). *Coming of age in New Jersey.* New Brunswick, NJ: Rutgers University Press.

Moreno, V. (2002, June). *I say lesbian, you say leebian, Or: slang, double standards, and insurance in a dormitory setting.* Unpublished term paper for Sociology/Anthropology 110, Carleton College.

Newman, D.M. (1999). Three faces of relevance: Connecting disciplinary knowledge to the "real world." In B.A. Pescosolido and R. Aminzade (Eds.), *The social worlds of higher education: Handbook for teaching in a new century* (pp. 309-317). Thousand Oaks, CA: Pine Forge Press.

Olson, A. (2002, June). *Two become one: An anthropological study of the Carleton College Aikido Club.* Unpublished term paper for Sociology/Anthropology 110, Carleton College.

Rice, P.C., & McCurdy, D.W. (Eds.). (2000). *Strategies in teaching anthropology.* Upper Saddle River, NJ: Prentice Hall.

Speigner, C. (2002, June). *Attention Ragstock shoppers, does this make me look fat? An investigation of the insecurities of shopping in groups at Ragstock.* Unpublished term paper for Sociology/Anthropology 110, Carleton College.

Turner, V.W. (1967). *The forest of symbols: Aspects of Ndembu ritual.* Ithaca, NY: Cornell University Press.

Wikan, U. (1989). Managing the heart to brighten face and soul. *American Ethnologist, 16(2),* 294-312.

Seeking the Other in Early Modern Literature

Cathy Yandell

> *"L'histoire, comme tu peuz entendre,*
> *est chose de soy fort chatouilleuse."*

[History, as you can imagine, is a very tricky subject.]

Estienne Pasquier, *Dialogues,* 1560

> *"Je trouve qu'il n'y a rien de barbare et de sauvage en cette nation,*
> *à ce qu'on m'en a rapporté, sinon que chacun appelle*
> *barbarie ce qui n'est pas de son usage."*

[I don't find anything barbarous and savage in that nation,
from what I've heard, except that all of us call
barbarous what is not our practice.]

Montaigne, "Of Cannibals," 1580

A few years ago, students in Carleton's Department of Romance Languages and Literatures had the ingenious idea of making a T-shirt for French majors with the purpose of building community spirit. A winning entry in the competition for a slogan quickly emerged: "French at Carleton: Seeking the Other since 1866." The in-joke would be readily apparent to any reader of the college's website or catalog, in which almost every upper-division French class that is listed there treats in some way the other, the outsider, the exile, the immigrant, the transplant, the transgressor, the outlaw, or the eccentric.

This unbridled frenzy for studying "otherness" is not restricted to a particular discipline, of course, nor can it be found only in the humanities and

CATHY YANDELL, the W.I. and Hulda F. Daniell Professor of French Literature, Language and Culture, joined the Carleton faculty in 1977. She earned her B.A. at the University of New Mexico and her M.A. and Ph.D. at the University of California, Berkeley.

social sciences. Carleton, like many colleges and universities throughout the country, has instituted a one-course requirement for the "Recognition and Affirmation of Difference" (the "RAD Requirement"), which addresses among other things "the experience of being different." Specifically, students are required to study areas outside Europe or the United States and/or issues of gender, class, race, or ethnicity anywhere in the world.[1]

As valuable as these studies in diversity are, I believe that our students need to examine another area rich in difference, one that incorporates a more temporal perspective: the historical other. This form of otherness is the principal focus of my class on literature of the French Renaissance, which in addition investigates yet other manifestations of difference. Titled "Love, War, and Monsters in Early Modern France," the course unites the three apparently disparate subjects by their relationship to the concept of the other. Conceived as an introduction to the literary and social culture of the French Renaissance, the course also aims to allow students to encounter some of the linguistic ambiguities, the political instabilities and the philosophical controversies of the 16th century.

> As valuable as these studies in diversity are, I believe that our students need to examine another area rich in difference, one that incorporates a more temporal perspective: the historical other.

It occurred to me about two years ago that although the French Renaissance is the area I am most passionate about, as well as the field of my research and publications, my upper-division Renaissance course proved paradoxically to be the most difficult to teach. Both the readings and the class discussions were often stimulating, yet something was lacking in the course as a whole. It seemed to me that the students were not sufficiently engaged in their learning. They would complete the assignments but were often unmotivated to go beyond a superficial understanding of the texts. To explore Renaissance culture, ideally, should be to view the world through several different lenses. Upon reflection, I identified at least one major problem of the course: My pedagogy was not sufficiently attuned to the subject itself. In other words, if I was serious about the students' discovery of historical difference in the literary texts, I needed to devise assignments that required more critical probing, more confrontation, and more originality on the part of the students.

In the process of redesigning this course, I have learned what could be called pedagogical "lessons" or a few eclectic ideas on teaching. I offer them here as a document-in-progress, since classes continually change and teaching is inevitably a dynamic, ongoing endeavor. Pedagogical ideas do not originate in a vacuum, of course; in my case, they have arisen from the classroom itself, as well as from extensive pedagogical discussions with colleagues.[2] At the least, I hope that these ideas will generate discussion; at best, perhaps colleagues in related fields will find them useful for their own teaching. In writing these reflections on pedagogy, I continually recall the celebrated aphorism attributed to Michelangelo, "*ancora imparo*" [I am still learning].

Lesson number one: It is my responsibility as a teacher to help students become continually vigilant readers. Language itself can serve as a metaphor for the initial confusion students encounter as they enter into the early modern period. Sometimes what looks familiar is indeed familiar, and at other times the familiar can lead one astray. In middle French, for example, the verb "*cognoistre*" looks much like the modern French "*connaître*," which is an accurate reading. However, the word "*aucun*," meaning "someone" in middle French, signifies quite the opposite ("no one") in modern French. To the students' bemusement, "incontinent," today a cognate in French and English, in middle French means simply means "suddenly." Readers of Renaissance English are faced with similar problems: The word "silly" (or "*sely*") in middle English can encompass meanings of happy, innocent, good, kind, poor, and hapless. Finally, the term "booty," meaning "guerdon" or "mede" (a precious stone) in middle English, often elicits giggles from 21st-century students.[3] Thus the language is at the same time familiar and different, reliable and untrustworthy. The heightened attention to language prepares both teacher and students for the work of deciphering meaning in the literary texts.

Interestingly, I originally intended to spare drudgery early in the course and hoped that the students would acquire the necessary vocabulary through experience as the term progressed, yet students often complained of the linguistic difficulty of middle French. I now hold students accountable for a fair amount of vocabulary (and the reading of Roman numerals necessary for locating sonnets in a collection!) quite early in the term, which then liberates them to concentrate on the text and its social context. Now that we devote attention ton to mastering the technically difficult aspects of vocabulary straight away, students seemed to find the language less daunting.

Lesson number two: Intellectual rigor is dependent not on the quantity of works read but rather on the depth of the critical analysis. What was once known as "coverage" is perhaps a figure of our collective professorial or educational imagination. Indeed, "coverage" is an intriguing word: What would it mean to "cover" French Renaissance literature? In my particular course, it seems more fruitful to imagine ourselves "uncovering" important works from 16th-century France, some of which are known today whereas others were frequently read in their day but have since disappeared from circulation. These sorts of statements have become truisms in contemporary pedagogical discourse, but how exactly does one go about creating a course in which this ideal is realized?

The study of historical "difference" requires particular attention to detail on the part of the students. When I first taught the Renaissance course, I wanted to ensure that students had the broadest possible understanding of the poet Ronsard's works, so I assigned between 10 and 20 poems per class for close analysis (my reasoning, although feeble, was the following: Ronsard did, after all, write over 2,000 pages of poetry!). Under this system, with everyone held responsible for all of the poems assigned for each class, students' understanding was sometimes good, but often not.

Since students were doing too little with too much, it seemed that the solution would logically be to devise a way to do more with less. But it wasn't quite that simple. Not being convinced that cutting down on the number of poems to be studied would be useful unless the reduction were accompanied by more attention to the process of explicating a poem, I began requiring a short book on poetic analysis in French and distributing sheets I had prepared for students with many suggestions for the critical reading of poetry.

Further, since there remained arguments for the students' exposure to a larger number of poems than those we could reasonably analyze during the class period, I noted in advance a few poems that we would discuss at length in class. While these steps brought some improvement in class discussions, individual engagement was still not what I had hoped it would be.

Enter the problem of the relationship between individual assignments and class discussion. I had previously asked students in pairs to give oral presentations of poems, but too often each presentation became a *vox clamans in deserto*—other students tuned out. My plan for the next course (yet to be implemented) is to assign one poem per student for written analysis outside of class and to suggest a few extratextual leads in each case (for example, Neoplatonic philosophy, Petrarchism, Renaissance uses of particular mythological characters). In class, rather than making formal oral presentations, students who have prepared poems for that day will contribute to class discussion and raise questions for their colleagues. With the addition of the extratextual categories, I hope that the students will be continually reminded that even poetry—arguably the most self-contained of discourses—takes place within what Michel Foucault terms an "epistemological space" or a cultural code of a given society at a given time.[4]

> Since students were doing too little with too much, it seemed that the solution would logically be to devise a way to do more with less. But it wasn't quite that simple.

In a final change in the course that privileges depth over quantity, I limited the number of anatomical poems that students read, while adding a critical exercise intended to heighten students' awareness of the period. Since the French poet Clément Marot launched a poetic contest in the 1540s and asked Renée of France to serve as judge, I challenged students to recreate the contest by imagining that they were a committee advising Renée (needless to say, the winner of the historical contest was not revealed in advance). Each of them was to choose the most ingenious of the poems and to be prepared to defend it using contemporaneous criteria. The debate proved to be quite illuminating, with the discussion ranging from *gaulois* humor to Neoplatonic philosophy; the students ended the discussion in a draw between two of the poems, one of which in reality Renée had chosen as the winner.

Lesson number three: If a class is being taught for the second time or more, it seems to me essential to continue to "problematize," to ask another question, to go beyond what was studied the last time the course was offered. This principle, a *sine qua non* for teachers in higher education, is particularly important in looking at questions of difference. Like all teachers of literature, I attempt to bear in mind that it is not only what the text says that matters but also how it says what it says, be it through figures of speech, dialogue, poetic techniques, and even implicit resonances within explicit language. These elements often make the text mean more than what it first appears to say or even imply something contradictory to what it appears to say. Renaissance writer Catherine des Roches, for example, in an overtly moralistic dialogue, appears at first glance to follow the traditional teachings of Plutarch, Erasmus, and Vives, all of which specifically discourage dancing for women. Yet as the two young women characters of the dialogue discuss the importance of study, one of them recites love poetry and offers to play the lyre while the other dances. One must ask how these artistic interventions in the text change not only the shape but indeed the message of the dialogue.

To help students discover such subtle textual plays and to sharpen their critical skills, each time a short essay is due I have begun inviting four or five students to post their essays to a class folder; another group of students then reads them carefully and evaluates them on a prepared form, which includes such questions as "What is the author's thesis?" and "What specific suggestions would you offer for clarifying or tightening the argument?"[5] The query "In which ways does this essay further your understanding of the text?" reminds both writers and their critics that analysis involves explanations that a first-time reader might miss: In a poem, for example, what is the relationship between the strophes? How does the structuring of the text reveal its meaning? What references (e.g., historical, mythological, political) should be sought in other sources? This peer-based process inevitably enlivens the discussion in the next class, and students seem to appreciate both having a larger audience and receiving comments from their colleagues. Most important, through this new addition to the course, students are invited to read on several different levels and to establish their own critical voices.

Lesson number four: Since a literary text is produced within a social context, students should be encouraged to research aspects of that context and to contribute them to class discussions (rather than having all paraliterary material introduced by the professor). Whereas in previous years I presented the primary conflicts of the French Civil War, I now ask students to research and provide that information in class discussion. Half of the class (in groups of two or three) is assigned topics related to the Protestant point of view (e.g., the right to read and translate the Bible in the vernacular, the corruption of the Catholic church, Henry IV's perceived role as a Protestant future king) and the other half subjects related to the Catholic position (the importance of maintaining a united France, the heretical position of the Protestants regarding transubstantiation, Henry IV's perceived role as a converted Catholic future king). This "sharing of the burden" also makes for a far more complex and more spirited discussion of the polemic poetry by Protestant and Catholic writers. Moreover, the exercise subtly reveals to the students how it is possible to "take sides" simply because of a better understanding of a certain position and also how the strength of rhetoric can sometimes carry an idea even if the speaker disagrees with it. Students occasionally find themselves genuinely arguing a position that in no way corresponds to their religious background (or lack thereof) simply because they have understood the reasoning behind the belief—the reasoning of an other.

Lesson number five: Creativity, rather than simply providing an outlet or an agreeable detour, can play a fundamental role in the course. Ideally, of course, all class work calls in some way upon the creative capacities of students. Even the ostensibly driest research paper can benefit from creative ideas, but some assignments require more overt creativity than others. I now include a number of explicitly creative assignments during the course of the term. Near the end of the section on poetry in the last Renaissance course, I asked the students to write a French sonnet in one of the commonly used forms of the period ("Marotic," classical, or Italian), including accurate rhyme scheme, strophes and versification. Many students, who had never written a sonnet in any language, remarked that before undertaking this exercise they had never before understood what was involved in the making of a sonnet, even though they had studied sonnets for a number of years. When the sonnets were revised with the help of other students, the professor, and the French assistant, one of the students then assembled the sonnets to "publish" a booklet (replete with student artwork) as a *memento vivere* for the course.

Another of these creative assignments derived from a student's idea.[6] A few weeks before the final exam, I often ask students to submit an essay question that they believe will induce serious reflection on the questions addressed by the course, and I distribute some of these questions (along with a few of my own) to the class to supplement their preparation for the final. One suggestion struck me as so excellent that I chose it as a take-home question for the final: "In the autobiographical style of Montaigne, write an essay discussing some aspect of what you have learned in this course." Since Montaigne frequently quotes from literary sources in his essays, this was a particularly felicitous question. It produced a number of thoughtful essays—so much so that I plan to use the idea again (or a similar idea) in future courses.

A final assignment inviting the students' ingenuity, unimaginatively titled "the creative project," came at the very end of the course, approximately two weeks after the major research paper for the course was due. It was conceived to some extent as an antidote to the formal, academic paper (which to my mind is an essential component of this upper-division course) and also as a means of demonstrating that responses to literary texts can be manifested in multiple registers, both academic and artistic. After all, virtually no work of art would exist today if it were not in some sort of dialogue (explicit or implicit) with other forms or works of art. The assignment was simply to create a project (visual, temporal, spatial, or aural; written, visible or audible; plastic or conceptual) that in some way furthers, interprets, or responds to at least one of the works we have read during the term.[7] Projects included composing a French madrigal and performing it with other singers; researching and performing a Renaissance dance; constructing a maquette of a 16th-century village replete with rack as mentioned in one of Montaigne's essays; writing a collection of anatomical poetry that parodies a similar collection from the 16th century; and making a video of updated scenes from Rabelais' *Gargantua*. Not only was the process beneficial for the student-artists in encouraging them to work creatively within

> A final assignment ... was conceived ... as a means of demonstrating that responses to literary texts can be manifested in multiple registers, both academic and artistic. After all, virtually no work of art would exist today if it were not in some sort of dialogue (explicit or implicit) with other forms or works of art.

the early modern period, but the presentations also generated further discussion and delighted both fellow students and professor.

—

The pedagogical "lessons" outlined above are both ephemeral and eternal issues of teaching to be grappled with, weighed and debated. Fortunately, also, as professors (especially in the humanities) our "lessons" in the classroom are not restricted to pedagogical ones; we also gain philosophical, literary, and historical insights through our students. In the Renaissance course, for example, I explained to the class my understanding of an Old Testament reference and its applicability to an epic poem we were studying. During the next class a student brought notes from her annotated Torah and provided a very nuanced interpretation of the same passage that at once complicated and illuminated our discussion of the 16th-century text.[8] In the best of circumstances, by the end of the Renaissance course, students are equipped, if not to "find" the historical other, at least to be able to pose some questions that make such a search worthwhile.

"Seeking the other," much like teaching itself, is an asymptotic process: we get closer and closer without ever fully arriving. The ultimate lesson in otherness that the Renaissance course attempts to teach can perhaps be best described by a metaphor from the period itself. Machiavelli noted in his preface to *The Prince* that in order to paint a mountain, an artist must stand on low ground, or to see a panorama of the valley, the painter must climb to the mountaintop.[9] Similarly, as students become ensconced in deciphering reflections of the historical other in early modern literature, they almost inevitably glimpse a clearer image of themselves. ■

ENDNOTES

[1] For a more complete description of the RAD requirement, see Carleton's Catalog at http://www.carleton.edu/campus/registrar/catalog/AcademicPrograms.html

[2] I have benefited from a number of sessions sponsored by the Perlman Learning and Teaching Center at Carleton. For illuminating discussions about teaching, I am also grateful to Deborah Appleman, Scott Carpenter, Heather Dubrow, Marshall Olds, Susannah Ottaway, Éva Pósfay, John Ramsay, Dana Strand, and Carl Weiner. I am especially indebted to Susan Jaret McKinstry for her contributions to a continuing pedagogical exchange.

[3] I am grateful to Timothy Raylor for these examples from his English Renaissance courses.

[4] Foucault uses the term "episteme" [from the Greek word for knowledge] or "epistemological space" to describe a paradigm of language, attitudes, ideas, and science of a given people—in other words, the ways in which knowledge is acquired, ordered, and disseminated in a particular historical period. See Foucault, p. xi.

[5] These are translations, since all readings and discussions in the class take place in French.

[6] Chandra Friend proposed this topic.

[7] This assignment was inspired by a similar one given to me in an undergraduate English course at the University of New Mexico by Professor David Johnson. His "final exam" gave me the opportunity to do some of the most rewarding work of my undergraduate career.

[8] The student in question was Shira Weidenbaum.

[9] Through this metaphor, Machiavelli assures the Medici prince to whom his work is addressed that although the author is of lowly social status, his distance from royalty allows him to make astute suggestions for the prince. Machiavelli, p. 4.

REFERENCES

Foucault, M. (1994). *The order of things: An archeology of the human sciences.* New York: Vintage.

Machiavelli, N. (1997). *The prince* (A. M. Codevilla, W. B. Allen, H. Arkes, & C. Lord, Eds.). New Haven, CT: Yale University Press.

Teaching Film Theory in a Post-Film, Post-Theory Era

Carol Donelan

Self-contained: having all that is needed in oneself; independent; uncommunicative, reserved or restrained in behavior.

That's how I would describe the students in my senior seminar this term. Images of the strong, silent type come to mind—The Duke, Clint, Arnold. Self-containment is valued in our culture—at least in the stories we like to tell ourselves about who we are or would like to be. And yet, there is something troubling to me about this particular group of students. They are terrific thinkers, many of them, and sweet, but they are also sad, manifesting little fire, little passion. In front of them, seeing myself in their eyes, I see old newsreel footage of Lenin or Trotsky haranguing a crowd, arms waving, carrying on. When self-containment is a value, enthusiasm in any form looks absurd. Making a spectacle of oneself is the ultimate social *faux pas*. The goal is to blend in, look right—*be cool*. Recognize this worldview? It is that of consumer culture, wherein you are what you buy. Identity is assembled out of the contents of a shopping bag. Contrary to the exhortation of the Brad Pitt character in *Fight Club*, you *are* your bleeping khakis. If those khakis happen to be flat fronts from the GAP, so much the better.

> For me, it was as if film theory was a mountain to be climbed for no other reason than because it was there. I was aware that developers were leveling the mountain. Why was I still asking students to climb it?

CAROL DONELAN, assistant professor of cinema and media studies, earned her B.S. degree at Iowa State University, her M.A. degree at the University of Iowa, and her Ph.D. at the University of Massachusetts, Amherst. She joined the Carleton faculty in 1999.

It is to a group of cool customers, then, that I market my goods: film theory. That's right, film theory—at a time when the specificity of film as a medium is being digitized out of existence and theory is considered by many to be much less central than it once was to the discipline of cinema studies. Film, in the words of Robert Stam and Ella Shohat (2000), is "dissolving into the larger bitstream of audio-visual media" (p. 394). To the extent that film is digitized, it will no longer be distinguishable from the content of other media such as the television or the computer. Marshall McLuhan's famous statement must be revised: The medium is no longer the message. Whatever "messages" are implicit in the "medium" are homogenized by digitization. A medium is merely one possible embodiment of a message that can have multiple embodiments, all derivable from the same data. One day soon, film as a photochemical medium will no longer be the primary aesthetic object anchoring the discipline of cinema studies.

Meanwhile, much of film theory is being called into question. Film scholars David Bordwell and Noël Carroll (1996) have mounted a campaign against so-called "Grand Theory," which includes the two most influential contemporary theory movements in cinema studies—screen theory and cultural studies.

Screen theory gained prominence in the 1970s in the British film journal *Screen*, but it is rooted in French theory of the 1960s, in the structuralisms of Saussure and Lévi-Strauss and the poststructuralisms of Lacan and Althusser. There is a tendency in structural and poststructural theory to "bracket the referent," to privilege the interrelations between signs over those between signs and the real, material objects to which they refer. Consequently, screen theory has been taken to task for its ahistoricism, for detaching films from their social and historical contexts.

Cultural studies offers itself as an alternative to the ahistoricism of screen theory, shifting the focus from film as film to the uses people make of all kinds of media representations. It gained prominence in the 1980s via the writings of scholars associated with the Birmingham Centre for Contemporary Cultural Studies in the United Kingdom, but its theoretical roots are also in the 1960s, in the writings of British leftists Richard Hoggart, Raymond Williams, E. P. Thompson, and Stuart Hall.

Whatever beef exists between screen theory and cultural studies is beside the point for Bordwell and Carroll, however. For them, screen theory and cultural studies are top-down, doctrine-driven Grand Theories that frame discussions of cinema "within schemes which seek to describe or explain very broad features of society, history, language and psyche" (Bordwell & Carroll, 1996, p. 3). More "modest" alternatives are called for, they argue, including "middle-level research"—"tackl[ing] film-based problems without making overarching theoretical commitments" (p. 3) and "piecemeal theorizing"—"building theories not of subjectivity, ideology, or culture in general but rather of particular phenomena" (p. 29).

Given the post-film, post-theory era in which we find ourselves, it seems reasonable to expect that a question about the value of teaching film theory might arise. But when a senior colleague let loose with it recently, I was caught off guard. I fumbled my way towards an answer that seemed to satisfy him, but I felt unsettled by our exchange. I realized I hadn't *really* thought about why I encourage the current generation of students to study film theory. For me, it was as if film theory was a mountain to be climbed for no other reason than because it was there. I was aware that developers were leveling the mountain. Why was I still asking students to climb it?

My reflections on this question have led me to two conclusions. First, I agree with film scholar D. N. Rodowick (2001, p. 1404) that film theory is "the most productive conceptual horizon against which we can assess what is new, and yet very old, in the new media." Against this conceptual horizon, my students can recognize what is different about how new media mobilizes our vision and desire. Or what is cinematic ("old") about the architecture of video games ("new"). Or that the aesthetic touchstone for digital imagery ("new") is still, anachronistically, photographic realism ("old"). Dudley Andrew (2000, p. 342) writes that we can best prepare students to grapple with the implications of new media "by grounding them through cinema in traditions and theories of storytelling and image making that reach to the roots of modernity."

The medium to which my students now have access is digital video rather than photochemical film, but their objectives with regard to this "new" medium are in fact "old." They want to tell stories. They want to make images. This is why I continue to make a place in our curriculum for the 100+ year history of film as a photochemical medium *and for the theories that facilitate our understanding of this medium*. For it is "through cinema," as Andrew suggests, that we can best comprehend our digital present and future.

Secondly, I think there is value in film theory itself, in the study of it, as one path to take in the pursuit of a liberal education. My task, in coaching students along this path, is to provide them with opportunities to become better readers, speakers, writers, and thinkers. This process has the potential to produce some interesting side effects. Literary critic Norman Holland (1988) argues that when we read, we use texts to symbolize and replicate our own identities. Confronted with a group of bright but unusually self-contained students, I catch myself fantasizing about the opposite possibility: Can we use the experience of reading to replicate the self not as self but as other? Can our encounter with film theory be a means of liberation from the constraints of consumer coolness? What other constraints specific to my students' experience of self in contemporary culture are hindering their efforts to acquire an education?

> Confronted with a group of bright but unusually self-contained students, I catch myself fantasizing about the opposite possibility: Can we use the experience of reading to replicate the self not as self but as other? Can our encounter with film theory be a means of liberation from the constraints of consumer coolness?

In order to entertain these questions, I propose to begin where most students of film theory begin, by reading the canonical essays of Sergei Eisenstein (1999), Soviet filmmaker and theorist, and André Bazin (1999a and 1999b), French theorist and critic. I will then devote my attention to Roland Barthes' *Camera Lucida* (1981), a book I like to situate on my syllabus as a sequel to Bazin's writings. In my discussion of these pieces, I hope to evoke some sense of how students can be encouraged to "experience themselves otherwise" through their engagement with film theory—specially, as passionate producers rather than cool consumers (via the words of Eisenstein), as believers rather than facile skeptics (via the words of Bazin), and as embodied rather than disembodied thinkers (via the words of Barthes).

Before we proceed, I wish to beg the indulgence of my reader as I carve a path through the thicket of film theory in an anthology devoted to reflections on teaching. Reading film theory, a discourse which has been known to bring out the obscurantist in many a writer known for the clarity of his or her prose, may seem to be more trouble than its worth, especially for readers interested primarily in exploring the experience of teaching. But only by engaging with film theory itself can we hope to catch a glimpse of the transformative potential it holds in store for our students and for us, as teachers, specialists in film studies and nonspecialists alike.

We begin with Eisenstein. His manifesto-style writings evoke for my students the qualities of an online rant: fragmented sentences, capitalized words. In one essay, he manages to assemble his fragmented assertions into the following thesis: "The most varied branches of Japanese culture are permeated by a purely cinematic element—montage" (Eisenstein, 1999, p. 25). Skeptical, we turn back to the words on the page for supporting evidence. We delineate the montage potential in the ideogram, taking care to note that which is specious in his argument, and then track his more sophisticated examples in Japanese poetry, figurative art, and theater until—suddenly—Eisenstein abandons the thread of the argument, and therein, abandons us. He wants to say something other than what we might want or expect him to say at this moment, and he will not be denied (this, incidentally, is melodrama, which I intentionally cultivate as a means of encouraging students' engagement with the material). In a two-and-a-half page digression, he expounds on the idea about which he is most passionate: his theory of cinematic montage, how it differs from that of Lev Kuleshov, his former teacher. Upon comparing the two theories— Eisenstein's and Kuleshov's—and speculating on what role the "anxiety of influence" may have played in Eisenstein's theory, I venture the opinion that the best students will always synthesize and overcome, dialectically, the ideas of their teachers. In doing so, I implicitly challenge my students to become other, to "become" Eisenstein—passionate, rather than cool, and dialectically engaged with ideas, including mine.

Coolness is not the only attribute of contemporary selfhood impeding my students' efforts to learn. They are also skeptical of everything. Skepticism can be a positive thing, of course. In ancient Greece, a skeptic was someone who engaged in constant inquiry and reflection. My students are more in tune with the derisive skepticism of South Park and Conan O'Brien, however. An antidote is needed, something that will allow my students to experience themselves otherwise—as believers rather than skeptics.

For this, the writings of the French critic and theorist André Bazin seem made to order. In contrast to the analytical discourse of contemporary posttheorists such as Bordwell and Carroll, Bazin advances his arguments ambiguously, by way of metaphor or analogy. Here are some examples of Bazin in action, paraphrased: The impact of filmmaker Jean Renoir's style on the classical styles of the Hollywood and French cinemas of the 1930s *is like* the effects of geological movements on the equilibrium-profile of a river: imperceptibly causing serious erosion. Filmmaker Roberto Rossellini's orientation to reality *is like* that of Matisse or Hemingway, Faulkner, and Dos Passos: as a filterer of facts. Rossellini changes nothing about reality, but leaves some things out. What he selects and leaves out is the key to recognizing his style. Put differently: A filmmaker's style in relation to fragments of concrete reality *is like* a magnet in relation to iron filings: polarizing. And how do we find meaning in Rossellini's "image-facts" (which are more concrete than mere shots)? Our minds leap from image-fact to image-fact as one leaps from stone to stone in crossing a river. Here, I perpetuate Bazin's mode of expression, at the risk of annoying my students more than I already have, by comparing Bazin's elliptical writing style to Rossellini's elliptical film style: Paradoxically, both are complete, but it is up to us to make the meaning.

Groans are better than nothing. I'm thinking the students are with me, with Bazin, despite the unspoken message they've been sending me about the "bogus" nature of this exercise. They're hooked enough to wonder where I'm going with this. They're waiting for the moral of the story, the punchline in this joke. But we've only set the stage for telling the story of Bazin's film theory. The story we need to tell begins with yet another of Bazin's analogies, this one from the world of mathematics: The relationship of cinema to reality *is like* an asymptotic line approaching a given curve: ever closer, but never meeting.[1]

It is upon this analogy that Bazin bases one of his most provocative theses, which registers with my students like the tag-line of a TV commercial: *Cinema has not yet been invented.* Cinema existed in the minds of human beings as a Platonic ideal long before the technology of film was invented, like the wings of Icarus before the airplane made human flight possible. In its ideal form, in what Bazin calls "the myth of total cinema," cinema not only *duplicates* reality—"recreates the world in its own image" via an "integral realism"— but offers an added advantage over reality: control over time (Bazin, 1999b, p. 202). Every scientific invention takes us closer to the ideal of "total cinema"— from the addition of sound and color to film, to the creation of three-dimensional interactive virtual realities. But the ideal has not yet been achieved: Cinema has not yet been invented. A gap still remains between the asymptote and the curve, representation and reality, the image and its model.

So far, so good. The math majors have had an opportunity to clarify for the English majors the meaning of "asymptote," and our speculations on the utopic and dystopic implications of foreclosing on the distinction between reality and representation have fired our imaginations. We dive into Bazin's 1945 essay on the ontology of the image, only to be stopped short by the following startling assertion:

> No matter how fuzzy, distorted, or discolored, no matter how lacking in documentary value the image may be, it shares, by virtue of the very process of its becoming, the being of the model of which it is the reproduction; it is the model. (Bazin, 1999a, p. 198)

Say what? The image *is* the model? Doesn't this contradict the idea we've just explicated about there being a *gap* between image and model, between image and reality, that has not yet been bridged in the service of achieving total cinema? If students are to become converts to Bazin's film theory, here is where it happens, for implicit in the dilemma we outline together are the great themes of love and death. Bazin struggled with ill health through his adult life, until his premature death at age 40, of leukemia. One wonders if intimations of mortality were ever far from his mind. Perhaps his experience of illness intensified his love for reality—his love for life itself.

In any case, central to his film theory is what he describes variously as a "mummy complex" or "preservation obsession," the desire to rescue reality (and ourselves) from the corruption of time (and death) by capturing and preserving it (and ourselves) in representation. We no longer preserve ourselves in the literal sense—as mummies—but sculpture and painting, at their origins, functioned as "substitute mummies," allowing us to preserve life through representation. With the invention of perspective in the 15th century, reality could be represented three-dimensionally, fueling our obsession with likeness or realism. This obsession is not "satisfied" (to the extent that an obsession, which is by definition irrational, can ever be satisfied) until the advent of photography and cinema. For while the painting is always a subjective representation of reality, photographic and cinematic images are objective.

By objective, Bazin means objective *for us* as intending subjects, in the sense of philosophical phenomenology. In phenomenology, we can never know the world apart from how we intend it; we can never know the "thing-in-itself." To the extent that something is objective, this quality has been conferred upon it by us. It is objectivity, subjectively realized. And it is precisely because photographic and cinematic images are objective *for us* that they are more *credible*, as representations of reality, than paintings or drawings. Photographic and cinematic images have the "irrational power" to "bear away our faith" (Bazin, 1999a, p. 198), to make us believe in them not simply as representations of reality, but as reality itself.

This brings us back to the contradiction in Bazin's writings between, on the one hand, the failure of the asymptote of cinema to ever meet the curve of reality, and, on the other hand, the assertion that the image *is* the model, *is* reality. Of course Bazin *knows* that cinematic representation and reality are and will be forever distinct—the fantasy of *The Matrix* notwithstanding. He *knows* that cinematic images are only *like* reality—*analogous* to reality—and not reality itself. The analogy he chooses—the asymptote—expresses this knowledge. He disavows this knowledge, however, in his assertion that the image *is* reality.

In effect, the contradiction in Bazin's writings can be expressed as one of disbelief versus belief. To paraphrase the classic formulation for disavowal ("I know very well, but even so . . . "), Bazin knows very well that the cinema is not reality, but even so . . . he is willing to suspend his disbelief in cinema as mere representation, choosing instead to believe it is reality.[2] In a leap of faith, he bridges the gap between the asymptote of cinema and the curve of reality, rescuing both himself and his beloved reality from the corruption of time and certain death.[3]

Here, I remind my habitually skeptical students that a leap of faith is central to the experience of the cinema. Giving oneself over to the cinema entails a willingness to believe in the "reality" of the images, despite the evidence of one's senses. The contradiction at the heart of Bazin's film theory simply allegorizes the contradiction at the heart of all film spectatorship: Whether to believe in the images, or not, that is the question.[4]

If the writings of Bazin make it possible for my students to rediscover themselves as believers, the writings of Roland Barthes afford me an opportunity to render explicit a notion implicit in my conversations with students thus far: Theory is not divorced from feeling and personal experience. Theory is a product of mind and body; to consign it to the realm of abstract thought at the expense of emotion is to undermine its meaningfulness as well as some of the pleasure we might find in it.

We can take Eisenstein to task for his logical inconsistencies, but we can also admire how passionate he is about his topic—even if that passion is alien to my students in their consumer coolness. Eisenstein's passion may lead to leaps in logic, but it also sweeps us across those gaps, and therein is one of the pleasures we might find in his film theory: to be caught up, as he is, in a passion for film.

Similarly, we can criticize as naïve Bazin's willingness to invest belief in the image as reality, but we can also identify with a dying man's leap of faith, especially when we realize that it is essentially no different from our own everyday psychic and

> If the writings of Bazin make it possible for my students to rediscover themselves as believers, the writings of Roland Barthes afford me an opportunity to render explicit a notion implicit in my conversations with students thus far: Theory is not divorced from feeling and personal experience.

affective investments in the cinema. Theory comes alive for my students to the extent that I can locate it in the embodied experience of real human beings and render it a narrative. Narrative is not the only way to organize knowledge, but it can be one of the most effective ways, especially when it comes to reaching students who may be encountering these ideas for the first time.

Thus, my students encounter the differences in Eisenstein's and Kuleshov's theories of montage as a melodramatic face-off between a student and his teacher, and Bazin's argument about the ontology of the image as a love story that ends tragically, but not without hope. In Barthes' (1981) *Camera Lucida*, my students encounter a sequel to Bazin's love story, and an example of theory that is explicitly personal and emotional.

The object of Barthes' theoretical inquiry is the photochemical image. He remarks that when he looks at a photograph, he sees the referent, "the desired object, the beloved body" (Barthes, 1981, p. 7) rather than the photograph itself. How is he to locate the essence or "noeme" of this invisible medium?

His first step is to reject the typical modes of classification organizing photographic knowledge. In the context of his ontological inquiry, it matters little whether a photograph is taken by a professional or amateur or whether it is a landscape or portrait—these categories are external to the object itself. Critical discourses such as sociology, semiotics, and psychoanalysis also prove unsatisfactory: Too reductive, he concludes.

Instead, like Bazin, he chooses the path of phenomenology, but a "vague, casual, even cynical phenomenology" (Barthes, 1981, p. 20) that allows for an overtly emotional rather than strictly logical apprehension of phenomena. "Instead of following the path of a formal ontology (of a Logic)," Barthes (1981, p. 21) writes, "I stopped, keeping with me, like a treasure, my desire or my grief; the anticipated essence of the Photograph could not, in my mind, be separated from the 'pathos' of which, from the first glance, it consists." Selecting a few favorite photographs, the ones he is sure "exist" for him emotionally, he opts to make himself—his desire, his grief at the recent death of his beloved mother—the starting point for his investigation.

He begins by delineating the possibilities available to him as an embodied and intending participant in the practice of photography: He can take photographs, he can be photographed, and he can look at photographs. In each of these cases, he cannot shake the feeling that photography is a medium haunted by death, the image a trace of the passed away, silent and immobile. Having not engaged in photography himself ("too impatient"), he has the least to say about the desire of the photographer, although it is apparent to him that the photographer must struggle to "keep the photograph from becoming Death" (Barthes, 1981, p. 14). Despite the photographer's contortions to produce lifelike effects, when Barthes himself poses for the lens, he claims to experience a "micro-version of death" in the transition from living subject to photographed object (Barthes, 1981, p. 14). Furthermore, as the spectator of his own image, he sees that he has become, most disturbingly, "Death in person" (Barthes, 1981, p. 14).

Rather than surrender to these morbid initial impressions, he resolves to follow the dictates of his desire, to seek out images that resist death. These images, he discovers, are characterized by a duality, the co-presence of two elements: the "studium" and the "punctum."

The studium is the network of cultural habits and knowledges that prompts our polite, general interest in the image: It is "of the order of liking, not of loving" (Barthes, 1981, p. 27). Journalistic photographs often engage our interest in various ways—informing, surprising, even shocking us—but they are for the most part "unary" images, invested with no more than our studium.

Occasionally, however, in the "habitually unary space" of the public photograph, the studium is "traversed, lashed, striped by a detail which attracts or distresses" us—the punctum (Barthes, 1981, p. 40). In order to clarify what he means by the punctum, Barthes must let us in on his private and unconscious obsessions. The straps on a woman's shoes, a boy's bad teeth, a girl's bandaged finger: These are the partial features that linger in his fetishistic imagination after examining a series of photographs. The presence of the punctum does not depend on the skill of the photographer. Neither is it always possible to name why a particular detail is disturbing. Sometimes, the source of the disturbance is unlocatable: A photograph "holds him," but he "cannot say why" (Barthes, 1981, p. 51). Ultimately, the punctum is the detail in the image that engages his unconscious desire and "animates" him, but also the desire that he, in turn, invests in that image, animating it. To the extent that a photograph has a punctum, it has been endowed (by us) with the power of cinema to expand metonymically into the space off-frame, releasing everything in-frame (and us) from absolute death.

Whereas Barthes gains insight into the workings of his desire by examining public images, he turns to his personal collection of family photographs in the second half of *Camera Lucida* in order to locate the universal, "that thing which is seen by anyone looking at a photograph" (Barthes, 1981, p. 60). He begins by searching backward in time (in yet another retreat from death) for the image of his mother that coincides with her being and his grief at her recent death. He finds it in the famous (but unseen) Winter Garden photograph. This image of his mother as a five-year-old is the Ariadne's thread leading him to the noeme of photography. What he discovers at the center of the labyrinth is this: The photograph is a certificate of presence. More than any other system of representation, the photograph testifies to the fact that someone or something has actually existed. The painter can conjure up an image without reference to a model, but the referent in photography is *necessary*. The stubbornness with which the referent adheres to the surface of the image gives the photograph its astonishing evidential force.

In certain images, however, the recognition of photography's power of authentication is compounded with a secondary realization: The referent belongs to the past. What is seen in the image "has been here, and yet immediately separated; it has been absolutely, irrefutably present, and yet already deferred" (Barthes, 1981, p. 77).

The noeme of photography is therefore not only the expression of a reality, there-it-is, but the superimposition of reality with the past, that-has-been. The realization of the "that-has-been" is the "catastrophe" of every photograph, but we tend to experience it with indifference. The Winter Garden photograph rouses Barthes from indifference; out of his embodied experience of love and grief, he arrives at a theory of the photographic image.

Although my students' response to *Camera Lucida* varies—one student, outraged by the emotionalism of the prose, is dismissive of it; another, identifying with it, discreetly wells up in tears—our discussions of the book allow me to drive home an important point: Theory is the product of embodied experience. It entails the engagement of the mind as well as the body, logic as well as emotion. Through it, we seek answers to questions that actually matter to us. Is cinema a language like other languages (semiotics)? Can film, collectively produced, express the worldview of an individual (authorship)? Do genre films function ritualistically to express our collective desires, or are they structures through which Hollywood lures us into taking up its own ideological positions (genre theory)? Which films transmit ideology transparently, and which intercept it and make it visible (ideology)? How do the interlocking shots in film not only "speak" the film (semiotics again), but also us, as spectators (suture theory)? Is cinema rooted in unconscious processes such as mirror identification, voyeurism, and fetishism (psychoanalysis)? How, and why, are men and women represented differently in the cinema (gaze theory)? What are the historical roadblocks to theorizing the erotic objectification of the male body, and to conceptualizing the female spectator (gaze theory)? What reception practices do spectators use in relation to cinematic representations they perceive as racist (spectatorship and race)? How can fandom or queerness be understood as critical practices or modes of reception (cultural studies, queer theory)? And finally, how does current digital theory challenge the "critical distance" of traditional academic theory (digital theory)?

There are compelling narratives to be constructed out of the attempts of various theorists to answer these questions. My task is to tell the story of film theory and to engage my students in the telling of it, for it will ultimately be up to them to narrate the episodes of the future. ■

For Vern Bailey

An abridged version of this essay, with the same title, is forthcoming in Spring 2004 in *Academic Exchange Quarterly, 8*, 1.

ENDNOTES

[1] It is tempting to locate the inspiration for this analogy in the existential language philosophy central to Bazin's milieu: language, in relation to thought, must ever be regarded as an asymptote. One of my favorite reflections on this relation is in the French filmmaker Jean-Luc Godard's 1963 film, *Vivre sa vie*. Nana, the main character, can never find the right words to express her thoughts. Her experience is that when she expresses her thoughts, her words take on unintended meanings. She worries about offending people. Alone in a café, she strikes up a conversation with a stranger, played by the real-life philosopher Brice Parain, a protégé of Jean-Paul Sartre's. Sartre is famous for proclaiming "our powerlessness to think with our words the events of the world." Parain argues along similar lines that there is no necessary connection between events and words. He is disconcerted by the "play" in language, by what he calls the "giddy inexactitude of speech." Sartre himself describes his protégé as "word sick." This description could very well apply to Nana. Like Parain, she "cannot bear that [her] thoughts should become indefinite when they are expressed." In the first episode of the film, for example, she repeats an inane phrase four times, prompting another character, Paul, to ask her if she's sick. "I was trying to explain something to you, to make it very clear, but I don't know how," she says. Paul accuses her of being self-centered, of talking only about herself. She responds by accusing him of being mean. "I'm not mean," he insists, "just sad." Nana then capitalizes on the non-necessary character of language to undermine the meaning in Paul's statement. "I'm not sad," she responds, "I'm mean." This childish exchange, bordering on the nonsensical, foregrounds the "inexactitude of speech" to which Parain alludes in his writings. See Sartre, J.-P. (1967).

[2] The prototype for all splittings of belief is Freud's description of the male child's confrontation with the reality of sexual difference. The child persists in his belief that "all human beings are endowed with a penis" even though the evidence of his senses tells him that "some human beings do not have a penis." The child retains the old belief under the new one through disavowal. See Freud, S. (1973).

[3] It is tempting to turn to Gilles Deleuze's remarks on the special relationship between cinema and belief in this context. For Deleuze, what characterizes our modernity is that the link has been broken between humanity and the world, such that we no longer believe in the world: "It is not we who make cinema, it is the world which looks to us like a bad film" (p. 171). The cinematic image, like no other medium, reveals our link to the world and restores our belief in it. See Deleuze, G. (1989).

[4] "Any spectator will tell you that he 'doesn't believe it,' " writes Christian Metz, "but everything happens as if there were nonetheless someone to be deceived, someone who really would 'believe in it' " (p. 72). If we don't believe that the objects on screen are real, who is this someone who does? "This credulous [believing] person is, of course, another part of ourselves. He is still seated beneath the incredulous [disbelieving] one, or in his heart, [and] it is he who continues to believe, who disavows what he knows" (p. 72). Inasmuch as our credulous self disavows what it knows, our incredulous self disavows our

credulous self. "That is why the instance of credulousness is often projected into the outer world and constituted as a separate person completely abused by the diegesis" (p. 72). Among the examples of "credulousness personified" Metz cites are the historical spectators of Lumière's *Arrival of a Train at the Station* (1895), who were supposedly so terrified by the image of the approaching train that they fled their seats. Credulousness is also personified, in many films, in the character of the sleeping dreamer, who believes everything in the dream (the film) is true, then wakes up to discover it was all a dream (a film). See Metz (1977).

REFERENCES

Andrew, D. (2000, May). The "three ages" of cinema studies and the age to come. *PMLA, 115(3)*, 341-51.

Barthes, R. (1981). *Camera lucida: Reflections on photography.* New York: Hill and Wang.

Bazin, A. (1999a). The ontology of the photographic image. In L. Braudy and M. Cohen (Eds.), *Film theory and criticism: Introductory readings* (pp. 195-199). New York: Oxford. (Original work published 1945)

Bazin, A. (1999b). The myth of total cinema. In L. Braudy and M. Cohen (Eds.), *Film theory and criticism: Introductory readings* (pp. 199-203). New York: Oxford. (Original work published 1946)

Bordwell, D., & Carroll, N. (1996). *Post theory: Reconstructing film studies.* Madison, WI: Wisconsin.

Deleuze, G. (1989). *Cinema 2: The time-image.* Minneapolis, MN: Minnesota.

Eisenstein, S. (1999). Beyond the shot [The cinematographic principle and the ideogram]. In L. Braudy and M. Cohen (Eds.), *Film theory and criticism: Introductory readings* (pp. 15-25). New York: Oxford. (Original work published 1929)

Freud, S. (1973). Fetishism. In J. Strachey (Ed.), *The standard edition of the complete psychological works of Sigmund Freud* (Vol. 21, pp.149-157). London: Hogarth. (Original work published in 1927)

Holland, N. N. (1988). Reading and identity: A psychoanalytic revolution. In K. M. Newton (Ed.), *Twentieth-century literary theory: A reader* (pp. 204-209). New York: St. Martin's.

Metz, C. (1977). *The imaginary signifier: Psychoanalysis and the cinema.* Bloomington, IN: Indiana.

Rodowick, D. N. (2001, October). Dr. strange media; Or, how I learned to stop worrying and love film theory. *PMLA, 116(5)*, 1396-1404.

Sartre, J.-P. (1967). The journey and the return. In J. L. Hevesi (Ed.), *Essays on language and literature* (pp.146-185). Port Washington, NY: Kennikat. (Original work published in 1946)

Stam, R., & Shohat, E. H. (2000). Film theory and spectatorship in the age of the posts. In C. Gledhill and L. Williams (Eds.), *Reinventing film studies* (pp. 381-401). New York: Oxford.

Liberal Arts and the "Real World"

Is This "Real Science"?

Tricia A. Ferrett

About 10 years ago, I set out to transform my introductory chemistry classroom into one that honestly reflected—in concepts, rigor, topic, skills, and process—how "real science" is done.[1] I wanted to educate both future scientists and scientifically literate citizens to engage science in their lives.

Prior to the transformation, my courses were organized around a standard text that covered a group of chemistry concepts that had been mostly unchanged for decades. The goal of coverage drove the course. Text applications of chemical principles to real-world problems were rare, though some leakage via "Chemistry in Action" or "Chemical Impact" sections[2] could be found in colored boxes. Still, it was as if the real world and real science were offered as side dishes while isolated and unapplied concepts dominated the menu. Even more disturbing was the fact that scientific inquiry and an authentic critical perspective were entirely missing from the texts. However, in lab I routinely engaged my students in open-ended experiments and projects, following a long tradition at Carleton. The class work and lab were oddly out of synch.

> Teaching in a way that reflects the practices and values of "real science" made my own intellectual life temporarily rife with uncertainty and change. But even with all the risks and difficulties, the changes have been worth it!

The primary learning cycle for students centered on doing text problems and problems that I created. Text problems were mostly simple, "plug and chug," sometimes multi-

TRICIA A. FERRETT, professor of chemistry, joined the Carleton faculty in 1990. She earned her B.A. degree at Grinnell College and her Ph.D. degree at the University of California, Berkeley.

step and challenging, and occasionally slightly integrative of two or three simple concepts. Text authors worked to bring the real world into the problems, but rarely in a truly convincing and meaningful way. This lack of authenticity spurred me to invent more complex problems and little mini-modules on the chemistry of vision, solar cells, and the atmosphere.

On the pedagogy side, I lectured in a highly interactive way, hoping to draw students into the beauty, wonder, and complexity of the natural world. I wanted to converse with my students about chemistry in the world, and I wanted to know what they were thinking. I figured that feedback and conversation would give me a better view into their learning processes. I cherished my students' fresh viewpoints and challenging questions. I was convinced from my own experience that higher engagement with the world and with each other would lead to greater learning, long-term retention, and involvement by women and students of color, those who tend to occupy the margins of the scientific community.[3]

In addition to teaching courses, I also headed a scientific research group with Carleton undergraduates. In my chemistry lab, the research group stumbled along, working on questions with no clear answers. We were fully in charge of posing the questions and assessing which ones were worthy of study and why. We debated priorities and agonized over lengthy "to do" lists. We constantly marshaled all of our knowledge and skills to solve messy problems with no perfect solutions. Compromises were rampant, as were discussions about the risks of compromise. Guessing, testing, hypothesizing, negotiating, and refining steered the way once a challenge was defined. Tricky problems took more than one brain to solve.

Science content also sat center-stage. We learned tough subjects together on a need-to-know basis, many of them outside of chemistry: electrostatics, electronics, vacuum science, mechanical design, and classical mechanics. We called on other experts and the original literature as needed.

Students were involved in every aspect of the work, and they had true intellectual input into the project direction. Once in a while, we'd get something right and celebrate. More often, we'd relish the small weekly victories that represented incremental progress. We worked as a team, with some tasks delegated to individuals. We learned about each other's strengths and weaknesses and used this awareness to support each other and more effectively solve problems. We worked hard to maintain our sense of humor, purpose, and focus.

Students often remarked that this kind of learning environment was powerful—and nothing like learning in courses. They said that we were doing more than—"just chemistry." We were doing "real science," and it was miles away from my introductory chemistry classroom.

This lack of congruence between my research and teaching led me to work with dozens of chemistry faculty from universities and liberal arts colleges to make "systemic" changes in introductory college chemistry. Apparently others shared my growing unease. In 1993, the National Science Foundation (NSF) thought the time had come to overhaul these courses, and they were soliciting major curriculum development proposals spread over five years. NSF was convinced that grassroots discontent among college chemistry instructors had grown enough that systemic change was as inevitable as it was needed.

The faculty groups I worked with in the ChemLinks Coalition[4] and the Modular Chemistry Consortium[5] (MC[2]) decided that traditional introductory chemistry missed the boat on three counts: 1) It did not develop a wide range of scientific and critical thinking skills in our students, 2) the chemistry content was disconnected from students' lives, the real world, and authentic scientific inquiry, and 3) it was not providing a rich range of effective and active learning activities. We aimed to write topical modules as deep case studies driven by modern scientific issues. We hoped to teach the core concepts of chemistry through the windows of real science, linking naturally to interdisciplinary issues. We planned to infuse materials with a broader range of active class and lab activities, with a major focus on changing ourselves as teachers. We ended up using a

> I lectured in a highly interactive way, hoping to draw students into the beauty, wonder, and complexity of the natural world. I wanted to converse with my students about chemistry in the world, and I wanted to know what they were thinking.

"storyline" as the organizing thread and line of inquiry, stringing together authentic contextual questions that students would naturally want to answer.

After six years, many meetings and pedagogy workshops, thousands of emails, and approximately $6 million from NSF, consortia authors wrote over a dozen topical modules.[6-7] Published under the ChemConnections name, modules revolved around issues including global warming, dietary fats, star composition, airbags in cars, and automobile air pollution.[8] I co-authored one of the early modules on the Antarctic ozone hole and edited and tested many others.[9]

At first, I leaked new activities into my course. I did a little ozone chemistry, and the next year I did a little more. I taught an early version of the ozone hole module mid-way through my course, but it was sandwiched in with my older, more traditional text-based approach. Most students enjoyed the little real-world forays and breaks from my interactive lecture mode.

Finally, I took a gentle plunge and taught a new version of the ozone module from start to finish. Students spent more time in class working a problem or discussing in small groups. They worked more with real data sets, interpreting them as we built, tweaked, rejected, and refined atmospheric models. Student response was still quite positive, with significant numbers of students wishing we had spent even more of the term studying real problems in depth.

My fully modular course was launched in the spring of 1999. Thoughtful and sensitive students spotted the rough spots in the new curriculum and helped me work out the bugs.[10] Many students embraced the real-world context, the process of authentic inquiry, and the more active classroom. A small number objected to the inclusion of class activities and scientific writing in the course ("you need to lecture more" and "writing is for non-science classes"). Over time, I gained the perspective that some students were experiencing a scary shift in their own view of science. I had to learn to help students move along attitudinal and intellectual development curves—toward "real science."

After I had taught the modular course for three years, student resistance ebbed and I got much better at teaching with modules. I had raised the bar with a richer and more challenging set of educational goals, and it took a while for all of us to adjust. After bouts of uncertainty with new teaching methods, I eventually came to sympathize with the cliché "the third time's a charm." Student culture changed as students in my modular course moved on, quite successfully, to become science majors and graduate students. I recruited teaching assistants who had taken my new course. Their maturity and enthusiasm for this kind of learning helped support the new educational goals.[11] Colleagues around the country were also experiencing success.

Were my students really learning more or better, and what did this mean? I noticed gains in students' ability to demonstrate and integrate their knowledge of chemistry and to apply this knowledge in context. For example, when presented with new reactions in the earth's atmosphere, they reasoned in sophisticated ways about which ones must be fast and dominant, based on what they already knew about ozone hole chemistry. Students suggested calculations that were needed to address additional chemistry, and some of them just went ahead and did these calculations as part of their final project. Students were starting to do math upon their own initiative because they saw value in the outcome—a real step forward in quantitative literacy. A few students started to act more like junior and senior chemistry majors.

They all started acting more like real scientists; they posed new questions and worried about tricky effects we had not yet considered. They worried about the global issue of ozone depletion. They started to play it forward, jumping ahead with proposals as if they were truly engaged in inquiry and solving a serious problem. Many were inching their way into sophisticated systems thinking. Students were routinely demonstrating a deeper conceptual understanding of chemistry.

In short, my students were developing a critical perspective. Students also did as well or better on my traditional chemistry exam questions as they had before; no obvious compromises had been made in the chemistry content arena. For me, there was no going back in light of these gains.

Amidst all the learning gains, some stubborn student resistance remained. A small portion of my students persistently wondered if they were learning enough "real chemistry." It was a fair question—with all this other stuff going on, were students getting less of something important? They knew my course was different from what they had experienced before, and they were not sure if they were being well prepared for the future. I knew their concerns were sincere, justified, and understandable. Many college chemistry teachers voiced the same worries.

At the same time, I found this "real science" concern ironic and even amusing. Module authors had designed this holistic and rather radical new college chemistry curriculum with the aim of better educating introductory students by doing "real chemistry." Modules raised the bar by asking students to learn and then apply concepts in real situations. Many students got it and were thriving. The curriculum was more cognitively demanding, and most students appreciated this and rose to the challenges. But a few did not, and they were vocal and sometimes angry. Overall, a number of students articulated a common gut resistance to a new kind of science education unmatched to their past experiences and proven success strategies.

With the help of the outside evaluation team on our project, we were able to surface and separate some of the issues behind student resistance to learning with modules. What follows is based on my own experience, but it is consistent with research results from in-depth focus interviews with hundreds of students across the country who have learned with ChemConnections modules.[12]

Much of the student resistance can be traced to young students' lack of understanding that "real science" is more like learning with the new modules. Context-rich modular problems are better examples of how science works than the simplified textbook examples. Real problems require modeling, analysis, estimations, lucky guesses, and deeper conceptual understanding. It is harder to get correct answers in the messiness of the real world, and that raises anxiety.

I was trying to break down students' oversimplified notion that a "plug and chug" textbook problem solved with complex formulas constituted real science. For example, in addition to asking students to derive a molecule's 3D geometry or calculate the heat released in a chemical reaction, I also asked them to undertake harder tasks, and many were filled with natural ambiguity. They were designing new experiments, interpreting real and sometimes conflicting data sets, taking imperfect data, designing better refrigerant gases, and ultimately struggling with complex policy questions (what should we do about global warming or the fats in our diet?).

> Many students found the new curriculum both interesting and doable and this sometimes produced anxiety. The statement "this can't be real chemistry because I like and understand it" captures a common student response.

Doing real science requires an appreciation of the uncertainty inherent in original inquiry and maybe even a delight in it. My research students were naturally mired in ambiguity. Some undergraduates have not yet achieved this acquired taste, particularly if their stage of intellectual development and certain forces in American culture dispose them to expect "right" and quick answers.

Some students feared that they might not be learning "enough real chemistry" to carry them forward. Module authors worked hard to include the traditional core chemical concepts in the modules, often in even more depth. The content is still very central, but it is now wrapped in context and inquiry. The chemistry emerges more naturally on a need-to-know basis and often in the same logical "chunks" as in the texts.

For example, I include about 80-90% of the chemistry I used to "cover" in my course by using three carefully selected modules. I now include a quick module-text comparison exercise in my course that helps students see how much we are still "covering." I still assign traditional text problems; many students find this comforting.

Students (and some faculty) also tend to assume that because a topic is "covered" in a lecture class, effective learning will ensue. All of my experience and the research literature on learning indicate that deep learning is not simply transmitted from speaker to listener. Learning that "sticks" requires steady inquiry, personal struggle, reflection, and refinement of ideas. Learners must self-construct their understanding and build upon what they already know.[13] The learning path is frequently messy and nonlinear. In addition, lasting learning often occurs in a particular context where an important problem is solved, a question is tackled, or a complex topic is analyzed. Content divorced from context can leave ideas hanging without an organizational framework, freer to slip away over time.

Many students found the new curriculum both interesting and doable and this sometimes produced anxiety. The statement "this can't be real chemistry because I like and understand it" captures a common student response. More accessible and relevant material was one of our goals, but some students do not expect such a virtue.

Yet a different group of students missed the notion that modules aim for more depth to help them gain a deeper understanding. These students may, out of habit, passively skim the surface of material and never dig in, resulting in a learning experience that feels superficial. I have learned to guide students on how and why an in-depth approach is valuable.

Overall, I have had to work with students to help them understand that effective science learning can occur when their work feels interesting, challenging, accessible, and even doable.

Digging even deeper, the statement that "this is not real science" may also reflect a desire for an intellectual scaffold on which to hang ideas. A number of students asked me for help in building a framework of key chemical ideas. They wanted to "see the chemistry forest through the trees," even in introductory courses. More students were now asking for the forest.

In a traditional chemistry course, the intellectual scaffold is the chapter headings—the logical traverse through topics in a chemistry text. Effective or not, the text organization is a chemistry scaffold. It also has the advantage of being accepted by the community of college chemistry teachers. However, the elegant textbook structure is of most immediate use to faculty and is seldom dealt with by students, who are busy working their way through memorizing "the chemistry trees." The security blanket of the text organization may be just that for students—a powerful illusion.

More thoughtfully, some students and instructors work to make connections between chemistry ideas and to place them in an overall framework. Themes of micro/macro, statics/dynamics, structure/function pervade valiant efforts to do this. It is essential that teachers convey the broad utility of thermodynamics, atomic and molecular structure, kinetics, equilibrium, and elementary periodicity. Our best students work to build this scaffold for themselves by self-organizing the chemistry ideas. Courses and instructors can help do this explicitly.

Mature students often voice a major risk associated with teaching in context. In dealing with particular applications, students may not fully decipher the generalities and their broader applicability. Some of my best students asked for a chance to generalize principles across contexts, testing for range of applicability. The act of applying chemistry ideas in a different context is critical in reaching this higher cognitive level. This transferability concern is now active in the revision of our curricular materials.

Finally, change of any kind is simply hard. The writers and adapters of our curricular materials had to remind themselves constantly about how long it takes substantive change to take hold. The careful assessment evidence on our project shows that teachers simply need to be patient, waiting until a new course is perceived as more "normal" and less "experimental" within a department or institution. We also need to wait until students reach a developmental stage that allows them to appreciate what "real science" really is. It helps to talk openly with students about the natural difficulties they face in confronting new educational expectations.

Some instructors have also found ways to help students understand what it takes to learn something deeply. For example, I now talk with students about how various types of questions (factual, logistical, probing, integrative, synthetic) encourage more advanced levels of cognition. The conversation about metacognition is now on the table, and this seems to help students better appreciate the less obvious developments in their own cognitive skills.

My introductory chemistry students now behave more like my research students. Learning requires the use of a wider range of critical thinking and "thinking like a scientist" skills. Students do more writing that aids their learning. They are asked to work in teams and communicate with others about their work.[14] The work is hard, satisfying, messy, analytical, critical, uncomfortable, and more relevant. Upon student initiative, we talk together more about how best to tackle environmental problems, how complex systems work, the ethics of caring for the planet, our own health, the tensions of technology development, and more. Students talk more openly, and with some self-awareness, about their struggle with skill development. The learning feedback loop now operates openly and quickly—I can much better see and adjust to where my students really are in their learning trajectories. I am a more authentic partner in life-long learning, side-by-side with my students, in the midst of problems that matter to all of us. The significant gains I see in student learning, both in content and skill areas, are confirmed by careful assessment of many modular students across the country.[15]

"Real science" has surely taught me that one answer always breeds more inquiry. Our project raised complex questions about resistance to change and the theories of change that reformers in education use as they attempt to make lasting improvements.[16] By far the toughest personal thing about all this change is that I have had to live with and learn from the risks that I took. Changing my teaching was a big deal that made me see things in new ways.

When I started to converse more and in different ways with students, I was faced with the reality of what they actually understood, and it was far less than I had assumed. I came to realize that this was my problem—I had been flying blind. My clearer vision, promoted by more active learning activities and conversation, allowed me to meet students where they were and help them move even farther forward. My relationship to students changed, mostly in very positive ways. I was brought closer to the experience and feelings of learning and to my students. However, different learning expectations also brought out the wrath of a few vocal skeptics. Dealing with the skeptics was a new experience in my teaching life, but it taught me about intellectual stages of development and student resistance that is rooted in being stuck at one stage.

Before I began this journey, my own identity as a teacher was pretty stable. I was comfortable with who I was, and what I heard at tenure was nicely congruent with my self image.

As I tried new teaching techniques, I regularly moved out of my comfort zone. At first, I thought I was actually changing my teaching strengths. A wise friend recently suggested that I have discovered a more authentic teaching persona and one that draws on a wider range of my personal strengths and values. My struggle with mid-life and a few health issues have not made this transition any easier, but the whole package has helped me come to a tighter focus on who I am as a teacher so I can give my best to students.

There was also the real risk of not getting tenure. I averted this risk intentionally by deciding, with the strong advice from mentors at Carleton and elsewhere, that I wait to teach with modules until after tenure.

I look back on all this with mixed feelings. I played it safe at a time when the stakes were high. But I also felt like the waiting game was unhealthy. At the same time that I was determined to have my students take more risks in their learning, I was told to put my passions on hold until I could tolerate the risk of failure. It was not clear to me then whether my colleagues sympathized with Boyer's notion that my curricular work was a legitimate "scholarship of teaching."[17]

I suppose one has to be savvy about timing. Yet, sending a message to untenured faculty to minimize risk prior to tenure is quite inconsistent with the realities of striving for excellence in teaching over a whole career. Fortunately, I had lots of experience in risk-taking prior to tenure, and I was encouraged by several college administrators to take more risks after tenure. I also had good departmental support for working in ChemConnections.

In making change, there is the risk of being perceived as marginal by colleagues. Since many of the participants in ChemConnections were lone reformers in departments that were neutral or negative toward the project goals, marginalization was felt strongly. A friend of mine who has made it her life's work to study change once remarked to me "Dear, change always comes from the margins." I learned to let go of what others think and follow my instincts. I had to focus on my own teaching strengths, not the expectations of others based on theirs and tradition. From the large network of teachers in the consortium I was able to get the support I needed to push forward to create the kind of science education I thought I could offer.[18]

The last bit about risk relates to my identity as a scholar. My own increased appreciation for environmental science and other science-rich issues have led me to examine my laboratory research agenda. This has been especially hard because at tenure, my mentoring of research students was highlighted as my greatest strength. I went to college and graduate school in the late 70s and mid 80s when interdisciplinary research did not exist, or at least its presence was not apparent to me. My teaching career at Carleton, combined with the decade-long journey

> The chance to learn with committed colleagues and students, both about new areas of science and about improving education, has been a gift.

into a new kind of teaching and learning, have honed my own skills of synthesis, integration, and systems thinking. In teaching more about scientific skills, I have come to better understand and develop my own. I have lost my youthful taste for simple problems requiring only a reductionist approach. I now yearn to work on real-world problems that are more complex and applied, and I want to do it as part of a collaborative team. The ongoing shift in my scholarly agenda honestly reflects this growth.

Of course, the struggle to learn and teach has merely shifted its guise. In order to move forward with my new aspirations, I will have to confront a few more of my own fears—and some departmental, institutional, and professional traditions. Teaching in a way that reflects the practices and values of "real science" made my own intellectual life temporarily rife with uncertainty and change. But even with all the risks and difficulties, the changes have been worth it! The chance to learn with committed colleagues and students, both about new areas of science and about improving education, has been a gift. It is not a trivial matter to sustain one's enthusiasm for teaching over a 30-year career. I have had one grand experience with how to build the process of renewal into my professional life. Ahead I see an intellectual and teaching life that is more meaningful, satisfying, and built upon truer passions. ■

ENDNOTES

[1] This essay, particularly the section on student resistance, is based partly on a shorter one co-authored by Ferrett, T., Schwartz, T., Lewis, E., & Spencer, B. (2000). *What do students really mean when they say "this is not real chemistry"?* Unpublished.

[2] a) Chang, R. (2002, 7th ed.). *Chemistry*. New York: McGraw Hill. See "Chemistry in action" sections.

b) Zumdahl, S.S., & Zumdahl, S.A. (2003, 6th ed). *Chemistry*. Boston: Houghton Mifflin. See "Chemical impact" sections.

[3] a) Seymour, E., & Hewitt, N.M. (1997). *Talking about leaving: Why undergraduates leave the sciences.* Boulder, CO: Westview Press.

b) Seymour, E. (1995). The loss of women from science, mathematics, and engineering undergraduate majors: An explanatory account. *Science Education, 79,* 437.

[4] The ChemConnections web site can be found at http://wwnorton.com/college/Chemistry/Chemconnections/modules.html and http://wwnorton.com/college/Chemistry/Chemconnections/index.html.

[5] The ModularCHEM Consortium web site can be found at http://mc2.cchem.berkeley.edu/.

[6] These materials were developed with support of the National Science Foundation grants DUE-9455918 (ChemLinks Coalition) and DUE-9455924 (ModularChem Consortia).

[7] Anthony, A., Mernitz, H., Spencer, B., Gutwill, J., Kegley, S., & Molinaro, M. (1998). The ChemLinks and ModularCHEM Consortia: Using active and context-based learning to teach students how chemistry is actually done. *Journal of Chemical Education, 75,* 322.

[8] a) Anthony, A., Brauch, T.W., & Longley, E.J. (1998). *What should we do about global warming?* New York: John Wiley and Sons. Currently published with W.W. Norton & Company.

b) Laursen, S., & Mernitz, H. (2000). *Would you like fries with that? The fuss about fats in our diet.* New York: John Wiley and Sons. Currently published with W.W. Norton & Company.

c) Drossman, H., Tikkanen, W., & Laursen, S. (2002). *How can we reduce air pollution from automobiles?* ChemConnections. Currently published with W.W. Norton & Company.

[9] Ferrett, T., & Anthony, S. (1998). *Why does the ozone hole form?* New York: John Wiley and Sons. Currently published with W.W. Norton & Company.

[10] Seymour E. (2000, July 31). *We know that science majors are lost because of poor teaching, but why do students resist our efforts to improve their learning experience?* American Association of Physics Teachers, Summer Meeting, University of Guelph, Ontario, Canada, Plenary Session. Results from our assessment

team indicate that one cannot take this kind of student behavior for granted. Students better tolerate reform, and even embrace and help with the endeavor, in climates that foster trust between students and faculty.

[11] Seymour, E. (2000, January). *The TA's role in classroom innovation.* Presentation to the Gordon Science Education Conference, Ventura, CA. Also forthcoming as a book titled *The role of teaching assistants in innovative undergraduate science education.*

[12] Seymour, E. (2001, May 5). *Sources of resistance to pedagogical change in undergraduate science teaching: faculty, TA's, and students.* Presentation to the Annual Symposium on Excellence in Teaching Undergraduate Science and Mathematics: National and Chicago Perspectives, University of Illinois at Chicago.

[13] a) Bodner, G., Klobuchar, M., & Geelan, D. (2001). The many forms of constructivism, *Journal of Chemical Education, 78,* 1107.

b) Bodner, G.M. (1986). Constructivism: A theory of knowledge. *Journal of Chemical Education, 63,* 873.

[14] Millis, B.J., & Cottel, P.G., Jr. (1998). *Cooperative learning for higher education faculty.* American Council on Education, Oryx Press.

[15] Gutwill-Wise, J.P. (2001). The impact of active and context-based learning in introductory chemistry courses: An early evaluation of the modular approach. *Journal of Chemical Education, 87,* 684.

[16] Seymour, E. (2002, January). Tracking the processes of change in US undergraduate education in science, mathematics, engineering, and technology. *Science Education, 86,* 79.

[17] a) Boyer, E.L. (1990). *Scholarship reconsidered: Priorities of the professoriate,* Princeton, NJ: Carnegie Foundation for the Advancement of Teaching.

b) Glassick, C.E., Huber, M.T., & Maeroff, G.I. (1997). *Scholarship assessed: Evaluation of the professoriate.* Special Report of the Carnegie Foundation for the Advancement of Teaching. San Francisco: Jossey-Bass.

[18] Many colleagues in ChemConnections contributed to the creation of the new curriculum and to my own development as a teacher. I want to thank especially Brock Spencer, Eileen Lewis, Sandra Laursen, Sharon Anthony, Joanne Stewart, Angy Stacy, Heather Mernitz, Jim Swartz, Susan Kegley, Truman Schwartz, George Lisensky, Joshua Gutwill, Elaine Seymour, Karen Harding, and Melissa Kido. At Carleton, Elizabeth McKinsey (then Dean of the College) has gracefully helped me negotiate through identity shifts, reminding me about what is of constant value in the face of change. I thank my Carleton Chemistry Department colleagues for inspiring me with innovative teaching, encouraging me to teach to my strengths, and for letting me take risks.

Experiential Learning Abroad

Martha Paas

When Harry Truman's economic advisors refused to predict what would happen to the economy, he is supposed to have said that he would give anything for a "one-handed economist." They had told him that, on the one hand, this could happen; on the other hand, if conditions change, that could happen. Economics is the study of scarcity, and scarcity implies choices. The analysis of the process of making choices generates economic theory, but the outcome of applying a particular theory to a real world problem depends on the variables in the model and the assumptions we make in the theory about how the variables interact.

My professional life has always revolved around this dilemma: How can I help students develop the skill and imagination to identify the relevant variables and to make assumptions that will give significant results in their analysis of problems? The relatively easy part is to study models and theorems in economics. Carleton students have the intelligence and usually the diligence to master this material. They learn how to apply economic theory with the standard stock of economic variables, and in our capstone "Comps" (short for "Comprehensive") exercise, they accomplish often excellent economic analysis.

> My professional life has always revolved around this dilemma: How can I help students develop the skill and imagination to identify the relevant variables and make assumptions that will give significant results in their analysis of problems?

MARTHA PAAS is the Wadsworth A. Williams Professor of Economics. She joined the Carleton faculty in 1976. She earned her A.B. at Randolph-Macon College and her Ph.D. at Bryn Mawr College.

Still, this process of teaching students to think like an economist has always left me somewhat uneasy. Perhaps it is because I hold up the humanistic end of our curriculum and teach courses in economic and intellectual history that I have always had a suspicion that our students do not really understand the nature of economic theory because they do not fully appreciate the range of variables on which the outcomes depend. For example, population changes slowly over time and is usually held constant in economic modelling, but it can be a critical variable over time. "*Ceteris paribus*" (everything else remaining the same) is a powerful tool in an economic analysis. It allows us to specify the effect of changing one variable holding all others constant. But what if *ceteris* is not *paribus*? What if a variable that we hold constant in the short run changes dramatically in the long run? These concerns are particularly important to an economic historian concerned with economic growth over time, and it is important in the education of a young economist to gain an appreciation of the range of variables that should be considered.

> **What if *ceteris* is not *paribus*? What if a variable that we hold constant in the short run changes dramatically in the long run?**

Heaven knows I've tried. I have taken them back in time in my courses in economic history and the history of economic thought to Renaissance Venice, to 17th-century Holland, to 18th-century Britain and 19th-century America and asked them to look at the historical context in which scarcity was confronted and economic theories were developed. I have challenged them to consider how this historical context changes the array of variables we must consider when we formulate economic theory. I have even confronted them with the idea that maybe the root causes of economic growth were not, in fact, economic, and that we must adjust our analysis accordingly.

For some of them, this is unsettling. Almost drunk with the power of economic analysis and the importance of things economic in society, it does not come easy to them when I suggest, as John Stuart Mill did, that a person is not likely to be a good economist who is nothing else. A knowledge of history, sociology, psychology, political science, geography, and even physics can often be critical in getting right the assumptions on which economic theory depends. A liberal arts education expands the imagination and multiplies one's vicarious experiences so that when it comes to figuring out which variables to consider and which assumptions to make in economic modeling, there is a chance of actually saying something useful as well as elegant.

Although I probably could not have formulated my ideas about the dilemma this way at the time, I am sure that a general belief in the value of the liberal arts for young economists was behind my desire to provide our majors with an off-campus study experience. In the 1970s, when off-campus study was in its infancy at Carleton and the campus coordinator was a faculty member who served part-time out of an office in the basement of a campus building, economics majors rarely went abroad. Students who majored in economics tended to be ambitious and goal-oriented, and they usually wanted to get on with the very important process of becoming an economist instead of being "diverted" by a trip abroad.

To counter this trend in 1980 I mounted the first economics seminar abroad. I took 20 students to Nuremberg, Germany, and we studied the German economy. They lived with German families, and we studied German economic institutions. We took trips to see first-hand how various institutions in the economy functioned. On the day that Ronald Reagan was elected, we were at the *Bundesbank*, the German central bank. Officials told us that the bank would not intervene in foreign exchange markets to help maintain the value of the German mark as it fluctuated in the wake of the election. Later the students learned that just a few floors above us, the bank was in fact intervening strongly.

But they also learned more fundamental things. Living with German families, they learned from conversations that Germans are much more worried about inflation than about unemployment. They learned that Germans are reluctant to move from their place of birth to take better jobs elsewhere. They learned that East German students they met in Berlin regarded the lack of a guaranteed job in America to be a huge price to pay for "so-called freedom." And they were incredulous. We were not on Mars. This was a culture that had become Americanized since World War II and that on the face of it resembled our own in more ways than not. Didn't the Germans know that unemployment is the major post-war problem facing Western economies and if you are always afraid of inflation you won't stimulate your economy enough to ensure full employment? Didn't they know that resources need to be mobile in order to maximize output? Didn't they realize that state socialism is inefficient and that market capitalism and democracy provide the greatest good for the greatest number? Yet, with Germany's history of hyperinflation following World War I, its late unification and strong regional traditions, and the eastern part's organization into a socialist state, they could not make the same assumptions about what motivates human behavior in their economic analysis that they could in the United States.

In 1983, I moved the program to Britain and Cambridge University where it permanently resides (and where our students all speak the language, more or less). (My brother is a physicist and Life Fellow at King's College, and he convinced the college that we would not steal the silver.) So we were the first American college to establish a program abroad at King's College. King's was the college of John Maynard Keynes, the father of modern macroeconomics, and other giants of economics, including Marshall and Pigou, and for that reason is as close to a place of pilgrimage as economics is likely to get.

I began by using a curriculum which examined the origins of the British economy, its current institutions and policy debates, and the process of theorizing that produced the Keynesian Revolution. And something miraculous happened: In England, which was more like America than almost anywhere else on earth, students learned that they needed to look with new eyes at this culture and its history if they were going to make sense of its economy.

Building on the experience of the students in Germany, I called this new learning process "experiential" and made them self-conscious about it.[1] When we go abroad as tourists, I said, we tend to assume that we know how things work because on the surface everything appears similar enough to lull us into those assumptions. I told them that they would be learning to learn in a new way which resembled more than anything else the learning process of their early childhood, when they questioned everything and how it worked because it was unfamiliar.

> Building on the experience of the students in Germany, I called this new learning process "experiential" and made them self-conscious about it.

And indeed, the Cambridge students did learn through their experience with an extended stay in Britain that if they operated on the level of a tourist, they missed information critical to a student of human behavior. They could not assume that the British have the same motivations and behave the same way that Americans behave any more than they could assume that they could walk on the grass at King's College because they could walk on the grass at Carleton. They were to learn that the river of culture into which they were wading was deep indeed.

They began to study the Industrial Revolution with new eyes. Earlier they might have skimmed over descriptions of early technological advances, saying "yes, yes, but that was all very early and primitive compared with the real advances in steam and turbines." It was the undisputed highlight of my teaching career to have had a 6-foot, 3-inch young man who had just reluctantly learned how to spin wool on a great wheel at the Helmshore Textile Museum in Lancashire, look up and say with unabashed wonder: "So that was what the industrial revolution was all about! Mechanizing the twist on that thread!"

Suddenly, things that they had never considered in economics became important. For example, they discovered that early entrepreneurs actually had to lock the first workers into factories because they were not used to working longer than they needed to for subsistence. How can economics account for that when we operate on the assumption that workers are "rational maximizers"? Here we were confronting the fact that medieval man did not even conceive of economic change and that itself was a barrier to change.

They were surprised to learn that Keynes was a member of the Bloomsbury Group, which included radical thinkers and artists such as Lytton Strachey, Virginia Woolf, and Duncan Grant. While Lytton Strachey was undermining the attitudes and mores of Victorian Britain in his biography of eminent Victorians, Virginia Woolf was breaking the mold of the novel form with psychological realism. Duncan Grant was painting murals and furniture and turning out designs like nothing that had been seen before. No wonder Keynes was questioning the very basis on which economic theory rested if his friends were turning history and literature and art upside down!

When we identified the antagonism which Bloomsbury had for the methodology of Jeremy Bentham, the students began to understand the intellectual underpinnings of the group's revolutionary approach. They knew that economics was founded on the notion that economic man is a rational maximizer and that Bentham had formulated a methodology for predicting how economic man would behave when confronted with choice. Bentham's approach was the basis for the development of the scientific method in economics in the 19th century.

Bloomsbury rejected Bentham's "felicific calculus" of pleasure and pain and put forward a new vision of society based on G.E. Moore's philosophy. Moore's ethics became the philosophical basis for Bloomsbury, and his philosophical method and epistemological realism had a profound effect on Keynes' economics. Moore insisted that the question should be analyzed before any answer was attempted so that the nature of the assumptions being made could be scrutinized. By applying this approach, Keynes discovered a critical flaw in classical economics and the reason it was ineffective in dealing with depression: the assumption of full employment. In 1933, three years before he published his monumental *General Theory of Employment, Interest and Money,* Keynes wrote

> . . . all our ideas about economics instilled in us by education and atmosphere and tradition are, whether we are conscious of it or not, soaked with theoretical presuppositions which are only properly applicable to a society which is in equilibrium with all its productive resources already employed. Many people are trying to solve the problem of unemployment with a theory which is based on the assumption that there is no unemployment. (Keynes, 1933, pp. 279-81)

This was not a trivial matter. The Great Depression was threatening the livelihood of millions of people throughout the Western world, and the failure to provide an economic solution to it put the very social fabric of democracy at risk, as was to become horribly evident in Germany and Italy. Keynes knew that he was embarked on an urgent matter, the outcome of which would determine the future of the Western economies. After we read Keynes' *General Theory* with this in mind and the students saw the social reconstruction it implies, the forest which they had always missed because they were struggling with the trees of the specific theoretical construct became clear. It was a heady summer.

Since that first summer in England, I and my colleagues have taken students to Cambridge for almost 20 years. The curriculum changes with the interests of the faculty member leading the seminar, but the central purpose remains the same: to open windows of the students' minds that are simply out of reach on campus. It has been our experience that by giving the students a concrete personal experience of the place where the Industrial Revolution happened and the milieu in which the Keynesian revolution occurred their learning is transformed. By making them self-conscious about the process of doing and knowing through experience, they reach a new depth of meaning.

In 2000, I directed the last Cambridge seminar of my career, and I implemented one final innovation in the seminar. It turned out to be a keystone experience. Rather than locating the seminar entirely in England, I decided to begin on the Continent. I took the students on a 10-day backpacking trip which began in Germany to visit sites which provided background for their studies in Britain later in the summer. If I ever underestimated the power of experiential learning, this trip was to make it clear once and for all. Just as they were to gain hands-on experience of the places and artifacts of the Industrial Revolution later in the summer, here they were to see the places that would figure in the background to that story.

We visited Rothenburg, Nuremberg, and Brughes, medieval and early modern towns which are representative of the preindustrial economy of Europe. The students were amazed by the small scale of the medieval cities and the extent of their defensive walls. We saw medieval fields and examined early kinds of grains with far smaller yields than later varieties which were part of the agricultural revolution in Britain in the 16th and 18th centuries. We sailed down the Rhine and saw where robber barons had swooped down from their hilltop castles on merchant caravans to disrupt trade and to extract draconian tolls in medieval times.

Because the world wars are so important in understanding the British economy, I took them to look at the ruined architecture of the Third Reich in Nuremberg and to stand where Hitler stood at the Nazi party rallies. We visited sites of World War I in Flanders and stood in the trenches at Paschendale, where the Allies sacrificed the flower of a generation over four years and a few hundred yards of muddy ground. We saw where the British shot deserters as young as 16 to "strengthen the troops' resolve." We attended the daily ceremony of the "Last Watch" at the Menin Gate for the over 50,000 soldiers of their age in the Great War who perished there without a trace. Later, when they saw the long rolls of the local war dead in village churches throughout Britain, that experience would have special meaning.

We were accompanied in Flanders by two guests: Stanley Graham, whose grandfather had died in Flanders, and Brigid Pailthorpe, whose father and father-in-law had both been decorated in Flanders during the conflict.

Stanley brought photos of his grandfather and showed the students the few possessions which had been returned to his grandmother. Brigid described the impact of the war on her father, who commanded a military unit, and on her father-in-law, who was a doctor at the front. Neither man ever talked about his war experience, and it was not until their deaths and the discovery of their diaries that they learned the agony of their years at the front. These eye-witness accounts made the experience real to the students in ways that even the scarred landscape, the monuments and cemeteries could not.

When we reached England and began our course of study, there was an entirely new level of understanding when we discussed the limitations of the early modern economy's scale of output, the economic effects of the lack of political unity in Germany , and the effect of the world wars on Britain. The students had actually seen the evidence of these things on the ground with their own eyes. Students who, studying this same material at Carleton, might have left their studies at the classroom door as a thing apart now walked to Grantchester to sit in the orchard for tea as Keynes had done to discuss being a conscientious objector with other members of Bloomsbury. They read poetry by Rupert Brooke and other war poets. They visited the archives at King's and held in their hands Keynes' notebook for *The Economic Consequences of the Peace* from the Versailles Conference. "Cool," they said.

They traveled to London in their free time to see the Impressionist collection at the National Gallery, which Roger Frye, a member of Bloomsbury, had with great vision procured for the nation and for which Keynes had allocated the money as a young Treasury official. They visited Charleston Farmhouse, which was the home of some of the members of the Bloomsbury Group, with its murals, furniture, paintings and decorative arts, and Monk's House, where Virginia Woolf lived and worked until she committed suicide in the face of what they all believed to be an imminent German invasion. They began to discover what my colleague Ada Mae Harrison used to call " the awesome interrelatedness of everything." Students who might have grudgingly taken an obligatory arts and literature class when they would rather have been in an industrial organization class now went back on their own to look at the ceiling at King's College Chapel one more time before leaving for the airport and bought a volume of Emily Brontë, Jane Austen, or Virginia Woolf to read on the plane. Dewey's belief that knowledge must be grounded in "the depth of meaning that attaches to its coming within urgent daily interests"(Dewey, 1916, p.8) was fully supported by the experience of the students in Cambridge.

I know that I will miss the Cambridge seminar and will feel a sense of loss now that it is no longer part of my teaching. I will miss knowing students as well as the director comes to know them on a program abroad. I will miss sharing with them ideas and places that have had been so meaningful to me intellectually. But the program takes enormous amounts of energy, and as I grow older I wonder how long I will be able to lead the way and be the first up on the moor. I also feel acutely the responsibility of taking students abroad, and part of me wants to quit with a perfect record of returning them all safely home. (One of my students was booked on the plane that went down in Lockerbie, but he missed it. How I felt until I knew he was safe defies description.) I also have several research projects I want to finish before retirement; they will not get done unless I make time for them in the summers to come.

> **What will endure is the expanded breadth of imagination of all the students who studied there ...**

My able young colleagues will take over the seminar, and it will continue, although they will not replicate my curriculum. Nor should they. They should lead their students to discover things that excite *them*, for that is where the spark in the seminar originates. (Having said that, I cannot deny that I probably will still feel a bit proprietary about what has been accomplished on this program. Maybe that is just another indication that it is time to pass on the torch!)

In 1992, unbeknownst to me, the Cambridge students obtained permission from the Cambridge City Council and Gonville and Caius College to put a plaque on the childhood home of John Maynard Keynes. It read: "Former home of John Maynard Keynes, Economist, 1883-1946, presented by Professor M.W. Paas and the Carleton College Economics Seminar." They surprised me with the mounted plaque on the last night of our stay in Cambridge. Last summer 14 of those students held a 10-year reunion in England to which I was invited, and they talked about the plaque and about the one and only time they ever saw me speechless. I think they regard that plaque as the lasting contribution of the Cambridge seminar. But I know better. What will endure is the expanded breadth of imagination of all the students who studied there and who, through experience, learned anew how to see the world with fresh eyes. ■

ENDNOTES

[1] Although I was not aware of it at the time, scholars in education were in the process of developing a full-blown theory of experiential learning in the late 70s and early 80s. Building on the tradition of apprenticeship and using Dewey's belief that knowledge must be linked to experience (1916), Kolb (1984) developed a theory of experiential learning which has been very influential in education.

REFERENCES

Dewey, J. (1916). *Democracy and education.* Toronto, Ontario, Canada: Macmillan.

Kolb, D. A. (1984). *Experiential learning: Experience as the source of learning and development.* Englewood Cliffs, NJ: Prentice-Hall.

Civic Engagement through Tragedy

Carol Rutz

T he most frequently quoted response to the trauma of September 11, 2001, was stark: "Everything has changed." But, of course, everything did not change. As firefighters, police officers, military personnel, and so many others worked at the World Trade Center site, the Pentagon, and the crash site in a Pennsylvania field, the rest of us paused, tried to understand, and eventually resumed our lives.

At Carleton College, a peaceful place geographically removed from the destruction, the events of September 11th were disruptive—for a while. The television sets in the student union and dorm lounges were tuned to CNN, rather than ESPN or the daily soaps. Faculty and administrators quickly organized special panels on Islam, politics in the Middle East, and other relevant topics, which were well attended by faculty, students, and staff. Those with direct connections to the tragedy were comforted, counseled, and supported. A wary swell of support for the Bush administration was leavened with chilling fear of the worldwide implications of a prolonged, armed conflict. Classes were conducted as scheduled, and the generally liberal, thoughtful ethos of the campus remained intact. The serious, yet upbeat tenor of the student body persisted, and the work of laboratory, discussion, lecture, and field trip continued.

> While engagement ... is one of my goals for every course and every class meeting, the shock and pain of September 11th produced a collective experience that accelerated the civic project implicit in our teacher-student contract.

CAROL RUTZ, lecturer in English, earned her B.A. degree at Gustavus Adolphus College, her M.A. at Hamline University, and her Ph.D. at the University of Minnesota. She joined the faculty in 1997.

So no, everything did not change. However, there were subtle changes that resist documentation, and this essay examines one such change after September 11th: my experience as a classroom teacher in a first-year writing seminar. While engagement—in the sense of connectedness in a shared educational enterprise—is one of my goals for every course and every class meeting, the shock and pain of September 11th produced a collective experience that accelerated the civic project implicit in our teacher-student contract. Acceleration was not the only effect; the terms of the course itself were redefined through trauma that was essentially sublimated into the rhetoric of problem identification and research on those identified problems—all of them with social/civic implications and proposed solutions.

THE PREMISE OF THE COURSE

First, a bit of context: As a rhetorician, I teach a writing course that differs substantially from the courses most of my students have taken in high school, where they have typically learned to write themes on assigned topics, reports based on library research, narratives derived from personal experience, and—if they have been lucky—a little poetry or fiction. Recognizing that my students have done well enough on these assignments to earn their way into a good college, I offer them a course designed to build on what they know. Although many of them would be startled to hear my goal for them in these terms, the course is designed to help them become rhetorical beings—adults equipped with the rhetorical skills required for citizenship and the world of work.

My students are savvy consumers of education who understand that most writing done in high school is literally *for school*. When else in life is one asked to write 500-1000 words on a Hawthorne short story or a report on the history of the Salvation Army and submit it to one reader for evaluation? Students recognize that the writing they do in school has pedagogical value. Reporting on one's knowledge through formal papers, essay exams, and in-class writing all adds up to a measure of learning. Students know how this works, and they readily comply.

As they prepare for college, students expect to do more of the same, even if they expect at some level that the standards will be higher and the tasks correspondingly more difficult and complex. Nevertheless, they tend to view this kind of writing as "school work"; their investment in that work is correlated to grades, teachers' approval, and success in a major. As a rhetorician in the pragmatist tradition, Kate Ronald (personal communication, February 25, 2001), once explained to me, "school writing has little or no real value to those who write it or read it—except as a measure of compliance." Regardless, neither Kate nor I would want students to miss the experience of school writing, because we agree with our students that practicing topical themes, library reports, and personal narratives really does serve pedagogical purposes. Students learn to form sentences and vary them; they experiment with vocabulary; they test some useful forms that become part of their rhetorical repertoire. And so on.

Nevertheless, the late adolescent who comes to college has rarely thought about the writing she will do as an adult. The same first-year student who confidently predicts he will enter law school (or medical school, graduate school, whatever) tends to conceive of the writing in that new situation as yet another helping of school writing—just at a more challenging level. For good reasons, some of them developmental, high school graduates fail to carefully observe the adults in their worlds. Among those missed observations is the amount of writing done on the job or as a function of being responsible adults. High school graduates have little sense of themselves as public beings—even if they work, they do not yet connect work with identity and self-expression. Moving beyond the employment environment, few of them imagine themselves preparing a presentation for the school board, the zoning commission, the local humane society, the League of Women Voters, or the county licensing board for daycare providers. School writing rarely directs their attention to the writing situations adults actually face.

> My students are savvy consumers of education who understand that most writing done in high school is literally *for school*.... As they prepare for college, students expect to do more of the same ...

My job as a rhetorician is to help students attend to some of the writing occasions that await them. I could accomplish this with a course based in service learning, where writing on behalf of some community group would focus the issues of audience, purpose, and rhetorical situation in a non-school setting. Some of my colleagues design courses that do just that. To help students prepare both for service learning courses and their own writing as adults, my first-year seminar is designed to produce public writing through a process of inquiry.

To structure the major writing assignments in the course, I use a version of David Jolliffe's methodology as detailed in his 1999 book, *Inquiry and Genre*. Students choose a topic (subject to a few practical considerations worked out in conference) and write about it for three papers.

The first paper is a reflective essay that positions the writer within the topic, differentiating what the writer knows from what s/he wants to learn and posing some questions about the topic that offer a basis for research.

The second paper essentially reports on the ways the writer has explored the topic, using the initial questions to launch research on line, in print sources, and through oral history. The inclusion of oral history—human sources—is particularly important. Whatever experience our students have with research before they come to college, they adhere to a belief that research for a classroom assignment translates into their combing the Web and (we hope!) the library, for text, images, and other sources. Until required to consult human beings with expertise in a given area, they seem oblivious to the reality that textual sources are produced by people who work, think, converse, and write. Posing their questions to people who may or may not have answers for them gives students a new sense of what research actually involves.

In connection with the second paper, students give a 15-minute talk to the whole class about their research in progress, with emphasis on the unexpected new questions that inevitably emerge from their research. A discussion period allows members of the class to ask questions as well, and further feedback takes place on an online conference. Frequently, students demonstrate through this talk that their initial formulation of the topic has metamorphosed through exploration. For example, I once had a student who was interested in a virulent type of strep infection, necrotizing fasciitis; as she learned more, she began to wonder about a common therapy that seemed to worsen the disease. Treatment of the disease had not been the basis of her original interest. However, as evidenced by her presentation to the class, she developed this focus for her research through studying the medical literature as well as by consulting emergency room workers who had coped with the disease as professionals. Like many students who undertake this project, this student reported that her new emphasis emerged from the research process itself.

Finally, having completed an exploration of the topic, following whatever rabbit hole seems most propitious for their purposes, students write a persuasive piece related to the topic. Here is where the public writing comes in. Whatever the form—brochure, op-ed piece, letter to a public official, formal article, sermon, grant proposal, bathroom stall ad—students must identify a specific audience and attempt to persuade that audience to act in a specific way. The student interested in necrotizing fasciitis wrote a grant proposal to fund a clinical trial with animal subjects to test her hypothesis that a particular therapy accelerated the infection. In her case, persuasive writing argued for funding for more research. Other students argue for political reform, policy change, improved public education on some issue, and so forth.

When given a chance to reflect on the work they have done during the term, students typically recognize at least two benefits from this sequence of assignments.

First, they appreciate the amount of research one must do before one is qualified to take a responsible, informed position on a topic. As they trace the movement of their own thinking toward accommodating new information, they respect the role of informed context in helping others learn new ideas, consider them, and become amenable to changing their thinking.

The second benefit relates to the social maneuvers required by the sequence. The involvement of human sources and the experience of giving a talk to a live audience both work toward a recognition that research comes out of human activity, and its results must be communicated in ways that human audiences can interpret and accept. They internalize the reality that human audiences read as well as listen. Students invariably report that facing a live audience—even a friendly, casual one—requires them to think about that audience's needs and organize their material accordingly. The final drafts of those exploratory papers show written results of that affective confrontation.

Given this structure, the civic nature of the course is completely on the table. Typically, the first few weeks are spent negotiating topics, working on related rhetorical tasks, and building a classroom community through discussion in large and small groups as well as on line. By the middle of our 10-week term, students are well acquainted with one another and are fairly clear on the topics as well. Engagement in the course itself parallels the students' engagement in their research projects. The more we

> **Given this structure, the civic nature of the course is completely on the table.**

share interests, research problems, searching for sources, and so on, the more we invest in the class itself as the vehicle for these activities. The course design reinforces social as well as pedagogical goals.

SEPTEMBER 2001

In the fall of 2001, our classes began on September 10th, a day that promised all of the typical back-to-school rituals. I gave my first-hour class of 16 brand-new freshmen an assignment to attend our opening convocation that afternoon, take notes, and write about their observations. Many had never seen an academic procession, and none had witnessed the institution-specific traditions that accompany this event. (For example, upperclassmen arrange themselves in the chapel balcony and blow bubbles on the faculty as we process below them.) The main speaker was Fay Vincent, former Commissioner of Major League Baseball, and the program also featured organ music, readings, welcoming speeches, and awards for student achievements. As usual, the program promoted a happy, go-get-'em mood. As I sat in my academic robe during the convocation, I looked forward to reading my new students' impressions of this occasion, wondering how they would decode the various levels of tradition and ritual.

The next day, September 11th, we were all back in the chapel under radically different circumstances in an entirely different mood. During our president's halting remarks, I scanned the room, thinking about my students, even though I had met them only once and strained to recognize their faces in the crowd. In light of the terrorist attacks, what would they do with the trivial assignment I gave them? What would I do tomorrow morning, their first class on The Day After? Would they even show up? Would they be packing for home? Who could blame them if they were?

At 8:30 a.m. on September 12th, 16 subdued first-year students joined me in our classroom. All of them had freshly printed papers with them. To begin, I said, "I don't want to ignore what happened yesterday. However, my guess is that many of you did at least some of your writing yesterday or last night, and I'd like to see how world events come up as we talk about what you wrote." They exhaled. I asked them to exchange papers with a partner and just read—no marking, no teacherly commenting. After reading, they were to talk to one another about what they wrote.

With a little shuffling around and general good will, the students found partners and got to work. Once the reading ended and discussion began, I wandered around, listening to some of the conversations and fielding a question here and there. As the discussion began to taper off, I asked if anyone had read a paper that s/he really liked—for whatever reason. Several hands went up immediately. One student's hand was waving wildly, so I called on him and asked him to read the paper that he liked so much. With a glance at Catherine, the writer of the paper, he began:

> The contrast between today and yesterday is most apparent in the clapping, or lack thereof. Yesterday, everyone's hands burned to applaud, to congratulate speeches and speakers. Today hands lay deadened or twitching in intense anxiety. The pews are definitely the same as they were yesterday, the podium, only slightly moved to the left, and the hymnals tucked in behind the pews haven't moved. But almost as if someone briefed the students before entering, we all knew not to clap.[1] (Courcy, 2001)

Catherine's paper proved to be a moving meditation on the differences she experienced in the chapel two days running. She wrote, "Taking notes during the convocation, I never imagined that my experience and reaction to the event would be easier to evaluate following a terrorist bombing, [sic] however that is the way it turned out." Throughout her paper, she moved from the somber Tuesday gathering to the "exuberant . . . start of a new year" on Monday, demonstrating how her notes from Opening Convocation took on new significance in light of disaster. "We were only a day away from seeing political strife manifest in tragic events. At the same time . . . I am so happy that we have an education to celebrate over, because . . . more education for more people is what the world needs more than anything."

Structurally, Catherine's paper mines her notes, using them as the basis of a meta-commentary on the social and educational phenomena that crystallized for her the day after the ceremony. At the time, however, she admitted to losing interest in the convocation while it was going on, not realizing the significance of what she wrote until later:

> All alone at the bottom of the page are the lone words in quotation marks, "it is our humanity we celebrate here." Apparently this was

the ending of [Fay] Vincent's speech. I understand so well now how necessary it is to continue doing just that. In a circumstance like this that feels so devoid of humanity, mercy, and celebration, I feel compelled to keep searching out that humanity, in individuals or nations . . . . I feel a surge of needing to do good in the world. (Courcy, 2001)

After the student finished reading Catherine's paper, I thanked him and asked the rest of the class for reactions. Many complimented Catherine on her skill at conveying the contrast in mood. Someone asked her how she chose the details to feature. She shrugged and replied briefly, noting in passing that her home is in Boston, where two of the hijacked planes had originated. She looked down as we all winced in sympathy. As the questions continued, she explained in more detail how she made decisions as a writer—decisions that governed the form, argument, and diction of her paper.

That exchange opened the door for another student to explain that while he chose *not* to write about world events, the seriousness of those events still affected him, raising the ante for him as a writer. To keep faith with himself and his budding higher education experience, he felt more responsible than usual for producing an accurate, detailed report. Toward that end, he took time to research the defining moment of Fay Vincent's tenure as baseball commissioner, the Pete Rose scandal. As he read his paper for the class, we all appreciated his juxtaposition of Carleton's opening convocation with a particular historical-cultural context—linking the world of major league baseball with Vincent's views on the objectives of higher education.

And so the class period continued, moving among rhetorical issues— "what I wrote and how I made those decisions"—and emotional responses to terrorism. Catherine's paper opened a way for us to be together in tragic, traumatic times and still do our work in the classroom. As a result, we reached a level of engagement in the class during that second meeting that would normally take three or four weeks to achieve. Once established, that mutual commitment remained a conspicuous feature of that class. Throughout the term, I witnessed a consistent level of care among the students and myself that was demonstrated unselfconsciously through our online environment, peer critiques, and feedback on oral presentations. Furthermore, the topics students chose for their research reflected the urge to "do good" that Catherine expressed in her paper. Because the world clearly needed better understanding and specific improvements, each student latched on to a project that could make a difference to the world as they understood it.

In many respects, the range of topics was not that different than what I was used to seeing in courses based in the inquiry model. Nevertheless, the students displayed an eagerness about their topics that translated into intentional investment in civic issues. All of their projects were aimed at making a difference in a world with obvious, painful defects in international relations, public education, health care, and more.

A further measure of their engagement was the attendance pattern, which was striking indeed. The class met at 8:30 a.m., three days a week. Carleton students regard 8:30 a.m. as early—painfully early. Of the 16 students enrolled, eight never missed a class; no one missed more than twice. My sense was that they attended for one another—not to curry favor with me. The class itself became a civic group that was committed to changing the world through research, discussion, and public writing. In many ways, they fulfilled the prediction of William A. Galston (2001), writing in the *Chronicle of Higher Education,* who observes that the "surge of patriotism" following September 11th is likely to energize students, pointing them toward civic issues and public service as sites of meaning for their lives. Whether this brand of civic engagement has lasting effects remains to be seen. Galston argues that we— teachers and administrators in higher education—should seize the opportunity to keep public service in the foreground of our students' thinking, lest their enthusiasm wane through insufficient application of their civic impulses.

ENGAGEMENT AND THE CLASSROOM

Meanwhile, we who would encourage civic engagement are part of a sociopolitical laboratory in these post-September 11 days. We came through the terrifying first days. We organized and attended teach-ins and programs on Islam, the conflict in the Middle East, U.S. foreign policy, and more. Yet the informative, learning side of education was only part of our experience. As colleague and theater professor David McCandless (personal communication, April 8, 2002) pointed out to me, the repeated video of the Boeing 767 colliding with the second tower forced a confrontation with an unbearable reality, yet simultaneously blunted our responses to that reality. In psychological terms, we all have "flashbulb" memories of those collisions, and the images themselves are only one component of the emotional hemorrhage congealed in that flash of pain (Neisser, 1982, p. 45). That surreal image was emblematic of a far-reaching terrorist plot and its associated political baggage. The shock and grief were turned to action for some, immobilized numbness for others, and to internalized agony for still others. Eventually, everyone had to make peace with the images, the enormity of the loss, and the associated trauma. For my students and me, trauma was at least partially sublimated into research projects, discussion, and a sense of taking on the unknown to master our feelings as well as our ignorance. Engagement in the course—and one another—helped us manage the larger context outside of our lovely rural ivory tower. Our geographical distance from tragedy lent our project a measure of safety, and the course itself served as a rehearsal space for civic activity.

Here I must confess that I have something in common with my students who regard their high school writing as "school writing." Until the fall of 2001, I regarded my work with students in the classroom as "school work," something set apart—in a special way, to be sure, but still separate— from the rest of my life.[2] The classroom itself, I now realize, is a social and political sphere that crystallizes experience that cannot be confined to the specific hours in the course schedule. Much of

> Until the fall of 2001, I regarded my work with students in the classroom as "school work," something set apart— in a special way, to be sure, but still separate—from the rest of my life.

what my students and I did on September 12th was in service of normalizing the trauma we all felt and struggled to articulate. In the classroom, we all complied with the expectation that everything, even the unspeakable horror of September 11th, is fair game for intellectual examination and analysis. Emotions have a place in the classroom as well, particularly if they are dressed in skillful rhetoric and graceful words. Furthermore, substituting a baseball scandal for hijacking is appropriate, even celebrated, because the classroom will accommodate the abstract and the historical as well as the concrete and the immediate.

For me, the sublimation of tragedy accomplished more than just getting through a tough time. I have to admit that I have never had a comparable classroom experience. The connections in that classroom sustained me personally and professionally, allowing me a physical and emotional space to work on my own responses to trauma with people I grew to trust—with whom I was truly engaged. After September 11th, I ask myself whether I can retreat to a previous level of engagement. I blush to admit that the class I taught the next term seemed lifeless and dull until I reminded myself that those students had an incredibly tough act to follow. I also ask myself whether I can withstand more of the trauma that produced the effects in my class this past fall. Obviously, I would not wish for similar inspiration just to recapture the rush of engagement and commitment that characterized that exceptional class. Still, as I see troops move out of Afghanistan, worry as the occupation of Iraq becomes a matter of status quo, and fret over detainees pacing in Guantanamo, I marvel at the degree to which the public (and I include myself) accepts these developments and resumes a life largely disconnected from them. As Galston (2001) warns, maintenance of a spirit of civic engagement is the key, but if sublimation of trauma takes the form of business as usual, what next? The answer may be to reconceive business as usual to accommodate a larger, more civic agenda, one that defines citizenship as a platform for problem identification and solution. I am more convinced than ever that a rhetorical approach to teaching writing benefits students as they begin to appreciate the social and political roles they will assume as adults.

The ongoing problems of human society—a volatile economy, poverty, troubled public education, malnutrition, degradation of the environment—offer plenty of fodder for civic engagement. Can we allow our students and ourselves to disengage? If we resist disengagement, can we expect ourselves to muster the energy to remain engaged? Having taught writing to first-year students within a model that offers practice in writing for citizenship, I now have to decide how much passion I can afford to expend as I challenge students to engage. Then I have to wonder about the post-course effects—for them and myself. Trauma inspires powerful motivation, but trauma also tends to enervate. I need to develop my own response to trauma that values its lessons, overcomes its damaging effects, and provides me with the means to engage my students consistently and respectfully toward civic ends. The classroom itself provides an appropriate arena. I am fortunate to inhabit that space (physically and metaphorically) with students who understand with me how a classroom works as a place to practice and enact our public lives. ■

ENDNOTES

[1] This and all excerpts from a student paper are quoted with written permission of the author.

[2] I am indebted to Bradley Peters of Northern Illinois University for insightful advice about the role of the classroom in this experience.

REFERENCES

Courcy, C. (2001, September 12). Untitled, unpublished paper. Carleton College.

Galston, W. A. (2001, November 16). Can patriotism be turned into civic engagement? *Chronicle of Higher Education*, B16-17.

Jolliffe, D. A. (1999) *Inquiry and genre: Writing to learn in college*. Needham Heights, MA: Allyn & Bacon.

Neisser, U. (1982). *Memory observed*. San Francisco: W.H. Freeman.

Finding Community through Civic Engagement

Mary Savina

I never thought so many people would be interested in what we were doing. (Keck Geology Consortium student, after presenting her water quality results to about 25 interested community members in August 2000.)

This essay is about the value—to students, faculty and community—of tying academic work together with community needs. Many of my courses and summer student/faculty research programs include community-based projects. Included here are quotations from the final reflective essays of students who took Introductory Environmental Geology in Spring 2002.[1] The class took many field trips to local farms, county and city planning offices, and more conventional geological sites (outcrops, streams, gravel pits). In addition, students worked either on a natural resources inventory for the city of Northfield or on a soil conservation assessment of the drainage area of a local lake.

> Classroom civic engagement projects provide a means for us to help our students overcome their cynicism by doing something that is worthwhile outside the bounds of the campus.

Many of the activities described in this essay fall under the broad heading of "service learning" or "community-based learning" (cf. Bringle and Hatcher, 1995, cited in Bringle and Hatcher, 2000; Weigert, 1998; Howard,

MARY SAVINA is the McBride Professor of Geology and Environmental Studies and Humphrey Doermann Professor of Liberal Learning. She earned her B.A. degree at Carleton College, and her M.A. and Ph.D. degrees at the University of California, Berkeley. She joined the Carleton faculty in 1978.

1998), that is, academic activities which also provide some kind of community service and an opportunity for reflection on that service. At Carleton, there are two main types of service learning: 1) the service learning component is one of many projects included in a particular class; 2) the entire class is focused around a single service learning project. Such projects have several purposes:

1) To show students that their work has interest and importance outside of the class and perhaps outside of the campus;

2) To make the boundaries between the campus and the community much more permeable, increasing the likelihood that individual students will design other service learning projects during their undergraduate careers, because they will see that it is possible and rewarding;

3) To use examples in the classroom that students can experience in all dimensions. Rather than drawing geologic examples from spectacular, but far away places, my classes focus on learning methods in the "here and now," the actual landscape that students are immersed in. Most of the methods they will use in studying the local area, are, of course, transferable, as are the habits of mind they acquire while acting as geologists.

A related purpose is to increase students' "civic engagement," defined by Campbell (2000) as "participation in voluntary associations of all sorts [including but not limited to] political organizations (p. 641)." I use the term somewhat more broadly to include participation in larger, civic activities, even if these are not connected with a pre-existing association of some kind.

Two major caveats on what follows: 1) My experiences (and therefore my examples) are mostly from rural, "peopled" landscapes, so there will be little here about either urban or completely isolated areas; 2) I will be speaking primarily from my own experiences and observations about what works for me and my students and not from the abundant educational literature about service learning and participatory learning (cf. Rhoads and Howard, eds., 1998; Giles and Eyler, 1998).

BACKGROUND—COMMUNITY AND STUDENTS

Carleton is a four-year, residential liberal arts college of about 1,850 students, located about 40 miles south of the Twin Cities of Minneapolis and St. Paul. Students come to Carleton from all over the United States and several foreign countries. Perhaps one-third come from Minnesota, Iowa, Wisconsin, and Illinois, but even these students from the Upper Midwest typically come from urban areas and first or second-ring suburbs. Northfield, a city of about 17,500 people (this figure includes 5,000 college students from Carleton and St. Olaf Colleges), straddles an urban-suburban-rural boundary. Residential growth in Northfield has come at the expense of productive cropland; some of the recent population growth in the community surely reflects expansion to the south of the Twin Cities urban area, though some reflects new residents' desires to live in a traditional small town. Like me, most Carleton students come from communities that experienced the rural-to-urban transition at least a generation ago. In a typical Carleton geology or environmental studies class of 25 to 45 students, two or fewer will have grown up on a farm and only four or five will have grown up in a community rural enough that agriculture is the major part of the economy. In a way, this is unsurprising, given the trends in census data which show that though the acreage of land used for agriculture has hardly changed in the past 50 years (about a 6.8% decline between 1947 and 1997; USDA, 2002) the number of farms has declined 62.7% in the same period (USDA, n.d.a). U.S. citizens listing "farming" as their principal occupation fell below one million for the first time in the 1997 Agricultural Census (USDA, n.d.b). The result is that most students come to Carleton with an urban or suburban lifestyle, familiar neither with small towns nor rural communities. However, they have opinions about agriculture and rural life, opinions which are seldom grounded in real experience or data.

> Rather than drawing geologic examples from spectacular, but far away places, my classes focus on learning methods in the "here and now," the actual landscape that students are immersed in.

Although different in many ways from urban and suburban areas, Northfield also has a microcosm of social issues characteristic of the early 21st century. The neighborhoods adjacent to the colleges are old and affluent; in other parts of town, low-income residents and immigrants to the Northfield area are concentrated in multi-family housing. (To a certain extent, students compete with low-income townspeople for inexpensive housing, because neither college has enough dormitory space to house all of its students). The Northfield Community Action Center estimates that 240 families in the community use the food shelf program in any given month (NCAC, 2002). Crime, while minor in both rate and type relative to more urban areas, nevertheless exists in Northfield. Perhaps more obvious, the community is split on many issues of governance and vision for the future. A recent referendum to allow a big-box retail store (Target) to build in Northfield was split almost evenly. Individual and group efforts to maintain a strong downtown (in historic buildings dating from just after the Civil War) are alternately obstructed or supported. The new superintendent of schools reportedly described Northfield as a community "with more opinions than people." These and other factors sometimes make it difficult to determine the "community" that one is engaging in—or encouraging one's students to engage in.

On many issues facing Northfield, a major challenge is lack of information. Elections and referenda are the common ways of determining citizen views about issues. Like most governments, Northfield lacks enough employees to investigate every important subject. The city hires consultants for major projects, but even those consultant studies commonly lack depth. At the same time, various city governments have had trouble phrasing the questions they would like consultants or citizen groups to answer. As a result, some issues are studied again and again, with a dusty bookshelf in City Hall filled with the 10 or so recent transportation studies and the five or so recent studies on maintaining a healthy downtown.

From the point of view of the community (or more properly, communities) in the Northfield area, then, there is no shortage of subjects for students to research that can assist Northfield-area residents in making decisions. The general heading of "environmental studies" is a particular rich vein to tap; recent student work at Carleton has a) defined a preliminary wellhead protection area to protect the community water supply, b) created an oversized flow chart of city development processes for the benefit of city staff, elected officials and developers, c) proposed minimum standards for riparian buffer zones to protect streams, d) presented alternatives to wholesale streambank reconstruction in the wake of a severe flash flood, and e) designed a preliminary natural resources inventory for the city, among many other projects. These studies don't substitute for good consulting or staff work, but they can fill in gaps, provide baseline data, summarize background, suggest questions that consultants can later focus on, and educate the community and its leaders. In many cases, these student projects are applications of knowledge or methods that are already widely known in academic circles. They are similar to those conducted by "science shops," many of which are associated with universities in Europe and the U.S. (Raloff, 1998). Through the student work, community members can gain access to the rich intellectual resources of the campus.

The need for a natural resources inventory of Northfield emerged during the revision of the city's Comprehensive Plan, an effort that began in 2000 and which was completed in early 2003, after which the zoning ordinances were revised to conform to the new plan. Originally, the natural resources inventory was to be compiled by a consulting firm in 2002, but budget constraints made this impossible. I thought that making a preliminary inventory would be an excellent student project for several reasons. First, students would quickly discover that there was not general agreement in the community about what were the important natural resources. Several prominent citizens told the students "That's what YOU are going to tell US." Second, having followed the earlier comprehensive planning process, I suspected that a consultant study would begin with assembling GIS-based information on wetlands, slopes, streams, etc. These data are readily available at Carleton; compiling them would engage the students in GIS (geographic information system) methodology that they might be able to use later in academic and professional careers. Third, since most students in the class were in their first or second year, I thought they would be surprised to find out that Northfield had such natural features as wetlands, endangered species, unique vegetation communities, and soil resources.

Northfield and Rice County are the backyards of Carleton students for four years. Carleton's history as an institution since the mid-19th century and its values are tied up in the local and regional history. Yet sometimes, Carleton's position as a "national" liberal-arts college means that it barely seems to be on the mental map of many Minnesotans. Through community-based academic projects, the college becomes a more integral part of the community.

VALUE TO FACULTY AND ACADEMIC INSTITUTION

Carleton colleagues and I have found that incorporating projects with real-world value into the curriculum, particularly when they connect students with the community, adds value to our teaching. For many years, students in technology studies and political science have completed white papers and case studies, for instance on Minnesota energy policy, national health-care reform, and comparing two countries as potential sites for new industries.

In a sense, the Northfield community-based projects build on these earlier examples. But the Northfield projects have somewhat different, perhaps additional, values to the academic enterprise at Carleton. That Northfield residents are commonly involved in the projects adds a layer of complex reality that some case studies and white papers lack. For instance, I find that when students meet local farmers, they are quickly disabused of the notions many of them have (remember, these are urban and suburban students) that farmers are uneducated, that all agriculture is corporate, and that "fixing" American agriculture is simple and straightforward. In other words, the problems emerge in all their complexity once they acquire individual human faces:

> Listening to Paul Liebenstein describe his work, day after day, with no vacations or breaks, was fascinating, but it was not the everyday logistics of the dairy business that left me with such a sense of humility and wonder. It was the tone of his voice and the look in his eye when he described to us, not his job, not his burden, but his life, his home. (Schultz, 2002)

One common problem that emerges particularly in environmental studies classes is that students come to feel powerless and cynical in the face of the overwhelming evidence that the global environment is deteriorating. Many faculty (and I am one) came of age during the Vietnam war, which coincided with colleges abandoning restrictive social policies such as curfews. Faculty in my generation are used to seeing connections between academic studies, the outside world, and our own lives. We are used to thinking that individual and community action can change the world or at least a small piece of it. Classroom civic engagement projects provide a means for us to help our students overcome their cynicism by doing something that is worthwhile outside the bounds of the campus.

I understood the implications of my own and others' actions on the earth and I became interested in doing something about it. Therefore, my most memorable experience within the past 10 weeks has been discovering that I understand what's going on around me enough that I care. (Moreno, 2002)

In addition to a sudden sense that I had actually had an effect on something, I was amazed at the power a group of people who share a common goal has to affect their surroundings. (Evans, 2002)

Most of all, I gained a true appreciation for Northfield and Rice County's real natural resource—the folks who live here . . . I was amazed at the enthusiasm of so many of the people who took time out of their schedules to teach us about John Deere tractors, lake watersheds, comprehensive planning, farming, raising cows, or the good old days before store-boughten fun in southwestern Minnesota . . . I left these classes with renewed optimism and a restored faith in mankind. (Maley, 2002)

Such considerations make it important to distinguish between civic engagement that aims for neutral presentation of research and civic engagement as advocacy. Despite my college roots in the late 1960s and early 1970s and a record of monetary support for state and national parties and candidates, I am uncomfortable using the classroom to advocate for a particular position. When I watch the Northfield City Council as an observer for the League of Women Voters, I look for instances of good (and not-so-good) process in decision-making. If the process is good, if all relevant information has been presented, and if there have been ample opportunities for the public to be heard and for council members to discuss the matter thoroughly, then I am comfortable with whatever decision the council makes, even if it goes against what I think is the key information and my own personal beliefs. The City Council, after all, is a political body and political decisions aren't always made on what a scientist would call a rational basis. I prefer to aim student projects at providing information that council members and the public may not have—such as what the scientific

> Such projects have a great deal of credibility, but heavy responsibilities go with them.

literature says about width and contiguity of effective vegetative buffers along streams. Such projects have a great deal of credibility, but heavy responsibilities go with them. At a recent meeting about the effects of big-box discount retail stores on established downtowns, a council member waved a copy of a study from Iowa State with the implication that because it came from an institution of higher learning, it had to be true. I work carefully with my students to maintain this credibility.

Those in the professional service-learning community remind us that we need to justify service learning on the grounds that students learn what we want them to better than they would without the service-learning component (Minnesota Campus Compact, 1996) and that the service-learning project should emerge from course and curricular goals. But incorporating real-world projects inevitably makes courses different (Howard, 1998). How would Introduction to Environmental Geology have been different without the natural resources inventory and lake projects? It's hard for me to say. Perhaps we would have taken some class time to discuss the text chapters on natural hazards (earthquakes, volcanic eruptions, etc.) that I barely mentioned. Perhaps our labs, almost all of which went to local field sites, would have included case studies from other parts of the world, so that students gained a more international view.

The reasons for choosing the other way come down to two basic elements in my belief system: that you can't understand the rest of the world unless you understand your own backyard and that practicing methods on small projects gives students tools to use these methods later on in different situations. My experience is that students remember the content of these projects and also the methods they employed more than almost anything else in the term, despite the lower "coverage" of content.

Like many academic departments, Carleton's geology department has both a goals statement and a list of values. The most recent version of the goals statement reads as follows:

> We believe that a broad, rigorous education [in the earth sciences], well grounded in the fundamentals of analytical and quantitative thinking, articulating and addressing scientific questions, and emphasizing clear communication, serves well both students who de-

sire to enter the world of science and students whose career interests lie elsewhere. (Geology Department, 2001, p. 2)

Thus, we believe that "learning to think like a geologist" will benefit all of our students. The heart of academic civic engagement in geology is applying the thinking of a geologist to community needs. This is what the students did as they designed and executed the natural resources inventory.

> I was extremely skeptical at the beginning of the class about our abilities as an introductory geology class to compile a useful document for the Northfield City planning council. However, as we worked on the project, I realized that the document that we were preparing served purposes that I hadn't even imagined when we began. (Evans, 2002)

> I'm very proud to have worked on this project and to have it turn out as professional and complete as it did. This was a project that again is something that taught me more about real life and our environment than any textbook could have. (First-year student, 2002)

One of the department values is particularly relevant to this discussion:

> RESPONSIBILITY OF KNOWLEDGE
> Knowledge is a privilege that carries with it the responsibility to act. Geologists should be active citizens in their communities (local to global), using their understanding of natural systems to assist policy-makers and other citizens. Geologic knowledge is relevant to the context and choices made by individuals throughout their life. (Geology Department, 2002)

VALUE FOR STUDENTS

Quotations scattered in the text so far, from students in the Spring 2002 Introduction to Environmental Geology course, show that students perceive some of the same values of this project that the community and faculty do, including developing a "sense of place" and reinforcing lifetime habits of civic engagement.

Carleton students typically refer to the "Carleton Bubble" to indicate the isolation they feel from the real world. This is despite the fact that the campus is two blocks from downtown Northfield. To many students, Northfield is a collection of pizza places, gift shops where one can furnish a dorm room, and groceries (this was the way I viewed Northfield as a college student in 1968-1972). Students transfer their perceptions from home, for instance about personal safety on the streets, to Northfield when they move here. Projects like the Northfield natural resources inventory start to make Northfield a real place. Like college presidents, incoming Carleton students come to understand Northfield and Minnesota to varying degrees (some of them never get it). For those that do, they gain insights both from observing the community as an outsider and then ultimately as an insider. (It is interesting to contrast Carleton students as they develop this

> I have identified four major challenges [regarding incorporating civic engagement projects in courses and curricula]: a) time, b) town-gown communication, c) record-keeping and institutional memory, and d) rethinking pedagogy and student assessment.

sense of place with summer research students who come to Northfield from all over the country and have to acculturate quickly to Northfield if they are to do fieldwork in environmental science. Sometimes I tell them to think of themselves as field anthropologists). Some adults claim that "their community is on the Internet." Perhaps so, but it is a depauperate community compared to the geographical community of a small town.

> Each of these events [farm panel, Dust Bowl panel, farm visits] equaled encounters with the Northfield/Rice County community, a community we at Carleton often become insulated from within our walls of learning. It seemed that environmental geology had opened the door to the idea of community and an actual community well worth discovering. (Loomis, 2002)

Many students come to Carleton with strong records of community service and volunteering. Civic engagement projects in the classroom augment this history by adding an academic side to commitment to service. It would be interesting to see if students who have been in classes that incorporate service-learning leave Carleton with different attitudes about civic engagement and service learning than those that do not have these experiences. Campbell (2000) reports that the volunteer activity of young people is a strong predictor of their level of adult volunteer activity. Giles and Eyler (1998) summarize many other studies which show profound effects of service learning on students, including stronger connections to communities.

> The final project helped to make me more familiar with my new college town and allowed me to give something back to the community. It was truly motivating to know that students like us are capable of compiling a dependable inventory of a county and that authorities will listen to us and use us as sources. (Oono, 2002)

CHALLENGES

Incorporating civic engagement projects in courses and curricula can be challenging, as many others have also noted. I have identified four major challenges: a) time, b) town-gown communication, c) record-keeping and institutional memory, and d) rethinking pedagogy and student assessment.

Carleton terms are 10 weeks long. Most projects related to individual courses need to be conceived, designed, executed, and finished within that period, including time for the students to learn necessary background. Students participating in a project need to get relevant information quickly from citizens and government sources. Closure is important, both for students and for the community. Fortunately, many professors are skilled at helping students design projects of reasonable size. In some cases, these class-size projects become parts of larger, longer projects. Work on these larger projects may come in short, intense spurts with long gaps when appropriate courses aren't being taught or as student interest in particular topics ebbs and flows. (These concerns are also addressed by Ward, 1999b).

Many students are concerned about possible negative responses to student work from the community, resulting both from the perception that students are "short-termers" in Northfield and from negative experiences citizens may have had with individual students. As an instructor, I want to be sure that future classes and their projects are welcomed. For a civic engagement project to be successful, there has to be a "getting to know you" step for both the students and citizens. My colleagues and I have been greatly helped by key contacts (such as one of the local Agricultural Extension agents) who have helped us find people who are willing to talk with college students. In designing the project, it is critical to make sure that everyone—instructor, students, citizens—agrees on the probable results. Student (and faculty) work can't substitute for professional work. For one, many professionals are registered and certain kinds of studies require a registered professional to sign off. But student projects can help define the focus for professional consultants later hired. It is also important to remember that these are *service* projects, designed to help someone else in the community and not create more work for them. In general, students desire and need more feedback from community members about their projects than they typically receive. I always try to arrange some sort of public presentation and a tangible written report that can be sent to interested citizens. Still, by the time the information is digested and perhaps acted on, the students are gone for the summer or scattered across campus, having moved onto their next set of courses.

As yet, we do not have a comprehensive way to collect posters and other products of students' work (nor a central place to keep them). We need a clearing house both for project ideas and for project results. There is little communication within or between academic departments, college offices, and the community about what the needs are, who is working on what, and who has done similar work in the past. Carleton is a very decentralized place. Bringle and Hatcher (2000) described institutionalization of service learning at a university or college as a complex process, involving students, faculty, administration, the academic institution, and the communities. Carleton seems to be about halfway along in this process, with a functioning student volunteer office (under the aegis of the Dean of Students) which promotes service learning along with other volunteer activities. Brown University (Ward, 1999b), Allegheny College (n.d.), and Occidental College (2002a, 2002b), three of the exemplary service-learning programs, all have centers devoted to coordinating community needs with academic projects. Should such a center be established at Carleton, there will be a continuous need to maintain and update data which is not easy with an intermittent set of student projects. Maintaining institutional memory is critical.

I found that as I developed civic engagement projects for many of my classes, my entire pedagogical approach changed. This is probably a subject for another essay, and, in fact, has been previously tackled by Howard (1998), but let me make a few points here.

I had to be willing to accept a loss of control over parts of the learning experience and the specific knowledge the students gain. Not all students come away from a project with the same specific knowledge. But in exchange, the students and I learn things I never imagined.

Some students need more structure than an open-ended civic engagement project may provide. It is always helpful to focus from the beginning of the assignment on the desired end product, such as a report or a map. This is also helpful in giving students the project closure that they need psychologically.

Most students work best in small groups, so often a larger project needs to be broken down into pieces that small groups can undertake. If small groups of students are each doing a project, the variation in the project topics will mean variation in the amount and type of work involved from group to group.

As in any assignment, it is important to take time to ask (and answer) questions like "Why are we doing this?," "What did we figure out?," "What just happened?" With the involvement of people from outside the institution, civic engagement projects add layers of unpredictability that aren't so common in other kinds of assignments (Howard, 1998). It is important to reassure students that it's okay to have a variety of reactions to these new situations.

> I had to be willing to accept a loss of control over parts of the learning experience and the specific knowledge the students gain. Not all students come away from a project with the same specific knowledge. But in exchange, the students and I learn things I never imagined.

I have found it important to recognize that the students in a particular class won't end the project (or the course) in the same place, because they don't all start with equivalent backgrounds and they don't all have the same level of maturity. My hope is that students will learn the skills and acquire the motivation to do similar projects again. There's never enough time for that repetition in a single class, so much of the payoff, for me and the students, comes later in the students' college careers and even after graduation.

Why do I do it? With students, I can be far more effective in the community than I could as a single individual. I simply wouldn't have time on my own to complete the civic engagement projects that I can fold into classes. And the insights students gain, along with the scientific knowledge and the skills, come more easily and more deeply through civic engagement than through practically any other kind of teaching method I might use:

> We project on to Rice County our ideas of nature; it is, in many ways, our training ground. Here we are actively learning to create and apply a land ethic, but we are only beginners. For long-term residents, for people who have lived and died here long before us, Rice County is home. It is not a template for study, but something that they rely upon each and every day and will continue to rely upon the rest of their lives. It is not my place to tell them how to think about Rice County. As much value as I feel in participating in the Northfield Natural Resources Inventory, I won't even be here in three years. Maybe I would like to dictate the future of Rice County based on my own land ethics, but I won't.

> Not that that bothers me. From what I can tell, Rice County will do just fine without me. (Stutz, 2002)

ENDNOTES

[1] Excerpts from student papers are quoted with permission of the authors.

REFERENCES

Allegheny College. (n.d.). *Center for Economic and Environmental Development.* http://ceed.alleg.edu/CEED/CEEDHome.html

Bringle, R. G., & Hatcher, J. A. (2000). Institutionalization of service learning in higher education. *The Journal of Higher Education, 71,* 3, 273-290.

Campbell, D. E. (2000). Social capital and service learning. *PSOnline (American Political Science Association), 33,* 3, 641-645.

Evans, R. (2002, June). Untitled, unpublished paper. Carleton College, Northfield, MN.

Geology Department (Carleton College) (2001). *Review Document.* Northfield, MN: Author.

Geology Department (Carleton College) (2002). *Response to Department Review.* Northfield, MN: Author.

Giles, D. E., Jr., & Eyler, J. (1998). A service learning research agenda for the next five years. In R. A. Rhoads & J. P. F. Howard (Eds.), Academic service learning: A pedagogy of action and reflection (pp. 65-72). *New Directions for Teaching and Learning, 73.*

Howard, J. P. F. (1998). Academic service learning: A counternormative pedagogy. In R. A. Rhoads & J. P. F. Howard (Eds.), Academic service learning: A pedagogy of action and reflection (pp. 21-29). *New Directions for Teaching and Learning, 73.*

Loomis, D. (2002, June). Untitled, unpublished paper. Carleton College, Northfield, MN.

Maley, C. (2002, June). Untitled, unpublished paper. Carleton College, Northfield, MN.

Minnesota Campus Compact (1996). Integrating service with academic study: Keys to success, 3 p.

Moreno, R. (2002, June). Untitled, unpublished paper. Carleton College, Northfield, MN.

Northfield Community Action Center (2002). http://www.northfieldcac.org/food.htm

Occidental College (2002a). *Center for Community Based Learning.* http://departments.oxy.edu/cvcs/

Occidental College (2002b). *Urban and Environmental Policy Institute.* http://departments.oxy.edu/uepi/

Oono, R. (2002, June). Untitled, unpublished paper. Carleton College, Northfield, MN.

Raloff, J. (1998). Democratizing science: Science shops are tackling research for and within communities. *Science News, 154,* 19, 298-302.

Rhoads, R. A., & Howard, J. P. F. (Eds.) (1998). Academic service learning: A pedagogy of action and reflection. *New Directions for Teaching and Learning, 73.*

Schultz, E. (2002, June). Untitled, unpublished paper. Carleton College, Northfield, MN.

Stutz, W. (2002, June). Untitled, unpublished paper. Carleton College, Northfield, MN.

U.S. Department of Agriculture, National Agricultural Statistical Service (NASS). (2002, April). *Track records, United States crop production.* http://www.usda.gov/nass/pubs/trackrec/track02a.htm#principal

U.S. Department of Agriculture (n.d.a), National Agricultural Statistical Service (NASS). *Agricultural statistics data base.* http://www.nass.usda.gov:81/ipedb/

U.S. Department of Agriculture (n.d.b), National Agricultural Statistical Service (NASS). *Summary of 1997 agricultural census.* http://www.nass.usda.gov/census/census97/highlights/usasum/us.txt

Ward, H. (Ed.). (1999). *Acting locally: Concepts and models for service-learning in environmental studies.* Washington, DC: American Association for Higher Education.

Ward, H. (1999a). Why is service-learning so pervasive in environmental studies programs? In Ward, H. (Ed.), *Acting locally: Concepts and models for service-learning in environmental studies* (pp. 1-12). Washington, DC: American Association for Higher Education.

Ward, H. (1999b). Evolving a service-learning curriculum at Brown University, or what we learned from our community partners. In Ward, H. (Ed.), *Acting locally: Concepts and models for service-learning in environmental studies* (pp. 65-75). Washington, DC: American Association for Higher Education.

Weigert, K. M. (1998). Academic service learning: Its meaning and relevance. In Rhoads, R. A. and Howard, J. P. F. (Eds.), Academic service learning: A pedagogy of action and reflection (pp. 3-10-72). *New Directions for Teaching and Learning, 73.*

Untitled. (2002, June). Unpublished paper. Carleton College, Northfield, MN.

Beyond "Pizza with a Prof": The Meat of a Liberal Arts Education

Scott Bierman and Mary Savina

I t is a crisp fall afternoon on a small liberal arts college campus and a junior psychology major is escorting three prospective students, their parents, and younger siblings around the quad. One of the parents asks about the quality of the faculty-student interaction at the school. The junior tour guide's face lights up and she says, "Just last week my seminar class was invited over to my professor's house for pizza. It was really cool. That sort of thing happens all the time here."

While the season, or the tour guide's major, or the menu offered by the faculty member may differ, this is a scene that, based on our personal experiences, is repeated on all tours at all liberal arts colleges (and many other academic institutions). Empirically, it is probably true that a high percentage of faculty at small liberal arts colleges feed a high percentage of their students once or twice a semester. Furthermore, students view this interaction as important. The fact that a faculty member fed a student, not what conversation might have occurred over dinner, is

> [Collaborative faculty-student interaction] ... is personally and intellectually challenging at a fundamental level—which means it is uncomfortable and difficult at times, the very antithesis of a pleasant conversation over dinner.

more, students view this interaction as important. The fact that a faculty member fed a student, not what conversation might have occurred over dinner, is

H. SCOTT BIERMAN, the Ada M. Harrison Distinguished Teaching Professor of the Social Sciences, joined the Carleton faculty in 1982. He earned his B.A. degree at Bates College and his Ph.D. degree at the University of Virginia. MARY SAVINA is the McBride Professor of Geology and Environmental Studies and Humphrey Doermann Professor of Liberal Learning. She earned her B.A. degree at Carleton College, and her M.A. and Ph.D. degrees at the University of California, Berkeley. She joined the Carleton faculty in 1978.

regularly cited as evidence of a teacher's effectiveness in student evaluations of faculty teaching at Carleton.

The prospective students on the tour and their parents have, of course, not received a particularly helpful answer to the question about the quality of the faculty-student interaction at that school. Who in their right mind would pay $30,000 a year to purchase an education based on a few evenings with Dominos and some dinner table banter, even with such luminaries as Carleton faculty? So when does important student-faculty interaction occur? Why is it important? In this essay, we provide our reflections on how two departments that believe that deep collaborative faculty-student interaction is central to their curriculum structure this collaboration so that it cuts to the core of the liberal arts objectives. This process is personally and intellectually challenging at a fundamental level—which means it is uncomfortable and difficult at times, the very antithesis of a pleasant conversation over dinner. Indeed, "dinner with a prof" in these circumstances may be a working meal, a peace offering, or a reminder that we are a community of scholars who can enjoy each other's company even after the intellectual battles. What makes the $30,000 per year of education a good investment comes from student-faculty interaction that may not be understood by a junior or sophomore because they have yet to experience it in its most profound form.

In her recent book *Cultivating Humanity*, Martha Nussbaum argues that at the center of the liberal arts approach to education is Socratic self-examination (Nussbaum, 1997, pp. 15-49),[1] that is, the willingness to subject one's world view to critical inquiry, discarding those pieces that fail to live up to logical and evidence-based scrutiny, and building on those pieces that remain. Education, then, relies on someone playing the role of a Socratic gadfly, to start the self-examination and critical inquiry. As Plato reports, Socrates defends himself in his "Apology" this way:

> And now, Athenians, I am not going to argue for my own sake, as
> you may think, but for yours, that you may not sin against the
> God by condemning me, who am his gift to you. For if you kill me
> you will not easily find a successor to me, who, if I may use such a
> ludicrous figure of speech, am a sort of gadfly, given to the state by
> God; and the state is a great and noble steed who is tardy in his
> motions owing to his very size, and requires to be stirred into life. I

am that gadfly which God has attached to the state, and all day long and in all places am always fastening upon you, arousing and persuading and reproaching you. You will not easily find another like me, and therefore I would advise you to spare me. [2]

The image of a liberal arts college faculty as a swarm of stinging gadflies may not be the best marketing tool, and we rather doubt it will make its appearance on the college tour circuit anytime soon, but it is, however, a very important piece of what takes place at a challenging liberal arts college. And, despite the apparent contradiction, the powerful symbol of breaking bread together provides another metaphor about the importance of an intellectual community in the process of learning.

The multidimensional objectives that liberal arts colleges strive to achieve can be hard to capture. For help we turn to John Sawyer's 1961 inauguration address as president of Williams College.

> The most versatile, the most durable, in an ultimate sense the most practical knowledge and intellectual resources which they [young people] can now be offered are those impractical arts and sciences around which the liberal arts education has long centered: the capacity to see and feel, to grasp, respond and act over a widening arc of experience; the disposition and ability to think, to question, to use knowledge to order an ever-extending range of reality; the elasticity to grow, to perceive more widely and more deeply, and perhaps to create; the understanding to decide where to stand and the will and tenacity to do so; the wit and wisdom, the humanity and the humor to try to see oneself, one's society, and one's world with open eyes, to live a life usefully, to help things in which one believes on their way. This is not the whole of a liberal arts education, but as I understand it, this range of goals is close to its core. [3]

We suspect that President Sawyer's remarks resonate deeply with most professors at liberal arts colleges. Though not as detailed as Sawyer's comments, Carleton's statement of purpose complements them nicely:

> Carleton College strives to provide a liberal education of the highest quality. The goal of such an education is to liberate individuals from

the constraints imposed by ignorance or complacency and prepare them broadly to lead rewarding, creative, and useful lives.[4]

These remarks point to a maturity of thought that liberal arts faculty expect of students by the end of their four years at college. In our opinion, a reasonable measure of the success of a college, or a program within a college, is the degree to which students actually achieve this intellectual growth. Few if any students possess this type of maturity at the time they enter college, so how do they reach it and what is the faculty's role? The sort of student/faculty social banter that takes place over dinner or a cup of coffee at the student union, while undoubtedly important at breaking down barriers, does not ultimately move students towards the quality of thought articulated by President Sawyer. Neither, we hypothesize, does class attendance alone. Instead we present the experiences of two departments with substantially different curricular structures who consciously believe the finest undergraduate education results from high quality faculty-student collaboration.

Since we are writing a drama instead of a mystery, we begin at the end of the story, with the central, culminating experience of each Carleton major, the Senior Integrative Experience. For most students majoring in economics or geology, the Senior Integrative Exercise, or as it is better known on campus, "Comps" (short for Comprehensive Examination, its historical name), culminates a student's intellectual experience in the department. The Carleton Catalog says this much about Comps.

> **Integrative Exercises** vary from department to department. Intended to help students relate the subjects they have studied in their major field, they sometimes take the form of comprehensive examinations covering the fundamentals of the discipline. In other departments, extensive research projects, papers or public lectures are required. A maximum of fifteen academic credits [most courses carry six credits] will be awarded for the integrative exercise.[5]

Carleton requires that every student pass this exercise in order to graduate. The blandness of the descriptive paragraph and the fact that there is no real justification for why it ought to be required belies the fact that most faculty at Carleton see "Comps" as importantly formative in the education of their students. The Geology and Economics Departments are two departments where Comps encompasses the most energetic and intellectually mature dialogue among students and faculty. Both departments expect students to engage in significant projects which, at their conclusion, add to the world's knowledge about their area of study (or interpret that knowledge for others) and are of near professional quality. Graduates of both departments go on to earn Ph.Ds. in large numbers

> Since we are writing a drama instead of a mystery, we begin at the end of the story, with the central, culminating experience of each Carleton major, the Senior Integrative Experience.

relative to virtually any comparison group (Carleton only grants B.A. degrees). Although neither department would argue that the goal of the Comps research project is the production of future professional researchers or faculty clones, these statistics are one piece of evidence of the character of the education provided by the two departments.[6]

To be specific, completing a Comps project in economics or geology at Carleton starts by requiring the ability to identify and articulate a problem, issue, or question that needs addressing and can be addressed. It requires the skills to understand and synthesize a complex and professional literature. It requires a plan to address theoretical and empirical issues that bear on the topic. It requires the creativity to see a way of addressing the question from a new and fruitful angle. It requires the communication skills to explain to an audience what place this research has in the professional literature, why it is important, what you are doing, and what you have learned. In fields such as economics and geology, it requires strong enough computer skills to analyze data moderately efficiently. It requires the willingness to take advantage of the community of scholars working in the area. Finally, it requires the stamina and tenacity to see the way to a completed project. These skills are, in our opinion, those that President Sawyer calls "most practical" when seen in the context of an ever-changing world in which graduates from institutions such as Carleton, Williams, and other liberal arts colleges are expected to be leaders. It is of course, fundamentally liberating to have in a graduate's hands hard evidence of her ability to be a full participant in the debate on which her research topic was based.

To reach this level of intellectual maturity in four short years requires substantial faculty-student collaboration. It is absolutely incorrect to imagine that Comps exercises in economics and geology are done independently. While these two departments employ different methods to help move students through the research process, a hallmark of both departments is the degree to which these collaborations are inseparable from faculty members' professional development. Indeed, in many cases, these collaborations *are* the primary part of faculty professional life. This is explicitly recognized by faculty in both departments.

COMPS IN GEOLOGY AND ECONOMICS

Carleton's geology curriculum is almost completely non-hierarchical; courses for the major may be taken in any sequence and only an introductory geology course is a required prerequisite for other courses. The open curriculum means that classes (with enrollments of 10 to 40) have a mix of students—sophomores, juniors, and seniors; majors and non-majors—with different levels of experience in geology and different levels of intellectual maturity. Most labs and many projects and papers are done in small groups with the groups intentionally designed to mix ages and experience levels. Thus, there is a lot of peer teaching. Faculty have identified the main skills needed for the Comps project (posing a reasonable question, designing a proposal, executing a project, and reporting the project), so that these skills are incorporated into most geology courses. The entire department puts high value on the kind of student learning associated with posing and researching real questions. Students complete "mini-research" projects in many courses, sometimes even in introductory geology. These differ from Comps in several ways: a) in many cases, the questions are posed by the faculty; b) in most cases, students use a combination of one field technique and one lab or computational technique, not many; and c) the aim is for a "first cut," not a definitive answer to a large question. (This is important and hard to articulate; faculty have to work hard to keep the class projects small—most questions could be expanded into graduate-level research projects.)

The small, tightly controlled research experiences that students encounter in many geology classes are really student/faculty research collaborations in geology. The faculty member ensures that these projects are "do-able" in the course of the final two weeks or so of the term, chooses questions that will allow students to use the skills they've learned earlier in the course, perhaps stretching them a bit into new techniques, and works closely with each student or small group of students as the research and reporting proceed. Results of these projects are typically reported as oral presentations and posters or papers—the same reporting mechanisms that will be used for Comps. At the same time, the students value the experiences highly: They have an opportunity to pick topics that interest them, they have partners, there is a sense of discovery because these are real questions and even the faculty member does not know what the research results will be, and they are part of an even larger group (the class) engaged in more-or-less the same enterprise simultaneously. The student questions at the presentations also show the value of the research process. Students will ask of each other, "But did you look at Factor X? Doesn't it affect your outcome?" and other thoughtful questions that demonstrate the positive effects of the research process.

In contrast to geology, the hierarchical structure of the economics major is worth noting.[7] A typical economics major at Carleton will have taken Principles of Macroeconomics and Principles of Microeconomics and one or two topic-oriented classes such as Labor Economics, European Economic History, or International Trade by the end of her sophomore year. In their junior year, while taking additional topic-oriented classes, students commonly take the required theory sequence of Intermediate Price Theory (called Intermediate Microeconomics at most schools), Intermediate Macro Theory, and Econometrics. A term of calculus is required for all the theory classes, and a course in statistics (taught by the Math Department) is also required for Econometrics. You should think of Econometrics as a kind of introduction to research methods in economics. The last big hurdle is Comps. Because students know almost nothing about research methods in economics until very late in their junior year, a true research project—even a highly directed one such as the Geology Department describes for its mid-level courses—cannot be undertaken before their senior year. Prior to that, students are getting a solid theoretic base and learning the hard task of thinking like an economist. While the department is trying to introduce assignments in earlier classes that hone some of the skills associated with developing a research project, the actual act of data-driven research is limited to Comps.

Important opportunities for student/faculty collaboration in geology come on the department field trips, where a group of 20-35 students and three to five faculty members travel to a region of great geologic interest for several days and tackle a series of mini-problems at roadcuts and other exposures. While some schools visit as many locations as possible each day with a tight itinerary, we spend more time at

> Listening to different [geology] faculty argue their case helps students learn to frame problems and construct protocols to answer them.

each of far fewer stops. When we arrive at an outcrop, students divide into small groups, the faculty sets a problem (e.g., "What's the relationship between the three kinds of rocks exposed here?") and suggests a strategy ("You might want to map them and carefully look at the contacts") before turning the groups loose. In an hour or so, we reconvene for a group discussion, often featuring the alternative hypotheses arrived at by different groups. Discussions are participatory, with contributions added from many faculty and students. Typically, once students present their observations and a range of interpretations, discussions conclude with an attempt to design a series of field and lab tests for the various interpretations that we would undertake with more time and some money. Throughout, the faculty are consultants to the student groups, asking questions, prodding for observations, acting like Socrates' gadflies.

Field trips are important for two other reasons. First, to solve a field problem in geology, one invariably needs information and skills from several sub-disciplines. This breaks down the artificial boxes that divide the curriculum in pieces. Second, faculty members, working together, model the investigative process for students. Few regular classes are team-taught, so students rarely have a chance to hear faculty discuss and debate geologic topics together. One faculty member may think the small box fold is an expression of the regional tectonic stress that uplifted the Black Hills. Another may interpret the same fold as something that occurred while the shale in it was being deposited, long before any mountain-building. Listening to different faculty argue their case helps students learn to frame problems and construct protocols to answer them.

The Economics Department also takes advantage of field trips, although in a very different way. Every year for the last 20 years, a Carleton faculty member has directed a group of Carleton students on a summer seminar in

Cambridge, England.[8] About two-thirds of the economics majors participate in this program during the summer following their sophomore or junior years. At its academic center is a course on the Industrial Revolution in Britain. The seminar accomplishes three important things. First, the students read a contentious literature where nearly every explanation of what *The Economist* magazine cited as "the story of the millennium" is an academic war zone. Economics, as a paradigm, becomes a working dialogue rather than truth handed down from someone with the keys to the kingdom. Second, the students engage a faculty member in a very different way—far more personally and far more collaboratively—than they would during a typical Carleton term. And, third, students become full-fledged members of a well-connected group of economics majors who have come to depend on each other.

Prior to their senior year, students majoring in economics must choose whether to write a research paper or take a series of exams to fulfill their Comps requirement. Those choosing the research paper must successfully complete a "senior" seminar and have a formal research prospectus approved before being allowed to proceed with their research. With only rare exceptions, the faculty who direct a senior seminar (sometimes the seminars are team-taught) will shepherd the student projects derived from that seminar.

It is worth emphasizing that students in economics self-select either the research paper or the exam. The research paper option is *not* designed only for honors students nor do students see it that way. In fact, the economics faculty is frequently pleasantly surprised by the fact that B students regularly turn in research papers that are among the very best. There would be little argument among the economics faculty that, all else equal, the research paper option is a far superior educational device than the exam. The reason for allowing students a choice is so faculty time can be allocated to those students who are more motivated to do the hard work necessary to complete a substantial research project. Since the department averages about 33 economics majors per year and we usually offer three seminars and about two-thirds of the majors choose the research paper option, a faculty member directing a senior seminar can expect to be working closely

> **Students majoring in economics must choose whether to write a research paper or take a series of exams to fulfill their Comps requirement.**

with five to ten students in the term subsequent to the seminar. This is in about as many directions as anyone can reasonably be expected to be pulled.

With this in mind, what does the Economics Department hope to accomplish by requiring that students complete a senior seminar prior to being allowed to continue with their research? While the seminars have an organizing topical theme, their primary focus is to move the students as rapidly as possible towards establishing an interesting, doable, original research agenda. But, remember that students have had no firsthand experience with economic research. This is an extremely scary and uncomfortable position for them. To get these students to a point where they can articulate a research question that is doable in the allotted time and for which there is a body of literature to draw on and some data that might be accessible requires a great deal of face-to-face time. The type of conversation that goes on in these seminar and individual meetings is foreign to undergraduates. They are used to asking faculty how to answer a problem set question, but they are not used to the sloppy give-and-take that developing a research question entails. A student typically imagines the creation of a research agenda is a linear process; the reality, of course, is markedly different and the tension between the two is palpable in these meetings. If the student also imagines there will be clarity each time she leaves the faculty member's office, the lack of that is profoundly unsettling. The culmination of these meetings is a research prospectus that the student submits to the department for approval.

The economics major taking a senior seminar is required to present to the rest of the seminar participants the seminal articles in the area the student is proposing to work on along with the student's prospectus. These presentations can easily consume 50% of the seminar's class time. The experience in the department is that student interaction in these sessions provides huge benefits. Some of these arise directly from pointed questions that are asked and helpful suggestions that are provided. But it is also very important that students get an appreciation for the existence of a research community where they can go for assistance (apart from the faculty). The fact that all the students are working in the same general area provides a degree of expertise that matters. At the end of the seminar students submit an extensive review of the literature on their topic area(s). Once editorial revisions have been made, these papers will stand as an important piece of their final Comps.

In geology, all students complete independent projects for Comps; there is no exam option. However, not all Comps projects are research projects. One major grouping of non-research projects can be thought of as "education and outreach," including high school textbook design, lesson plans, design of interpretive signs for parks, designs of displays, etc. While these projects aren't adding to the knowledge base of the field, they are important ways of linking scientific research with community needs.

When geology majors begin the Comps process as third-term juniors or first-term seniors, they identify a faculty member as advisor and write a proposal that is reviewed by the entire department faculty. Students work closely with their Comps advisors during the entire process, which stretches over most of the senior year from a proposal deadline early in the fall term to a due date for the paper in mid-March and oral and poster presentations in April and May. (Some students begin their projects earlier, with field work in the summer). The nature of the student-faculty interaction is largely left up to the student to design; it may include weekly or bi-weekly meetings, informal consultations, reading of sections of the paper or partial drafts, and, what students and faculty probably enjoy the most, discussions of the science behind the project, including the data interpretation.

Students also have other sources of advice for their project. The department faculty conducts three evening sessions during the first part of the winter term that are required of all seniors; at the first of these sessions each student describes his or her project. The result is that the members of the entire senior class essentially become collaborators in each other's projects. They can pass along information about resources and techniques to each other as they encounter them. With the strong emphasis on community within the department, which is established beginning in introductory geology, it is also common to see students reading each other's drafts, commenting on figures and graphs, etc. There is no sense of competition.

Because there is no restriction on subject for the Comps, students commonly undertake projects way outside the expertise of anyone on the geology faculty. Moreover, because the department graduates an average of 22 majors per year, individual faculty will have several Comps advisees each year (about the same range as economics faculty). Fortunately, students also have additional sources of support outside the Geology Department. Many students' Comps projects emerge from summer work done with Carleton geology alumni or in student/faculty research teams with faculty from other institutions. These alums and other faculty continue to act as mentors as the projects develop.

In both the Economics and Geology Departments the exciting stuff begins when the prospecti and proposals have been approved. The theory will usually need to be tightened, relevant variables identified, and testable hypotheses clarified. Data will need to be found and cleaned up. At each step the student will see the research project expand, contract, and generally morph into shapes unimaginable even a week earlier. Nearly daily the student will need advice and support. Nearly daily, the faculty member will need to try to figure out how to provide advice and support. Students will be experiencing frustrations they have never known (and faculty know only too well).

Once the empirical work starts, the level of activity triples. The student will find that early statistical or lab results are at odds with any reasonable theory. The faculty and student will look back to the theory to try to uncover hidden assumptions or back to the data to see what variables might be misspecified. Late evenings and weekend mornings will be spent with other seniors in the computer lab collectively struggling with each other's difficulties. More morphing, more frustration. With every iteration the project becomes more and more an original piece of work by the student. Ownership grows and grows. Maturity grows and grows. Toward the end of the project, the student has become the teacher and the faculty member just sits back and listens as the student presents the most recent set of results which by all accounts look surprisingly good. "Write it up."

CONCLUSION

The Geology Department has a long, rich track record of significant student-faculty research. This has allowed the curriculum to evolve into one where a culture of collaboration is built into the major very early and is imbedded deeply. Faculty in the department are aware that the significant time associated with these collaborations are appreciated by their colleagues and students (and, with any luck, by the president and dean). All this takes place within a curriculum that is proudly unhierarchical and where students are given great latitude in their senior year. The department sees it as a strength that it reaches out to the professional geological research community to help with the direction of senior projects.

The Economics Department has only fairly recently moved in the direction of serious student-faculty research collaboration. The department was reluctant to spend great effort on having a student do a senior thesis unless the student was highly motivated and there was a reasonable chance the student could do "real economics." Borrowing shamelessly from the sciences, the department has introduced a high cost/high reward model of faculty-student collaboration during the students' senior year. This model would be untenable if the faculty were not willing to modify research agendas so that they are more often accessible to students and if the faculty in the department were not explicit that their collaboration with students constitutes a significant piece of the faculty member's professional development.

Deans and presidents at liberal arts colleges, which are primarily teaching institutions, regularly employ the metaphor of faculty research as an investment generating benefits to future students. But they rarely take the metaphor much further. We agree with the spirit of this claim, but it is important to remember that not all investments yield the same returns. (Just ask people whose retirement plans were tied to the fortunes of Enron.) The geology and economics faculty have come to the belief that in their disciplines important research can be carried out

> Deans and presidents at liberal arts colleges ... regularly employ the metaphor of faculty research as an investment generating benefits to future students.... It is important to remember that not all investments yield the same returns.

collaboratively with current students and that this collaboration provides large benefits for future students while being professionally rewarding for faculty. It is not their only professional engagement, but it constitutes an important component, whether or not it results in peer-reviewed publications. Consciously pursuing research agendas that are accessible by future undergraduates and those in which undergraduates can participate generate, in our opinion, substantially higher future returns than other agendas. They should be sought out where possible and institutionally encouraged.

At the end of the day, how does the education a geology major or an economics major receives relate to the goals identified at the start of this essay by President Sawyer or Carleton College?

Recall that Sawyer argued that, among other things, "the disposition and ability to think, to question, to use knowledge to order an ever-extending range of reality; the elasticity to grow, to perceive more widely and more deeply, and perhaps to create; the understanding to decide where to stand and the will and tenacity to do so" was at the heart of the practical side of a liberal arts education. Comps in both our departments could not be completed at the level they are without these skills. Employers (here, we are not talking about graduate schools) return to our departments for new hires year after year because these practical skills produce practical benefits for their firms or agencies.

But Sawyer also talks about "the wit and wisdom, the humanity and the humor to try to see oneself, one's society, and one's world with open eyes, to live a life usefully, to help things in which one believes on their way." It is a little hard to see how both the Geology and Economics Departments achieve these objectives without going into a bit more detail about the motivation students bring to their Comps projects.

In geology, science is understood as a human enterprise, with close connections between many earth science problems and humanity, but in all cases pursued by humans. The Geology Department values—responsibility and sharing of knowledge, cooperation and fostering a community of personal and intellectual respect, open-mindedness and humility, the joy of learning and discovery and the value of a scientific mode of inquiry—permeate the curriculum, at least we hope and strive for that. Students emerge through the geology Comps process with a concrete product that represents their individual ideas and efforts and the values of the departmental community.

In economics, nearly all Comps research projects are motivated by a policy question and policy questions are motivated by a compassion for the human condition. Social science is, at its core, about understanding human behavior and how human institutions affect that behavior. Economics is a powerful collection of paradigms and tools that help to shed light on some of these interactions. The economics curriculum, particularly when it culminates in a Comps research paper, provides students with potent evidence that they have the tools to participate in a fundamentally useful life.

This is, we argue, radically liberating. It also is worth a celebratory dinner with the prof once Comps is all done.[9] ∎

ENDNOTES

[1] Martha Nussbaum, Cultivating Humanity (1997, Harvard University Press), pp. 15-49.

[2] http://www.pagebypagebooks.com/Plato/Apology/APOLOGY_p10.html

[3] http://www.williams.edu/admin-depts/registrar/geninfo/mission.html

[4] http://www.carleton.edu/campus/registrar/catalog/HistoricallySpeaking.html

[5] http://www.carleton.edu/campus/registrar/catalog/AcademicPrograms.html. Fifteen academic credits corresponds to a total of 2.5 normal trimester courses.

[6] Between 1996 and 2000, there were 30 Carleton graduates who earned Ph.Ds. in geology. Among liberal arts colleges the next highest was Oberlin with 18. Among all private colleges only Harvard, with 31 baccalaureate recipients going on to earn Ph.Ds. in geology, produced more. Over that same time period, 22 Carleton graduates earned Ph.Ds. in economics. Swarthmore was the only liberal arts college to produce more, with 29. Among all private colleges, in absolute numbers Carleton was the 13th largest producer of Ph.Ds. in economics and only behind Swarthmore in the percentage of graduates that go on to earn a Ph.D. in economics.

[7] Carleton offers no business major.

[8] For a more detailed perspective on this program, see the essay in this volume by Professor Martha Paas on Experiential Learning.

[9] Information in this essay is informed by frequent discussions of the major and pedagogy among the Geology Department faculty and students. Several publications and talks have emerged from these conversations, including:

Boardman, S. J., & Berglund, C. (2000). Undergraduate learning through investigation and research: The geology program at Carleton College. *Proceedings of the Annual Meeting, Sigma Xi, The Scientific Research Society*, 73-79.

Buchwald, C. E. (1997). Undergraduate geology education: The Carleton College experience. *Journal of College Science Teaching, 26*, 5, 325-328.

Buchwald, C. E., Bice, D. M., Savina, M. E., Boardman, S. J., Haileab, B., Cowan, C. A., & Vick, T. D. (2001). Values statement and "robustly useful ideas" as geology department planning tools. *Geological Society of America, Abstracts with Program, 33*, 191.

Savina, M. E., Buchwald, C. E., Bice, D. M, & Boardman, S. J. (2001). A skills matrix as a geology department curriculum planning tool. *Geological Society of America, Abstracts with Program, 33*, 191.

Williams, J. M. (1994). *The Carleton College Geology Department: A successful builder of women scientists?* Unpublished report.

On Being "Rigorous"

Kathleen M. Galotti

Since my high school graduation, I have studied and worked in "elite" institutions. I attended college at a top-10 rated liberal arts college and teach now at a competitor school; the years in between were spent in graduate study at an Ivy League university. Throughout these years, one administrator after another has spoken about the general level of talent surrounding us. We were (in my student days) frequently reminded that we were "the cream of the crop," the next generation of the world's leaders, the finest minds being trained for tomorrow. That fact obliged us to exert ourselves in mastering the knowledge and skills we'd need in the future.

Today, at the job I love very much, I often remind myself how privileged I am to be able to teach and guide tomorrow's future movers and shakers. I also am reminded frequently by administrators here of my enormous obligations to my students. In this essay, I want to explore the responsibilities I think I have as a teacher of such talented students and how those responsibilities need to be and should be balanced against a respect for and welcoming of student diversity. In particular, I want to explore what it means to be rigorous and to have high standards, how grading practices relate to these qualities, and whether broadening teaching practices to honor students with different cognitive or learning styles will necessarily un-

> **What does it mean to have high standards? Does broadening teaching practices to honor students with different learning styles necessarily undermine a commitment to rigor?**

KATHLEEN M. GALOTTI, professor of psychology and cognitive studies, joined the Carleton faculty in 1983. She earned her B.A. degree at Wellesley College and her M.A., M.S.E., and Ph.D. degrees at the University of Pennsylvania.

dermine a commitment to rigor. I should say at the outset that I don't think the points I make below apply only to elite places—any institution of higher education has its share of bright and motivated students, and faculty everywhere have (or should have) the desire and obligation to serve them. In fact, I believe my arguments apply, *mutatis mutandis*, to any teacher of any student.

RIGOR AND HIGH STANDARDS

One of the biggest responsibilities I think any teacher has is to set clear and high standards for her students, then to develop curriculum, assignments, and experiences that allow a student to meet those standards. Often, "good teaching" is associated only with the curriculum development aspect of pedagogy. In my view, this misses the mark.

Students, like other people, work for incentives. Rational students prioritize their time and energy in accordance with payoffs. When they are in a fairly non-demanding situation, where mediocre or "okay" work is acceptable, they will eventually find themselves meeting that standard. If they are bright, that standard will be all too easy to meet and little intellectual "stretching" or development will take place. Conversely, if only their best efforts are enough, students will find themselves developing new skills, new abilities, new ways of knowing and thinking. Of course, the level of rigor has to be calibrated to the general ability of the relevant student body: Asking people to do more than they are capable of leads inevitably to a great deal of frustration. The trick, the art of teaching, is to learn how to achieve this calibration and how to individualize it for different students.

Now, students don't always immediately appreciate being pushed. And, as I remember all my experiences with learning, it isn't necessarily "fun" in the middle of the process, especially when facing a new and daunting challenge. It's hard, it's scary, it's tempting to give up, it's frustrating more often than it is exhilarating and invigorating. The "fun" part comes after the challenge has been mastered—it's often a retrospective sort of thing.

Students at Carleton complain a lot about the stress of classes and assignments and how much is expected of them. Until, that is, someone makes a real move to reduce that stress. Then, students resist more than any other constituency (faculty, staff, administrators) stress-reduction initiatives such as reducing the number of courses required for graduation, dropping the idea of academic distinction in the major, instituting a "common time" during which no classes are scheduled each week. The stresses they face are seen as defining characteristics of their experience, ones worn proudly as badges of achievement. Whether this reaction is one common to most college students or not is hard to say, but I sometimes worry that we (faculty, administrators, parents) implicitly push the "you are top-notch and therefore able to carry superhuman workloads" message far too often at Carleton.

GRADING AND ASSESSMENT

One major mechanism for both enforcing rigor and high standards is, of course, the practice of grading. Not surprisingly, one general source of stress for many students is grades. Concern over the assessment of one's performance, and one's relative standing, are as common today as ever. Most of our students are used to being in the top percentiles of students (e.g., in their high school class), and it comes as a great shock to many that half will be "below average" in this new environment.

Perhaps in response to signs of student stress, there has been an issue of grade inflation throughout most institutions of higher education, Carleton included. When top-rated universities are graduating over half their students with Latin honors, it is a natural worry that the "honor" starts to lose meaning. And if every student who puts forth minimal effort can come to count on receiving at least a "B" (as is the case in many classes that I've taken or heard about), the very notion of grades as indicators of achievement or mastery becomes hollow (Rosovsky and Hartley, 2002, explore the problem and consequences of grade inflation in a thought-provoking essay).

If grades cause stress, or else give rise to inflation that undermines meaning, maybe it is time to question why we give grades at all. The standard answer offers two reasons: 1) incentive to meet standards, and 2) information about how well standards are being met.

As a teacher, I've found that grading work typically elicits better performance from students than not grading it. Papers students know will be graded typically are better written and organized; likewise with oral presentations, quizzes, etc. This phenomenon is understandable, and goes back to the idea that a rational student will align his behavior with the payoffs for that behavior—nongraded work has only the payoff of personal satisfaction, while graded work offers, in addition, more visible and perhaps public affirmation of a job well done. Grades seem to lend more importance to assignments.

Some colleagues make additional arguments that grades provide crucial information to students, allowing them to more accurately diagnose their strengths and weaknesses. A professor who gives out "charity" Bs, then, is seen in this view as doing a grave disservice to her students. By not accurately assessing their work, she gives false encouragement and information to them.

Of course, there are counterarguments to the utility of grades. One is that providing external incentives, even symbolic ones, can undermine an activity's inherent appeal. Psychologists Lepper and Greene showed this result in a study of preschool children who liked to draw and spent a lot of their free time doing so. When the investigators started giving "good player awards" for drawing, the activity suddenly became less fun for the children. By analogy, it can be argued that providing grades as an incentive for academic work makes that work inherently less fun.

A second argument has to do with the meaningfulness of the discriminations made by grades. This argument goes as follows: Separating the A students from the B, C, D and F students may make sense when you are dealing with a large and diverse population. However, imagine taking all the A and B students only, enrolling them in a program, and again trying to sort them into five groups: the As, Bs, Cs, Ds and Fs. Now cull, and sort again. At some point, the distinctions start to lose their meaning.

> A professor who gives out "charity" Bs, then, is ... doing a grave disservice to her students. By not accurately assessing their work, she gives false encouragement and information ...

The difference between an A and a B (or an A- and a B+) start to become miniscule and unreliable—the evaluator needs to start finding fairly small nuances to accomplish the sort. It has been argued that, at the "elite" schools where I've been, we are in this situation and the differences between students receiving different grades are negligible.

"Grade eggs, not people!" was a banner cry I remember from my own college days in the 1970s. The protest was against providing any kind of labels to people at all, against reifying a number (such as a grade point average, an SAT score, an IQ) and imbuing it with importance. Grades in high school were seen (cynically) as providing validation for entry into college, grades in college as validation for entry into graduate, law, business, or medical school. The sense was that all these institutions of higher learning ought to find a better, fairer way to select their applicants than by making feeder institutions use grades to sort.

MULTIPLE INTELLIGENCES AND LEARNING STYLES

Another argument against grades can be derived from the arguments advanced against the use of IQ scores—that they reduce performance unreasonably to a single number. This means that important aspects of performance are ignored or given short shrift.

Psychologist Howard Gardner broadened the concept of "intelligence" a few decades ago when he introduced the concept of multiple intelligences—noting that there are very distinct realms of achievement in which people can and do excel. For example, in addition to the traditionally prized academic intelligences (linguistic and logical-mathematical), there are the following: musical intelligence, bodily-kinesthetic intelligence, spatial intelligence, interpersonal intelligence, intrapersonal intelligence, as well as the recently added naturalist intelligence. Gardner's recent book (1999) presents detailed descriptions of each of these and makes the arguments for their existence.

Though certainly not without controversy, Gardner's claims have a lot of intuitive appeal. Who hasn't encountered the student who excels in one domain (say, using computers or statistical analysis) but struggles mightily with another (say, writing papers or delivering oral presentations)? Or the student with mediocre performance on tests and papers, who gives a brilliant piano recital or delivers a stellar athletic achievement?

Related claims about the existence of important individual differences come from researchers studying learning styles (see Sternberg, 1997; Rayner, & Riding, 1997 for overviews). The idea here is that, in addition to differing in terms of physical characteristics (e.g., hair, eye, or skin color, height, weight) and in terms of intellectual ability (e.g., intelligence or intelligences), people also differ in reliable and predictable ways in how they use their intellectual abilities, the way they approach situations or problems. These approaches may relate more to personality differences than to ability differences and have come to be called cognitive, thinking, or learning *styles*.

For example, we have heard proposals about visual versus verbal learners, the idea being that different learners find different approaches to acquiring information—either through viewing spatial depictions versus hearing linguistic explanations—more comfortable, intuitive, or natural (e.g., Edwards & Wilkins, 1981). There are proposals for whether people are extraverted or introverted, approach information judgmentally or not, in some of the work on the Myers Briggs Type indicator (Myers & McCauley, 1985). Other investigators adopt the concept of "need for cognition" to discuss individual differences in motivation to engage in cognitive tasks such as problem solving (Klaczynski & Fauth, 1996; Stanovitch & West, 1998, 2000).

The point here is that there exists documented evidence of apparently stable, personality-related traits, that seem to impact the way people learn, acquire or interpret information, make decisions, and perform other higher-order cognitive tasks. Although the evidence is not without its critics, once again there is some good reason to believe that people approach learning differently and in ways having to do with qualities other than their intellectual ability. Indeed, it's not a far-fetched idea to believe that some learning styles may be gender or perhaps socioeconomically or ethnically related (e.g., Belenky, Clinchy, Goldberger & Tarule, (1986/1997); Galotti, Clinchy, Ainsworth, Lavin, & Mansfield, 1999).

So the dilemma I see boils down to this: On the one hand, we want to adopt and maintain high expectations and high standards. We want to insist that our talented students "stretch" themselves intellectually. To do less is a disservice to any student, but perhaps particularly to the "elite" students who choose institutions such as ours *because* of the intellectual challenges we purport to offer. On the other hand, many recent and credible proposals suggest that a "one-standard-evaluates-all" model of assessment will not equally benefit (or honor) students with different styles. At the limit, forcing everyone to one standard may be unfair and discriminatory.

What to do? Do we hold fast to traditional standards of rigor, insisting that if the students are bright and motivated enough, they'll be able to adapt (and will, in the long run, benefit from developing the traditionally prized and assessed abilities and skills)? Do we abandon the traditional standards, accepting the argument that they unfairly privilege some cognitive or learning styles over others? If so, are we willing to risk abandoning the intellectual challenge to stretch?

Is there a way to customize our standards for every student, trying to match our expectations with his or her work? Thus, could we ask a "high verbal" student to continue to produce the traditional term papers and oral reports, but maybe develop new assignments and assessments for students who have other gifts? Of course, then the issue of comparability of standards arises—how

> Rigor *is* very important to me as a teacher; but I'm becoming more convinced that good teaching *also* requires sensitivity to diversity of various sorts.

would we know if the alternative assignments were as demanding, as comprehensive, and as well assessed as the originals?

Perhaps we should ask all students to assemble a portfolio of work—showing their performance across different types of tasks (making sure that the portfolio contains a product relevant to each major type of learning we hope to see). But again, how are rigorous standards to be applied to the assessment of the portfolio? Is customization, at the limit, equivalent to an abandonment of standards? If the "assessment" of the portfolios becomes so individualized, at the limit, then no comparisons can be made between one portfolio and another. This process would lead to a situation where every student is deemed to be "special" in "his or her own way"—in other words, the Barney (the dinosaur) view of assessment, where nothing is better or worse.

PERRY'S EPISTEMOLOGICAL MODEL AS A METAPHOR

I don't, unfortunately, have definitive answers to any of the above questions. I have mainly an uncomfortable feeling that some middle ground needs to be found. Rigor *is* very important to me as a teacher; but I'm becoming more convinced that good teaching *also* requires sensitivity to diversity of various sorts. Yet the "we need to find a middle ground" answer seems dangerously empty and hackneyed—I feel, as my students say, like a "wuss" simply to end with that idea.

So here's an analogy I want to present, one that I think is meaty and non-wussy. It comes from the work of William Perry, a researcher who ran the Harvard University Bureau of Study Counsel for several years in the 1940s and

1950s. Perry worked with undergraduates (most of them male) at Harvard, and published a report of the qualitatively differing patterns of thought he noticed in them as they proceeded through their undergraduate years (Perry, 1970, 1981). Only a brief summary of the results is possible here.

Perry identified three major structures of thought, which seemed to form a developmental progression. Younger college students were often found to make meaning of the world from a dualistic orientation, dividing the world into dichotomies: right vs. wrong, true vs. false, good vs. bad, we vs. others, what They (teachers) want vs. what They don't want. Students at this level attempt to place newly learned theories into these categories and to "learn" through simple "obedience" and adherence to instructor assignments.

The second major structure Perry called "multiplism." It involves a "live-and-let-live" orientation to new or foreign ideas: Anyone has a right to any opinion, and no one else is really in any position to judge or evaluate the validity of those opinions because they haven't had the same life experiences as the person holding a different opinion. Perry notes the liberating feeling this structure provides to many students: No professor or teacher can really comment, fairly, on a student's view of a piece of literature or an experiment—for the student's sincere opinion is just as valid as the professor's.

In the optimal case, students eventually construct a third, more synthetic structure, one that Perry called "relativism." In this structure students remain convinced that very few absolute answers exist. Nonetheless, they come to appreciate that not all answers have equal status, but vary along different dimensions: e.g., internal coherence, explanatory power, plausibility. Thus, standards can be discovered or constructed that allow one to make distinctions among better or worse answers. So, although there is no "right" theory of (say) child development, no "right" interpretation of *Hamlet*, existing theories can be assessed along different dimensions, and overall goodness can be assessed (at least with respect to certain assumptions). I should note that some of Perry's work was later challenged by feminist psychologists who discovered some differences in developmental progression when they studied female undergraduates (Belenky et al., 1986/1997). Nevertheless, for our purposes, the general Perry scheme seems to me to have sufficient generality as a model.

Let me now try to connect Perry's proposal with the idea of what it might mean to be rigorous. An analogy can be made, I think, between Perry's dualism and a rigid adherence to only traditional methods of assessment. Clinging to *only* one method of assessment, and including *only* traditional topics and assignments in a course because they are the "right" ones, is quite analogous to the first-year student who seeks to sort theories and ideas into only two categories, "right" and "wrong."

Similarly, I am struck by the similarities between Perry's description of the outlook of a multiplistic student ("one opinion is as good as any other") and the notion that all methods of assessment are as good as any other or that no assessment is necessary or possible. Because there is no one true, "right" way to assess student work does not necessarily imply that all methods of assessment are equally good, or equally flawed. Nor does it mean that radical customization (everyone just assemble whatever work is representative of your learning into a portfolio, and we'll all appreciate it) is the only possible response.

Just as good teachers push, nudge, or cajole their students toward Perry's relativism—a position where certain standards are constructed or adopted to assess ideas—so to do we as teachers need to grapple with a never-ending quest to find ways of constructing good assignments *and* good assessments. Certain ones *are* better than others, and we need to be prepared to develop and debate standards to be used to determine the relative worth. This will likely require that our assessments themselves be subject to periodic and rigorous assessment and revision.

> Because there is no one true, "right" way to assess student work does not necessarily imply that all methods of assessment are equally good, or equally flawed. Nor does it mean that radical customization (everyone just assemble whatever work is representative of your learning into a portfolio, and we'll all appreciate it) is the only possible response.

Recognizing that there are many paths to a goal is one way of honoring diversity. For example, we want fluent, articulate writers at the end of college. But many different approaches to developing writing skills exist. Having students jointly author (and edit) papers is one way of honoring students with a more extraverted learning style—just as having students independently author a paper honors a more introverted approach. Where appropriate, faculty could assign more hands-on assignments—being part of a theater production, for example (see Weiner and Hardy, this volume), or creating a piece of furniture (see Clark, this volume). The general point is to make sure that a course's assessments don't draw disproportionately on just one skill, ability, or intelligence. Figuring out the right mix of assignments, and the right mix of assessments, is the key.

So, can or should we be rigorous, especially if we are in elite places? I believe that we must. If we don't adopt and commit to high standards, few of our students will achieve as much as they are capable of. But being rigorous does not mean rigidly clinging to a single way of teaching or assessing. Indeed, the best teachers I know are quite flexible in their work, trying always to diagnose each student's current level of understanding and skill and tailoring a series of assignments and experiences to bring this level up a notch. Our challenge now is to extend that commitment to rigor to the development, design, and assessment of those assignments and experiences. ▪

REFERENCES

Belenky, M. F., Clinchy, B. M., Goldberger, N. R., & Tarule, J. M. (1986/1997). *Women's ways of knowing: The development of self, voice, and mind.* New York: Basic Books, Inc.

Edwards, J., & Wilkins, W. (1981). Verbalizer-visualizer questionnaire: Relationship with imagery and verbal-visual ability. *Journal of Mental Imagery, 5,* 137-142.

Galotti, K. M., Clinchy, B. M., Ainsworth, K. H., Lavin, B., & Mansfield, A. F. (1999). A new way of assessing ways of knowing: The Attitudes Toward Thinking and Learning Survey (ATTLS). *Sex Roles, 40,* 745-766.

Gardner, H. (1999). *Intelligence reframed: Multiple intelligences for the 21st century.* New York: Basic Books.

Klaczynski, P. A., & Fauth, J. M. (1996). Intellectual ability, rationality, and intuitiveness as predictors of warranted and unwarranted optimism for future life events. *Journal of Youth and Adolescence, 25,* 755-773.

Lepper, M. R., & Greene, D. (1975).Turning play into work: Effects of adult surveillance and extrinsic rewards on children's intrinsic motivation. *Journal of Personality and Social Psychology, 31,* 479-486.

Myers, I. B., & McCaulley, M. H. (1985). *Manual: A guide to the development and use of the Myers-Briggs Type Indicator.* Palo Alto, CA: Consulting Psychologists Press.

Perry, W. G. (1970). *Forms of intellectual and ethical development in the college years: A scheme.* New York: Holt, Rinehart & Winston.

Perry, W. G. (1981). Cognitive and ethical growth: The making of meaning. In A. Chickering (Ed.), *The modern American college* (pp. 76-116). San Francisco: Jossey-Bass.

Rayner, S., & Riding, R. (1997). Towards a categorisation of cognitive styles and learning styles. *Educational Psychology, 17,* 5-27.

Rosovsky, H., & Hartley, M. (2002). *Evaluation and the academy: Are we doing the right thing? Grade inflation and letters of recommendation.* Cambridge, MA: American Academy of Arts and Sciences.

Stanovich, K. E., & West, R. F. (1998). Individual differences in rational thought. *Journal of Experimental Psychology: General, 127,* 161-188.

Stanovich, K. E., & West, R. F. (2000). Individual differences in reasoning: Implications for the rationality debate? *Behavioral and Brain Sciences, 23,* 645-726.

Sternberg. R. J. (1997) *Thinking styles.* Cambridge, United Kingdom: Cambridge University Press.